THE ART OF KAYAKING

THE ART OF
KAYAKING

Everything You Need to Know About Paddling

Nigel Foster

FALCONGUIDES

GUILFORD, CONNECTICUT

FALCONGUIDES®

An imprint of Globe Pequot
Falcon and FalconGuides are registered trademarks and Make Adventure Your Story is a trademark of Rowman & Littlefield.

Distributed by NATIONAL BOOK NETWORK

British Library Cataloguing-in-Publication Information available

Library of Congress Cataloging-in-Publication Data
Names: Foster, Nigel, 1952- author.
Title: The art of kayaking : everything you need to know about paddling /
  Nigel Foster.
Description: Guilford, Connecticut/Helena Montana : FalconGuides brick, an
  imprint of Globe Pequot Falcon and FalconGuides are registered trademarks
  and Make Adventure Your Story is a trademark of Rowman & Littlefield,
  distributed by National Book Network, [2016]
Identifiers: LCCN 2017001071 (print) | LCCN 2017003149 (ebook) | ISBN
  9781493025701 (pbk. : alk. paper) | ISBN 9781493025718 (ebook) | ISBN
  9781493025718 (e-book)
Subjects: LCSH: Kayaking--Handbooks, manuals, etc.
Classification: LCC GV783 .F789 2016 (print) | LCC GV783 (ebook) | DDC
  797.122/4--dc23
LC record available at https://lccn.loc.gov/2017001071

∞™ The paper used in this publication meets the minimum requirements of American National Standard for
Information Sciences—Permanence of Paper for Printed Library Materials, ANSI/NISO Z39.48-1992.

CONTENTS

ACKNOWLEDGMENTS

How on earth did I come to learn enough about something I love to write a book about it? Thanks. Mum and Dad. You, my earliest inspiration and guidance, still never cease to amaze me with your wisdom and great example. Without you kindling the fires, I would never have gone exploring by kayak or otherwise, or started designing or writing.

And following on in time, my wonderful daughter, who first kayaked at the age of four and long ago far surpassed my expectations and hopes, and Alex, her husband, also inspire me to continue.

Thanks to Sharon, my first wife, who always encouraged me in my business of kayaking and writing, who joined me on many adventures and shared my love of outdoors. Without your support I may never have finished my very first book. This now is my eleventh.

I have the best siblings: My sister, always suggesting gems of places I should go to paddle with glowing descriptions that tempted and intrigued; my younger brother, always the creator of great questions; and my older brother, the role model I chased from behind. I am extremely lucky to have such a great family.

I am also blessed with a great network of friends around the world, without which I surely would have long ago stopped traveling and exploring, and may have lost my dreams.

Of many dear friends, I would like to specifically thank Roland and Britta Johansson, Tomas Öhman, and Joel Rogers for their unhesitating help in getting me the photos I needed for this book. I would also like to thank my close friend Drew Delaney, a true explorer and adventurer whose images may still appear, although sadly he cannot.

Among the friends I am fortunate to have, or have outlived, I count a number of influential characters from the kayaking world whose books you may have read, whose opinions you may have heard, whose ideas may affect how you paddle, or whose kayak or paddle designs you have seen, if not used. Among them too are those whose exploits are incredible and groundbreaking; paddlers who will surely continue to inspire from generation to generation. For my own part, I have often paddled against the tide of current opinion, style, or trend, seeking a path that seemed true only to me. I love it that every one of the characters I mention has at least the same passion, sensitivity, and obstinacy as I do, and seldom the same approach. The world is better off for the different opinions and different styles. Although I do not agree with all the opinions, I recognize that clones do not drive progress. Thank you all for your steering influence, whether by like poles or opposite. Your influence helps shape our sport.

The production of any book takes much more than writing. Thanks to all at Globe Pequot and FalconGuides for your belief in me. It is your persistence through the tedium of fact-checking, graphics, copyediting, and production that make my ideas appear in the form of a cohesive book. While I have had the pleasure of meeting only a few of you, I do sincerely appreciate your contribution.

Finally, I have a wonderful wife, Kristin, who believes in what I do and shares in what I do. Kristin, you have no idea how much that means to me. Thank you.

Nigel Foster
June 2016

Introduction

"Nigel kayaks: It's what he does."

I began as a teenager, inspired by my older brother and encouraged by my parents. Wheeling our kayaks two miles downhill to reach the sea was just the start to our challenges. We little knew how little we knew.

Acquiring a new skill was like finding a fossil on the plowed, flint-cobbled fields we passed on our way to the sea. A rare occurrence, for although we passed fields on our way we had other matters to mind. When I launched my kayak I wasn't thinking about learning, I was thinking about paddling. I managed to roam in my kayak without learning anything much of value about paddling at all. Kayaking simply seemed very accessible.

Of the many ways to learn kayaking, mine was mostly error and trial. I laid down a wonderful foundation of poor technique that took years to unravel. While trying to establish better habits I began to see how useful the details were and how they all worked together in a stroke. I also discovered how quickly habits form, and how difficult it is to change them later. These were key concepts that helped me when I began instructing.

Early in this book I introduce basic elements that will get you afloat without bad habits. Although you can work fine with just these main points, you can add flavor to them as I dissect each technique, add finer detail, and introduce more complex moves. I also explain why and when you might find such moves and details useful.

Everything you do in your kayak should be made to measure. Very few techniques are "ready to wear." You must adapt techniques to suit your physique, your flexibility, your confidence level, your equipment, and your needs. I offer alternative approaches that achieve similar results, so you can develop your own preferences and paddling style, which will differ from mine.

I am driven by curiosity and my mantra: "Minimum effort for maximum effect." There are many nuances that can each improve performance. I enjoy paring down what I need to do to the absolute minimum required to do what I want to achieve. This demands groundwork and understanding not only the skills involved, but also the equipment and the environment. Some technical moves will only work in certain conditions, while others require specific equipment. You cannot expect the same result from one paddle as from another, or with one kayak versus another. I have enjoyed using my understanding of how I use equipment to help me design kayaks and paddles,

Kayaking on the milky blue water above a volcanic vent, Turtle Island, Taiwan.

which in turn has helped me further develop my paddling skills.

Control of your kayak and application of skills is just one aspect of paddling. You also need to know about the environment you paddle in. I will talk about waves and how they work, about shores and wind and weather, and about how to plan journeys and what can go wrong. Planning includes what you might choose to take with you; learning includes what we wished we had taken with us.

The section on "skills breakdown" arguably could have been first or last in the book. I included it primarily for instructors, but it is pertinent to any paddler. The ultimate goal in my teaching is to impart how to learn from experience. Learning from experience is what you do when there is no teacher. It is what you must do before you can become better than your teacher. And to progress, the sport needs paddlers to become better than their teachers.

One aspect of paddling, in particular, that I have grown to love is how water exudes endless energy. Its surface has a pulse with a complex rhythm. Work against the rhythm and you create

The dark blue water of the Kuroshio current turned milky blue in the foreground by an underwater volcanic vent, Turtle Island, Taiwan.

splash and splutter. Work in harmony and your kayak takes off and glides freely, riding with the energy from a hint of a wave here, turning to surge forward on another wave there. I hope that whatever you learn, you will develop the awareness and sensitivity to find joy in the movement of kayak and paddle.

Reading the water and moving with it rather than against it brings me back to my mantra of "minimum effort for maximum effect." It is where kayaking changes from sport to art. Kayaks truly offer us a very special kind of freedom, a gateway into living art.

In kayaking, as in life, there will always be more to learn, always more to discover, and always ways to improve. For me, that makes the journey worth continuing. It can only be the journey for me, because the destination will always be a little out of reach. By seeking perfection, by seeking harmony and effortlessness on the water, I am discovering the art of paddling. I hope you too will enjoy your journey.

Glossary:

An Introduction to Kayaking Terms

I have compiled this abbreviated glossary to clarify what I mean by terms you might use differently, or may be unfamiliar with. Elsewhere in the book I explain technical terms when I first introduce them, but when you dip into a section at random, you might miss out on an explanation that occurred earlier. For this reason I have included a full glossary near the back of the book (page 297).

Explaining with diagrams in the sand, Ærø, Denmark

Distinguishing One Side of a Kayak from the Other

When one paddle blade is being used in the water, this blade is *active* and the other is *inactive*. The side of the kayak with the active blade is the *onside* of the kayak and the other is *offside*. The hand closest to the active blade is the onside hand. The other is the offside hand, even when it is moved to the onside of the kayak.

For ease of description, the front hand is the one closest to the bow and the other is the back hand. Likewise, when the paddle is held upright there is a top hand and a bottom hand.

Edging Terms

I refer to *edging* the kayak as "heeling" the kayak (one gunwale held higher than the other) within the body balance you can maintain without your paddle. *Leaning the kayak* is heeling your kayak beyond that point of balance.

The kayak is said to be "edged" toward the low side, so I am edged to the left when I hold the left

These terms are used when distinguishing one side of a kayak from the other.

kayak is edged
from the paddle

high side

low side

Kayak is edged
to the right

Kayak is turning to the left:
kayak is edged from the turn

the right edge is engaged

These terms apply to "edging" a kayak.

side lowest. You *engage an edge* by holding that side down. Once edged, I refer to the *high side* or *low side*.

When edged "into a turn" or "into a wave" or "into the wind" or "toward the paddle," the low side of the kayak is toward the center of turn, the wave, the wind, or the paddle. The opposite would be *edged from*.

Blade Alignment Terms

The *blade face* (also the *power face* or *drive face*) is the side used to pull the kayak forward, and the back is used for pushing and reversing. The blade face of a Greenland paddle may be identical in profile to the back of the blade, so differentiation between face and back occurs as soon as the blade is held for use. The side aligned for pulling is the face and the side aligned for pushing is the back.

I divide the blade edge into two at the tip, or end. To *slice the blade* means to slide it edge-first in neutral, with the least possible pressure on the face or the back unless otherwise indicated.

When the blade is sliced through the water, one edge will lead the way. This is the *leading edge* and the other the *trailing edge*.

Greenland blades are usually symmetrical front to back and side to side

Euro-blades typically differ from face to back and are often asymmetric from side to side

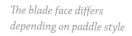

The blade face differs depending on paddle style

To *skim the blade* means to slide it almost flat across the surface, so it stays on the surface or climbs back up if slightly submerged. The blade must have a slight climbing angle—the leading edge held slightly higher than the trailing edge—for the blade to skim or plane. When the blade is skimming the surface, that angle between the water and the blade may alternatively be called a *planing angle,* or a *skimming angle.*

If the blade is held vertically in the water with the face toward the stern, and moved sideways from the hull with a slight climbing angle, that means the face is lightly pressing the water and the leading edge is closer to the bow than the trailing edge.

With pressure on the blade face, the face is engaged. With pressure against the back, the back is engaged.

Wind References

A *tailwind* blows at your back. You can make better speed with a tailwind because the wind helps you along. *Downwind* is the direction the wind pushes you. If you sit and drift in the wind you will be blown downwind, regardless of which way you are facing and which way you wish to travel. A tailwind helps you in the direction you want to go when that is downwind.

A *headwind* will blow in your face as you paddle. Upwind is the direction you travel when you paddle with the wind in your face.

Kayakers here are crossing from a weather shore toward a lee shore.

A *side wind* blows from the side.

Wind direction refers to the origin of the wind. A north wind comes from the north and pushes you south. A west wind, or westerly, comes from the west.

An *onshore wind* blows from the sea onto the shore. When you are on the sea, the shore with an onshore wind is known as a *lee shore*, because land will be on the sheltered, or "lee side," of your kayak. A lee shore is an exposed shore.

An *offshore wind* blows from the land onto the sea. When coming to land, the shore with an offshore wind is known as a weather shore.

There is sometime confusion between *leeward side* and *lee shore*. Islands have leeward (sheltered) and windward sides. But from a kayak, you differentiate between a shore seen over the side, or end, of your kayak from which the weather approaches, (weather shore) and a shore over the side, or end, of your kayak that is sheltered (lee shore). The lee shore is on the windward side of an island.

Sea Condition References

A *head sea* comes from in front. You paddle into the approaching waves.

A *side sea* comes from the side, when the kayak is broadside to the waves.

A *head-* or *bow-quartering* sea comes at an angle between the front and the side.

A *following sea* comes from behind. You could surf the waves.

A *stern-quartering sea* comes at an angle from behind and one side at the same time.

Waves coming from the stern quarter cause a kayak to *broach*. Broaching is when the kayak is pushed around broadside by a wave. Usually, when kayakers talk of a *quartering sea,* it is understood to mean from the stern quarter, which is the direction that usually causes the most reason for comment, with the kayak constantly trying to broach.

Wave References

When a kayak is carried sideways by a wave, the *up-wave side* is where the top of the wave is situated. The trough running ahead of the wave is on the *down-wave side*. When a wave approaches a beach, the down-wave side will be the shore side and the up-wave side will be to seaward. The front of the wave is the face. The back of the wave is the slope that follows behind the crest.

Turning Terms

A *skid turn* is when the stern of a kayak (when you are moving forward) loses its grip on the water to slide sideways, making the kayak turn. (Similarly, when reversing, skid turn is used to describe how the bow slides sideways.)

This kayaker is edging toward the up-wave side.

A *carved turn* is when the stern is edged to the side that locks it, preventing it from skidding out sideways. The stern more or less follows the path of the bow along a curved path.

Equipment
Basics

This chapter outlines the basic gear you need for your first time afloat, and what the different parts are called. For details about the different kinds of kayaks, paddles, and equipment that work best for specific purposes, refer to the Equipment Detailed chapter on page 243.

The names for the parts introduced here will be used throughout the book, so refer back here when you need to.

The Kayak

Kayaks come in different shapes and are made of different materials depending on what they are designed to do, but they all should have a hull, a deck, a cockpit with a seat, foot braces, flotation, and end grabs.

The hull is the underside of the kayak, with the deck covering the top. The top edge of the hull, where it meets the deck, is called the gunwale.

The cockpit is the opening in the deck where the seat is positioned. The deck around the edge of the cockpit usually has a rolled-over lip—the cockpit rim or coaming—over which a spray deck (also called a spray skirt) can be secured to keep out splashes.

A sit-on-top kayak has a lower, flattened deck. There is no cockpit so you sit on the deck rather than under it, although the seat is often recessed

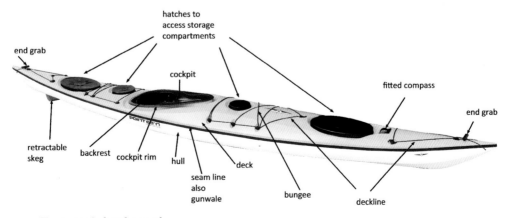

The parts of a kayak named.

down low for stability, with the sides a little higher all around creating a cockpit of sorts.

Flotation is essential in both ends of the kayak, so if filled with water it will float level on the surface. The flotation may be in the form of watertight compartments, fixed closed-cell foam, or float bags (air bags). Fill extra space in the ends with air bags to keep water out and make emptying easier. Sit-on-top kayaks are typically sealed units full of air or other flotation material.

Foot braces allow you to maintain foot contact with your kayak for better paddling control and power. They are usually adjustable, and may take the form of a pedal on either side, or a single fixed plate.

The kayak should have convenient handholds to use when lifting, emptying, and for on-water

Foot braces on this sit-on-top kayak are built in.

rescues. End grabs of some sort are essential. Most kayaks have deck lines as well, if the deck is too long to reach easily from the end grab to the cockpit. For safety, deck lines must not be able to foul the cockpit area, and should be kept sufficiently taut so that they cannot entangle you.

Extra carrying handles are especially useful for tandem kayaks, so the heavier load can be conveniently carried by several people.

Multiple handles make carrying a tandem easier and safer.

The Paddle

A kayak paddle consists of a shaft (loom) with a blade at each end. When both blades are aligned in the same plane the paddle is said to be non-feathered. It will rest with both blades flat on the ground. A feathered paddle has the blades set at

Here is a nonfeathered paddle.

different angles to reduce the air resistance against the upper blade, so you use less energy to cover the same distance.

Each blade has a face, used to pull the kayak forward, and a back, used to push the kayak in reverse.

Paddles often come fitted with rubber or plastic drip rings to deflect water running down when you lift a blade.

Most paddles for touring and general recreation measure between 200 and 230 centimeters in length. Paddles for whitewater kayaking are usually shorter.

Essentials

A *float vest* is an essential piece of equipment for paddlers. This must conform to the safety standards and laws of the place you paddle. Also, importantly, the vest should fit well so that it does not float up around your ears should you find yourself in the water. When correctly wearing an appropriate float vest you will be supported in the water at the surface, without wasting energy just keeping afloat. Should you spill, this can be very helpful. In extreme circumstances it may be lifesaving. Fasten

Your PFD should fit your body size and be correctly fastened to function appropriately in the water.

all the attachments and cinch up the adjusting straps before you set off.

A float vest is also commonly known as a personal flotation device (PFD for short), a buoyancy aid, or a life jacket, although technically a life jacket must have additional properties to be sold as such.

Be aware that local, regional, or national regulations may stipulate the color and type of PFD

A spray deck or spray skirt fits around your waist and the cockpit rim to seal out splashes. Keep the release tab (in this image, the red handle at the front) outside when you seal the spray deck. If you seal it inside by mistake, release the spray deck by grabbing the looser fabric at the side of the cockpit just in front of your hips and easing the elastic free. joelrogers.com

This is a personal flotation device (PFD).

you use, and the amount of flotation in it. They may also specify other items to be carried, the most common being a whistle. A spray deck/skirt is a useful addition to your gear. This makes a seal between your waist and the cockpit rim to keep out splashes.

Other Considerations

Kayaking is a water sport, so you may get wet. Wear something that will remain warm when wet, such as wool or polypropylene, rather than cotton. A windproof jacket will cut down wind chill, especially if you are wet. It is important to wear footwear such as running shoes, trainers, or water

Consider the water temperature and the sun when deciding what to wear kayaking.

shoes to help protect your feet if you need to wade. You cannot always see where you step.

If you stay close to your launching place, you will not need to carry much with you, but if you venture farther, think about your creature comforts. Will you need water to drink, or a snack? Did you remember sunscreen? Make plans for likely

eventualities. A dry bag could be a useful investment to keep your stuff dry.

Water splashing onto a sit-on-top kayak should self-drain through scuppers (holes through the hull of the boat), with any remaining too little to be of concern. A kayak with a cockpit will hold water in the cockpit, so it is useful to carry a hand pump or sponge to bail it out.

Carrying, Lifting, and Transporting a Kayak

More kayak-related injuries happen on land, lifting and carrying kayaks, than happen on the water. It is easier for two people to carry a kayak than one, and it is easier for four than two. Crouch down and lift with your legs to avoid bending your back. Empty your kayak before carrying it whenever practical. Kayak carts are a great alternative to carrying if the ground is fairly even.

To transport your kayak on a car, check to see what the vehicle's weight limits are, and find a roof rack designed for the vehicle. Pad the roof rack to protect your kayak, or use cradles. Strap or tie your kayak securely to the rack, and tether the bow and stern to the front and back of the car so you will

A kayak cart offers an easy option over carrying.

A padded roof rack with upright stacker bars offers a stable place to load your kayak. Tie down to both ends of the roof rack, add bow and stern lines, and hang a red flag at the back.

not lose your load should your roof rack ever come adrift. A red flag at the back will remind you how far your kayak overhangs the vehicle, and will also warn following traffic. Different regions have different laws regarding carrying a load on the roof of a vehicle, so check your local regulations, and plan ahead if you intend to travel to a different area.

Basic Care

Rinse your gear in fresh water after use to keep it fresh and extend its life. You will find more details about care, maintenance, and storage in the Equipment Detailed section on page 243.

Paddling along a sand beach,
Penghu Islands, Taiwan Strait.

Flat Water

Skills

Flat Water Skills 1, 2, and 3 cover kayak skills on flat water, from the easiest to the most complex. You can apply these basic techniques with kayak and paddle for efficient control in wind, waves, and current. Mastering just a few of the skills might be all you need to cope in basic conditions, but there is a difference between coping and being in complete control. There is also a gradient in how difficult it becomes to apply skills depending on the severity of the conditions.

It takes time to master a single skill, and to learn how and when to use it for best effect. So it is good to revisit the most basic skills from time to time. Adding nuances and then testing them out in conditions will improve how you paddle. Details make a difference, but they are incremental. You may pick up on one but fail to appreciate the value of another until your paddling creates context for it. On the other hand, an explanation may make sense of something you do naturally.

Flat Water
Skills 1

Paddling past Skanskaskrapan, "The Lipstick" building and the barque Viking at Lilla Bommen, Gotheburg, Sweden.

From getting in and out to paddling straight.

Getting In and Out

It seems as if more capsizes occur while launching and landing than at other times. You may be quite stable sitting, but when you lift your weight higher you become unbalanced. So it is worth spending some time experimenting with different options for launching and landing, and practicing the ones that seem most appropriate for your needs. It also pays to spend time working on balance exercises, as described in the section on balance (page 39).

Also consider timing. Wait until that wave passes before you lift yourself out of your seat, or until after the wave sets so you launch at the beginning of a lull.

A Simple Shallow Water Launch

Possibly the easiest way to get in and out is in shallow water. Stand astride your kayak, grasp it behind you at either side of the seat and sit down. Bring your legs into the cockpit afterward. Get out legs first, to then stand up astride your kayak.

Launching a Surf Ski or Sit-On-Top Kayak

Float your craft, and stand beside it holding both sides just in front of the seat, holding your paddle in the far hand along the side of the kayak. Sit in the seat and then swivel your legs into position.

A group of paddlers stand beside their surf skis waiting for the right moment before getting seated.

Launching from a Dock

Launch from a dock is a good starting exercise in balance and control. Sit at the edge of the dock above the cockpit of your kayak and rest your feet on the seat. Swivel slightly toward the front of your kayak. Place one hand on centerline of the deck about a foot behind the cockpit and your other hand on the dock roughly level with your first hand. Lean your body out over your kayak, and then lower yourself from the dock down to sit on the back deck of your kayak with your weight centered. Move your feet forward to clear the seat. Keeping your hands in position, lift yourself forward and down into your seat. Keep your hold on the dock while you bring your feet to the foot braces and settle comfortably.

Getting Out at a Dock

From a seated position with your hand on the dock, place your other hand behind you on the back deck, far enough back for you to be able to sit on the deck. If your cockpit is long enough for you to lift your knees out, position your feet close to your seat. Pushing down on the back deck, lift yourself up to sit on the back deck.

Bring your feet back onto your seat and lean forward. Move the hand from your back deck to grasp the front of your cockpit. Pull yourself gently forward and with your weight directly over your feet, stand up. Grasp the dock with both hands and lift yourself onto the dock. How you do this final stage will depend on how high the dock is from the water.

Remember to retrieve your kayak before it floats away.

Practice getting in and out of your kayak at docks of different heights.

Keep your weight low and in the center of the kayak when getting in.

Alternatively, hold the dock with your offshore hand, with the hand nearest the dock on the back of your cockpit at the midpoint, fingers on the deck, thumb down. Push down on the back deck and swivel in your cockpit to kneel on your seat. Hold the dock with both of your hands, stand, and step up onto the dock.

You can get into your kayak by reversing this procedure.

Keep your weight centered when getting in or out of your kayak.

A dock serves as a straightforward practice place, but you can adapt the same techniques to embark and disembark from rocks at different heights from the water.

Getting In and Out from Shore

It is a good idea to place your paddle on the dock or other kind of shore, where it will be within easy reach once you are afloat. Likewise, when disembarking, first place your paddle on the shore.

Some paddlers like to use a paddle as a bridge between kayak and shore while getting in or out. It offers an easily explained solution, but I prefer not to do that as it is too easy to damage your paddle, either by putting too much weight on it, or by scuffing the handgrips against the shore, dock, or cockpit rim. It is one of the easiest ways to bend aluminum paddle shafts, snap plastic blades, or crush or make hairline cracks in carbon fiber shafts. Better to get in or out first, and then take up your paddle.

Launching and Landing a Single from Shore

There are different techniques for every situation, but here are some common principles. If possible, float your kayak before you get in. Stand astride your cockpit and sit down, stowing your legs afterward. This quickly puts you in a stable position to paddle. You can paddle a few strokes forward to clear the shore before you seal your spray deck to avoid being blown back onto shore.

Alternatively, you can secure your spray deck onshore before sliding into the water, to avoid being swamped by a shore break. This is known as a seal launch. When seal launching, look for a launching place where your kayak will slide easily, without getting stuck on rocks. Sometimes driftwood or seaweed can be used to reduce damage to your hull. Anticipate which way the wind, waves, or shore current will turn your kayak when the bow is afloat but the stern is still on the beach, and allow for that when you line up to launch.

Seal launching works well, but if you have a retractable skeg, you will likely jam it with sand or small pebbles when you seal launch. A short loop of cord secured through a hole in the back corner of a skeg will make it easier for someone else to pull the skeg down if it does become jammed. Best check as soon as you have launched so you know your skeg will work if you need it.

Launching and Landing a Tandem from Shore

Launching a tandem requires more coordination than a single, but sometimes launching is easier. One paddler can steady the kayak while the other gets seated and ready to paddle. The first seated can hold the kayak from shore while the second paddler puts on the spray skirt and gets ready.

Landing is the reverse. Each paddler gets out while the other steadies the kayak. Onshore there are two to carry the kayak. Tandems tend to be heavy, so unload before carrying, and enlist the help of as many helpers as possible.

In calm water, hold your tandem parallel to shore to get in from the shallows.

Launching Two Kayaks Together in Shallow Water

When paddling with others, why not ask for and offer help getting in and out? One person can steady a kayak for another to get in, but you can also work in pairs.

This sequence illustrates launching two kayaks together.

Rest the kayaks side by side, with each paddler standing beside their own kayak. Rest both paddles across behind both cockpits. Face forward with your hands behind your backs, so that each grips the paddle against his or her own cockpit. The two kayaks now make a single stable platform. Each paddler sits in turn. This is a simple yet effective way to avoid an inconvenient spill.

Place the kayaks side by side, paddles behind the cockpits.

Grasp the paddles and backs of cockpits behind you with both hands.

When stabilized by the paddles, get seated.

Finally, retrieve the paddles.

BASIC TIPS FOR GETTING INTO A KAYAK

- Seek help if needed.
- Float the kayak first if possible.
- Keep your weight centered and low, if possible.
- Hold the kayaks together for stability.
- Question if timing is important.

Capsize and Wet Exit

Sooner or later you'll find yourself upside down, so you should know what to do when that happens. Better still, try capsizing deliberately a few times till you get used to getting out of the kayak smoothly and calmly. Practice in water shallow enough for you to stand up to empty your kayak, and where there are no hazards in the water or on the bottom. Have someone stand by in case you need help.

Before you go upside down, check to make sure you can find your spray deck release tab. With your paddle in one hand, bring your hands to your hips and run your fingers around the perimeter of the cockpit toward the front until you find the release tab. Try with your eyes closed till you are sure you can find it.

To release the spray deck, grasp the release tab and use it to lift the elastic from under the coaming. Then run your fingers around to release the elastic all around the spray deck.

This assumes you have secured your spray deck with the release tab outside where it is accessible. It is a common mistake to seal the release tab inside the cockpit where you cannot reach it. Make it a habit to check every time you seal your spray deck.

If you cannot find the release tab, grasp the fabric at the side of the cockpit, where the

curvature is minimal and the elastic grip is weaker, and lift the spray deck free. Practice this release also before you go upside down.

Practice your wet exit with a friend standing by, just in case.

Getting out of the kayak is easiest when you are completely upside down, rather than while you are capsizing, so wait, and take your time. When you are underwater, release your spray deck, then bring your hands to just behind your hips, relax your legs, and lean slightly forward. Push against your kayak with your hands to ease yourself out, rolling forward as you exit. Your legs will follow the curve of your upper body. Your PFD will float you up, so try to avoid hitting your head on your kayak.

Keep hold of your kayak and your paddle as you exit and surface. You will need both items again. Even a breeze can blow your kayak away faster than you can swim. Training yourself to keep hold every time, even when there is no wind, will likely reward you in the future.

Once you have completed your exit, empty your upturned kayak in shallow water by lifting the front end, leaving the back end floating. Grasp the kayak on either side a couple of feet from the bow, where you can prevent it from rotating. Lift until the cockpit clears the surface and water drains from it. Once the draining stops, keep the cockpit clear of the water and rock the kayak a little from side to side to shake out any water that might be trapped. Then upturn the kayak.

Personally, I was terrified at the idea of going upside down. It was not so much fear of being trapped as a fear of having my head underwater, but if either sounds familiar to you I recommend you find a patient instructor who can gently accustom you to the water. It is worth the time and effort to overcome that challenge. All your subsequent paddling will be more relaxed when you know you can exit underwater if you need to.

KEY POINTS FOR CAPSIZE AND WET EXIT

Before capsizing, practice releasing the spray deck from the cockpit, then practice releasing using the release tab with your eyes closed, then without using the release tab. To practice a wet exit, take your time to go upside down.

- Hold your paddle in one hand.
- Run your fingers around the cockpit from your hips forward to locate the release tab. Lift the elastic from under coaming to release the spray deck. Lift away from you; do not pull toward.
- With both hands just behind your hips, push the kayak away gently.
- Roll forward to exit.
- Keep hold of your kayak and paddle.

Forward Stroke

The forward stroke drives your kayak forward. It is what you do most of the time in a kayak, so make it your most efficient stroke. Focus on the details that will save you energy, and those that give you more power and speed.

Some Basic Concepts

The idea is to plant your blade in the water and pull your kayak past it, rather than pulling the paddle through the water.

When you pull gently for a moment on your paddle, it tends to stay in place. When you pull harder it will either flutter from side to side, or it will drag noisily through the water. Both these effects occur when you are wasting energy to move the blade and/or water back, instead of using energy to move your kayak forward. You will only experience flutter if you relax your handgrip. Keeping a relaxed or open grip is better for your joints and tendons.

I will focus on the three basic parts of the forward stroke: the power source, the transmission, and the traction. You can relate these to a car's motor, transmission, and the grip of the tires on the road.

Your power comes from muscles in your torso, through rotating your torso. Just as a car engine is braced so it does not turn around inside the car when you try to accelerate, you also need to be braced in your kayak to prevent spinning in your seat when you apply power. Brace with your feet.

Your arms, wrists, and hands provide the link between your torso rotation and your paddle, forming the transmission.

Your paddle blade grips the water; this is traction. How well it grips depends on the blade shape and on how you use it. Just as you get wheel spin

KEY POINTS FOR THE FORWARD STROKE

- **The kayak should move, not the paddle.**
- **There are three parts to a stroke: power, transmission, and traction.**
- **Power comes from torso rotation; brace with your feet.**
- **Transmission is provided by your arms and wrists. Keep a relaxed handgrip.**
- **Traction is how the blade grips the water. Flutter and turbulence both indicate an overpowered paddle.**
- **Gearing comes from wider or narrower spacing between your hands on the paddle, or from using a longer or shorter paddle.**

These foot braces are positioned for comfortable paddling. When the heels move closer to the body than the toes, the knees are raised.

when you apply power too abruptly in a car, in a kayak the paddle blade will flutter or slip when you apply power too abruptly.

You can change from lower to higher gear when kayaking by adjusting your hand spacing a little on the paddle.

Foot Brace Adjustment

To adjust the foot braces, sit upright in your kayak with your feet lightly on the braces. With the balls of your feet touching and your toes pointing upward, you should be able to straighten your legs along the hull with relaxed calf muscles. When you move your heels closer to you, you should be able to grip with your knees or thighs under the deck and still have firm contact with the balls of your feet on the foot braces. With your braces in this position you can avoid unnecessary lower back

pain and leg discomfort while paddling, yet still be able to maneuver and roll.

Foot Brace Positioning in Detail

If you have ever paddled a whitewater kayak, you are likely familiar with a frog-leg seating position, where your knees are pressed out to the sides and locked down, and your feet are close together. You probably expect your foot braces to be tight. You may be able to sit like this for a couple of hours without getting out for a stretch, but not much longer without getting uncomfortable.

To be comfortable for the longer periods of time typically spent in a touring or sea kayak, adjust your foot braces so that when your legs are down, straight along the hull, your feet are pointing up and lightly in contact with the foot brace. This way, when you bring your heels closer to you, your knees/thighs come into contact with the knee/thigh braces or the deck while the balls of your feet press against the foot brace.

When you reach forward to catch the water at the start of a forward stroke, raise the knee on the

It is difficult to sit upright when your seat slopes back.

Consider using a pad as shown to help you sit upright. Position your foot brace so you can straighten your leg.

same side and straighten the leg or drop the knee on the offside. Keep your hip, knee, and ankle in as straight an alignment as possible, with knees fairly close together, to avoid sideways twist on your joints, which can get uncomfortable over time.

Your power comes with the straightening of your onside leg, which drives your torso rotation, while your offside leg relaxes and bends upward. This is a gradual straightening of the leg throughout the power phase of the stroke, just as the torso

KEY POINTS FOR LEG AND HIP POSITION FOR THE FORWARD STROKE

- Position the foot braces to allow firm foot contact yet relaxed leg muscles when your legs are straightened.
- Position the foot braces to allow firm foot contact and knee or thigh contact when your knees are bent.
- Your toes should be pointed up rather than sideways if possible.
- Have a finger space between your hips and the side of the seat.

rotation is a gradual application of power throughout the power phase of the stroke.

To permit good torso rotation, make sure you can slip your fingers between your hips and the sides of your seat. Your hips should move forward and back about 2 inches with every double stroke. If your seat is tight, your hips will lock against the sides and you will lose some of the freedom of movement you need to generate full power.

Likewise, good torso rotation means your back will rub against the back support if you are too close. Sit upright and away from the support when you paddle, and relax back when you stop. If you have difficulty sitting upright, try positioning a narrow pad across the back of your seat. This will tilt you forward and make sitting upright easier.

This seating position may feel loose if you are used to being clamped tightly into a cockpit, but you will be able to sit comfortably in your kayak for far longer, and you will also be able to generate more power.

Torso Rotation

To experience torso rotation outside a kayak, sit upright with your arms folded across your chest, facing straight forward. This is the starting point, or neutral position, from which you rotate your torso. Next, rotate your upper body as far as you can to one side. This is the full range of your torso rotation to that side. You will probably notice one knee drops a little while the other lifts when you rotate, the result of one hip rotating forward and the other back. You should experience the same leg movement when you paddle. Return to neutral, then fully rotate in the other direction and return to neutral.

When relaxing in your kayak you most often face forward in the neutral position. To paddle, tension up like a spring to one side, then power the stroke back into the relaxed position again. Stretch forward to the other side and power the stroke back to neutral again.

Imagine a vertical rod running from the top of your head to your tail bone. Your rotation should be around this imaginary rod. Remember to sit upright.

Blade Placement at the Start of the Stroke

Hold your paddle at arm's length, rotate, and reach forward to place the blade fully in the water as far forward as your reach will allow. Maximize your reach by bending your knee up on the catch side and straightening your offside leg. The point at which your blade is just fully immersed is known as the "catch." It is at the catch that you apply the power to your stroke from your torso rotation.

Apply power only until you reach the neutral torso position, so start fully rotated away from the side where you immerse your blade. Finish in midrotation position, when your chest faces directly forward and your paddle is just passing midcockpit or slightly beyond. Farther back the blade is too far behind to be of much use to your

forward stroke. Continue through neutral torso position until you are fully rotated to the other side, positioning the other blade above the water ready for the catch on that side.

Notes: Apply power the moment the blade is fully immersed at the catch. Your kayak will continue to glide forward between strokes, so if you delay applying your power after the blade is immersed, your kayak will quickly float past your paddle. Focus your attention on the first part of your stroke for power.

Also, try not to apply power beyond your body's midrotation point. Past this point your blade angle changes, so an increasing percentage of your energy is spent lifting water rather than driving the kayak forward. There is plenty of resistance still, so it may feel as if you are paddling powerfully, but you are wasting energy. Better to apply power at the start of the stroke, where you will get the most benefit.

KEY POINTS FOR THE CATCH AND POWER PHASE OF THE FORWARD STROKE

- Sit upright and rotate your torso fully for the catch.
- Bend your onside knee and straighten your offside leg for full rotation.
- Fully extend your top arm for the catch.
- Apply power immediately on the blade's immersion.
- Press with your onside foot to straighten your leg; relax your offside leg and bend that knee.
- Apply power until your torso reaches neutral position.
- Apply power through straight arms.

To help focus your attention on the catch, rotate fully and bring your blade into position above the water ready for the catch. Pinpoint this position relative to nearby deck fittings, or mark the position with a marker pen or a length of sticky tape. Repeat on the other side of the kayak. Do the same for the catch position, when your blade is just fully immersed. This mark will be closer to you.

When you paddle, pause for a moment before each new stroke while you position the blade. Stab the blade into the water at the farther mark, and apply the power of your torso rotation immediately as the blade reaches the closer mark. The catch should be quick.

Handgrip

When you apply power at the catch, your paddle grips the water at the blade, while the rotation of your torso applies a push through your straight top arm (the one that is higher) and a pull through your bottom arm. Your top hand does not need to grip in order to push. Your bottom hand can also maintain a loose grip, so the paddle shaft is captured by bent fingers. If you pull straight back with a loose handgrip, you will notice the blade

While your top hand pushes, your bottom hand pulls. Keep a loose grip.

flutter occasionally, especially under heavy load. It is an advantage to be able to spot when this happens so that you can adjust your stroke for better efficiency.

Traction

Flutter—when the blade quivers or shakes in the water—only occurs when you overpower your blade. This happens when you try to accelerate too quickly, when you paddle hard against the wind or the current, or when you have additional resistance (for example, when towing another kayak). At these times you can adopt the slice-away stroke, described below, to gain more traction. Most of the time, once your kayak is up to cruising speed, you can paddle using any style you choose and you will have good traction and rarely experience flutter.

Keep your grip loose on your paddle shaft if you want to feel flutter. If you grip too tightly you will see or hear turbulence around the blade instead.

Flutter in Detail

Flutter occurs only when you pull hard enough against the water to make the blade slip. Then water flows across the face and over the edges, and creates eddies, or vortices, behind the edges.

An easy way to see these eddies form behind the blade is to stand on a dock (or in the water), hold your paddle vertically, and pull the blade toward you face-first. Eddies will form behind each edge like little whirlpools.

If the little eddies would stay the same size behind each edge, the blade would drag slowly in a straight line as you continued to pull, but they don't. One grows larger than the other, and the imbalance causes the blade to slip edge-first away from the largest eddy. Once the blade has moved your pull is off-center, so the blade soon stalls. The

When the blade is dragged straight back under load, eddies form behind each edge. When these eddies become unequal the blade will flutter. This indicates you are losing traction and wasting energy. Roland Johansson

Pulled more powerfully the blade creates turbulence, an indication you are wasting energy. Tomas Öhman

When you slice sideways as you pull back, the blade becomes stable even when you pull powerfully. Eddying now only occurs behind the trailing edge, the edge closest to your kayak. This offers the greatest traction and the most effective use of power. The less water you move the greater your efficiency. Tomas Öhman vortex behind what was the leading edge grows, and the blade slices back in the other direction. The oscillations make the blade zigzag toward you through the water in a series of short curves, like the fluttering of a falling leaf. Your paddle feels as if it is shaking or quivering.

The same principle makes a moored boat or an anchored buoy swing from side to side against a current or the wind, and the same process makes your kayak move forward and backward when you sit at rest with a strong wind from the side. A reed standing in current will quiver for the same reason.

If you drag your paddle very hard, the flutter will stop and the blade will drag in a straight line with turbulent water churning behind. The clean vortices behind the blade edges have been replaced, broken up into multiple vortices of different sizes interacting chaotically. You can see the splash of the turbulence, and you can hear it.

Eddies only form behind your paddle blade when your blade reaches a critical velocity through the water, because they are created by the flow of water filling the space left when your paddle moves. This is why you will rarely notice flutter when you are already moving forward and only pull gently against your paddle. You notice flutter most when you accelerate quickly, when you paddle against wind or current, or when you tow another kayak: any time, in fact, when you overload your blade. If you grossly overload your paddle, you will create turbulence in the water behind the blade as you drag it in a straight line.

One way to reduce or eliminate flutter and turbulence when accelerating is by building up speed gradually. By eliminating flutter and turbulence you avoid overloading your paddle, and in doing so save energy. Efficient paddle strokes will also be quiet, because noise is a result of your hard work moving water instead of your kayak.

Slice-Away Stroke

Another way to avoid flutter and turbulence, and to apply more power with better traction, is to start your stroke close to your hull at the catch, and guide it edge-first from the side of the kayak. The paddle should exit naturally when it reaches a point level with your hip, or slightly behind. Your top hand follows a horizontal path across your kayak, more or less in line with the horizon. You still pull against the blade to move your kayak forward while slicing.

In making the sideways movement you ensure that water flows past both the face and the back of the blade, to be deflected past the blade edge closest to your hull. This water flow ends up being deflected toward the back of your kayak, pulling your blade in the opposite direction, the direction of your travel. You can accentuate this pull by angling your blade slightly, so the edge farthest from the side of the kayak stays a little farther ahead of you than the edge closest to the hull. The angle is a minimal *climbing angle,* the same as you might use for a sculling draw stroke, and the effect is similar, although sculling with the blade at this angle pulls your kayak forward rather than

THREE TIPS FOR IMPROVING YOUR FORWARD STROKE

- Slice your blade out from the side of the kayak so it stays on the line of your bow wake.
- Watch your top hand sweep along the horizon line through your stroke.
- In a side wind, your kayak will be pushed toward the wake on one side, distorting the symmetry: Model your stroke on symmetry.

This paddler has rotated his torso and the blade is poised for the catch. Roland Johansson

Power the stroke with your torso from the start. Roland Johansson

The blade path follows the line of the kayak's wake to exit the water level with your hip. Roland Johansson

In general, the blade follows the line of the wake through each forward stroke. Your top hand moves across in front of you, along the horizon line. joelrogers.com

sideways. If you keep a loose handgrip through the stroke, the blade will tend to assume this angle anyway.

The blade will leave the water quite naturally, edge-first, and level with your hip or slightly farther back. Use finger control to adjust the final blade angle to make the exit as quiet as possible.

Of course, slicing in this way will only work with a high-angle stroke. We need to modify the technique to benefit the low-angle stroke.

At a low angle, it is still an advantage to move your blade edge-first through the water to increase traction, although you need to make it dive edge-first and then rise to the surface again edge-first. At the catch, as the blade descends, the leading blade edge—the one that hits the water first—will angle closer to the bow than the trailing edge. When you start to bring the blade to the surface, the new leading edge—the one that will reach the surface first—will again be closer to the bow than the new trailing edge. The change in angle occurs when the blade changes direction, at its greatest depth in the water during the stroke. The change in angle will happen naturally when your blade changes direction if you keep a loose grip.

Greenland paddles present an exception, because your hands grip the shaped shoulder so the blade is always tilted (canted) in one direction. The hand-grip angle is the correct one to take advantage of the later, rising stage of the stroke, not the earlier, descending stage. It would be challenging for your wrists to reverse the angle for the first part of the stroke, so typically, with a Greenland paddle, your blade will slice rather quickly back during the descent, but will have more traction during the ascent. The reduced grip in the descending phase may be one of the reasons a Greenland paddle used at low angle is less powerful for accelerating than other blade types, and also why some Greenland-style paddlers extol the virtues of the ascending phase. You achieve greater traction and faster acceleration with a Greenland paddle when you use a high-angle stroke.

Blade exit

Your blade should leave the water quietly at the end of the stroke. Leave the water behind rather than using energy to lift it.

Catch: torso rotated arm straight, blade immersed

Power from torso through straight arm Blade tracks back and out from side of kayak

The path of the paddle through the power phase of a forward stroke.
Tomas Öhman

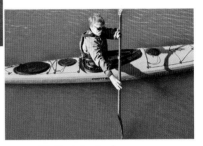

Exit: blade leaves water edge-first about level with hip

When you change from one type of blade to another, you may need to adjust how you exit the blade to avoid lifting water. Exit edge-first. If you find yourself lifting spray, it may be you are applying power until too late in the stroke. Try making your exit edge-first, and earlier.

AVOID OVERPOWERING

- Blade flutter and turbulence indicate an overpowered blade on a forward stroke.
- Avoid by accelerating gently.
- Avoid overpowering by slicing the blade sideways through the water while pulling against it.
- Exit quietly, earlier rather than later.

Gears

You can accelerate more easily and paddle more effectively under load when your hands are spaced slightly wider on the paddle shaft, effectively lowering the gear.

When you are cruising with little resistance, you can maintain your speed more easily by sliding your hands slightly closer together on the paddle shaft.

The extremes of hand position need only vary by an inch or two, but to fully understand the effect, compare a much wider handgrip to a much narrower one. With your hands very close together you will find it difficult to accelerate, but relatively easy to maintain cruising speed, especially downwind. With hands widely spread you'll find it easy to accelerate, even when towing someone, and easier to paddle against wind or current, but keeping a

TIPS FOR CHANGING GEARS WITH YOUR FORWARD STROKE

- Widen your grip on the paddle to accelerate, and when under heavy load.
- Narrow your grip when maintaining speed and under light load.

comfortable cruising speed in easy conditions will be more challenging.

Using Technology

Getting a good, efficient forward stroke is a key to fully enjoying your kayak trips. But aside from taking an occasional forward-stroke class with an instructor to fine-tune your efficiency, working on the instructor's advice day to day, reading, and watching videos, there hasn't been a really good way to work on improvements on your own. After all, in your daily paddling you can't watch yourself paddle. But times are changing.

The Motionize Paddle and Motionize Edge both use a sensor on your paddle and another on your kayak to relay data to an app on your cell phone. They track your paddle movement through every stroke, catching your difficult-to-eradicate faults and advising you in real time. You can choose to get feedback audibly, or watch your stroke in real time as it appears on your cell phone, which you can mount in front of you. Not only that, the app stores your paddling information until you decide to discard it, so you can focus on one detail of your stroke, such as the catch, the paddle path, or the clean exit, and then sit down with your coffee afterward to figure out if and how you are improving your stroke.

The Motionize system uses a small sensor with rechargeable battery that clips to your paddle.

This picture shows the Motionize Paddle deck-mounted control panel and paddle-mounted sensor. Motionize Edge operates with two small sensors, plus your phone. You can see how fast and efficient your paddling is, how much distance you get from each stroke, how far you've traveled, and where you have been. If you prefer to work with a coach, you can share your data and get feedback from the coach about what to work on, even if that coach is on a different continent.

The kayak-mounted part may differ. One option has a deck mount that attaches under your deck bungees. This houses the kayak sensor, its own rechargeable battery, a waterproof speaker that can offer advice on your stroke when you choose that option, plus your cell phone in its waterproof case. The cell phone case mounts so you can watch the path of your stroke on the app in real time. A second, newer option does away with the display mount, instead using a small sensor that mounts easily on your kayak. You can still access your data and watch your stroke on your cell phone in a waterproof case in real time, or wait to analyze it later. This more compact solution is more readily portable, so you might use it more.

The app is easy to use. I just pick the paddle type and length I use (for example, general touring, 210 centimeters), the boat type (for example, touring, 17 feet, 24-inch beam), enter my weight and height, and off I go. If I paddle a different kayak, no matter: I just enter the new info. When my friend wants to try, I tap in his or her details, and it's ready to go.

How much information can you really get from using the system? Let's say you are curious about how much difference a slightly wider or narrower handgrip would make, or if changing the feather on the blade really will improve your stroke or speed. Or you wonder how much extra distance you can get per stroke using a wing paddle blade instead of a dihedral. The system offers a way to discover that level of detail. On the other hand, you may appreciate a constant reminder to start and finish your stroke earlier for better efficiency. It can do that too. There are many ways to use Motionize to tweak your performance. Of course, the unit is waterproof.

Reversing

Kayakers reverse to stop, to hold our position against wind or waves from behind, and for backing out of tight corners. We don't often have

reason to reverse for long if it is easier to turn around and paddle forward, so normally the back of the blade is used. In most cases this is less efficient than using the face, but for a few strokes it is fine. The advantage to using the back is that you will be ready to apply a different stroke without confusion when you need to, without switching your handgrip. But you will benefit by using the face if you need to reverse for a long distance.

As with the forward stroke, the paddle must be upright when you apply power. When reversing, apply power only when the blade reaches your hip and not before, and with the paddle close beside your hull.

To position the blade, slice it sideways from just behind your hip, or slide it into the water beside the hull behind you and let it sink into position as the kayak glides past. The former is a more effective method, but both work.

Once the blade is in position, push with the bottom hand, and pull with the top. Keep both arms straight to apply maximum power from your torso. Press with your offside foot, straightening that leg and relaxing your onside leg.

Look behind to see what is there. If you favor looking over one shoulder, alternate occasionally or you will have a blind spot.

You will need to steer with your paddle, as neither rudder nor skeg will help when you reverse.

KEY POINTS FOR REVERSING

- Use the back of the blade to move in reverse.
- Slice the blade into position.
- Apply power when the paddle is upright.
- Press with the offside foot.
- Look behind.

Best raise your skeg, and center or lift your rudder. Steer by trailing the blade, face to the bow in neutral, then engaging the face or the back.

Steering

A kayak will not always go straight when you want it to. It is worth perfecting your steering technique otherwise keeping straight may unduly slow you down.

Steering When Paddling Forward

You must understand how your kayak moves in relation to the water before you can steer. Moving forward creates pressure against the bow as it pushes water apart. Low pressure and turbulence is created at the stern, where water refills the space where the kayak has passed. This difference in water pressure between the front and the back of the kayak means the bow is held steady while the stern can more easily wander sideways.

With few exceptions, it is the stern moving sideways that sends you off course, so you can correct by steering at the stern. This is the case in all boats, which is why a rudder is invariably placed at the stern of a boat, not at the bow. Neither a rudder at the bow nor a paddle stroke at the bow is sufficient to steer a boat or kayak when it wanders off course. All your correction strokes need to be made at the stern. The paddle blade can be used as a rudder to steer at the stern: This technique is called a stern rudder.

Stern Rudder

The stern rudder is used primarily to steer your kayak straight when it wanders off course. It is not the best way to make a turn. A stern rudder can be added to the end of a forward stroke to adjust your course when your kayak weathercocks. It is useful for steering downwind or running down a wave.

Here are three positions for the blade, each with a different effect on your kayak, followed by some useful variations.

Blade Alignment for a Basic Stern Rudder

Let your kayak drift past the active blade until the blade trails edge-up in neutral alongside the stern. Bring your offside hand across your deck to a position low over the water on the onside.

Straighten both arms and turn the palm of your onside hand toward the water. This turns the face of the active blade on edge with the face toward the hull. Hold your blade in neutral with the face perpendicular to the water surface, aligned toward the hull.

Held steady, your blade will now act as a skeg to help your kayak track straight. Minimize the drag on your blade. Keep your kayak upright, not edged.

From this position you can steer either way using mostly your front hand (the hand nearest the front of your kayak). Bring your front hand in toward your deck until the back of your blade engages, and hold the position to steer you toward your paddle. That is to the right when your paddle is on the right, as illustrated. Push your front hand far out from the side of your kayak until your blade face engages, and hold that position to steer from the paddle. That is to the left when the paddle is used on the right, as illustrated.

You can also steer using mainly your back hand (the hand nearest the stern of your kayak). From neutral position, angle the top edge of the blade a little farther from your kayak than the lower edge to steer toward the paddle. That is to the right if the paddle is on the right. Bring the upper blade edge toward your kayak by a few degrees to steer from the paddle. That is to the left when your paddle is on the right. Don't forget to think about

general direction of travel ⬆

Steer by engaging the face or back of the blade, or by holding the blade in neutral position.

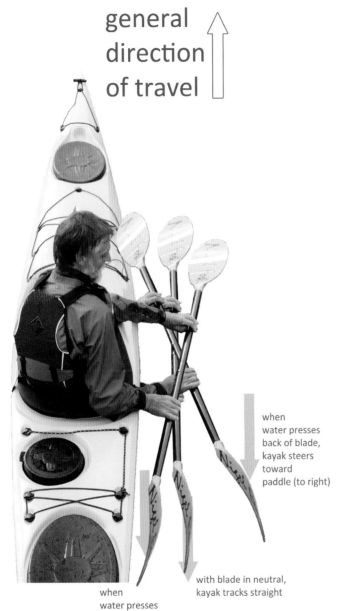

when water presses back of blade, kayak steers toward paddle (to right)

with blade in neutral, kayak tracks straight

when water presses face of blade, kayak steers away from paddle (to left)

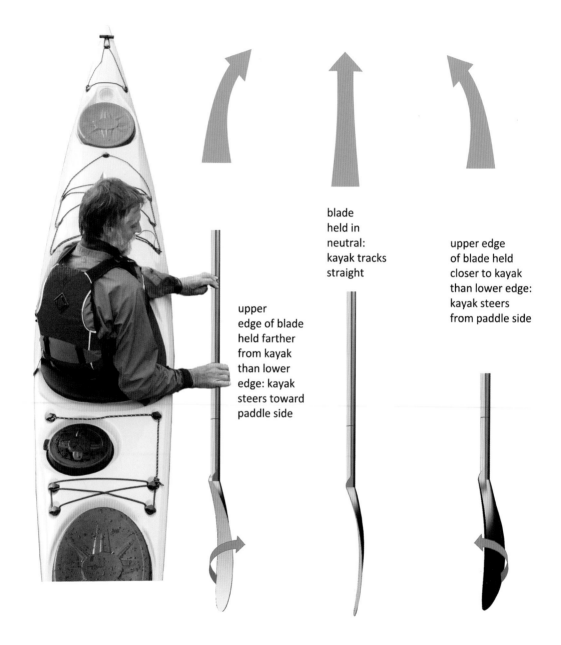

upper
edge of blade
held farther
from kayak
than lower
edge: kayak
steers toward
paddle side

blade
held in
neutral:
kayak tracks
straight

upper edge
of blade held
closer to kayak
than lower edge:
kayak steers
from paddle side

You can also steer by rotating the blade face a few degrees to either side from neutral.

Holding the paddle parallel to the kayak, you can apply a stern rudder by rotating the shaft to position the upper edge of the blade closer, farther, or the same distance from the kayak as the lower edge.

which face of the blade is engaged to achieve each result.

Edging with a Stern Rudder

Edging plays a significant part in the stern rudder. Sit the kayak upright when the blade is in neutral to track straight. To correct your course a little to the left, edge your kayak down a little to the right, and vice versa.

Variations on the Stern Rudder

The low-to-water stern rudder positions work well for steering, but a better position is used to blend into a stern rudder from a forward stroke, or from a bow rudder (see page 70), to maintain a course across the wind, or on a wave, or to maneuver around obstacles. In this high position, the face of the blade is engaged.

Keep your top hand at shoulder height at the end of a forward stroke, and push across your chest until your arm extends straight out across the water nearly perpendicular to your kayak. You will need to rotate your torso to get into this position. Bend your onside elbow to rest against your

Edge from your turn when using a stern rudder. Combine all the stern rudder elements for the greatest effect.

BASIC POINTS FOR STEERING

- When moving forward, steer at the stern. When reversing, steer at the bow.
- For a basic stern rudder, trail the paddle blade in neutral with the blade on edge and the blade face toward the hull.
- Pull or push against the blade to steer.
- Engage the blade face to steer away from the paddle. Engage the back of the blade to steer toward the paddle.
- Edge your kayak away from the direction steered.

hip and swing your hand back until your forearm is perpendicular to the kayak.

Find the neutral blade position with your top arm not yet fully extended over the water, and the forearm of your rear hand horizontal. Eliminate

Use a stern rudder on the downstream side, blade face engaged, to prevent turning when you cross an eddy line.

The stern rudder is used here to steer toward the camera, to prevent the current from turning the kayak.

Hold the stern rudder until the stern leaves the eddy.

pressure from both blade face and back. This is a version of the straight-steering position described previously. To steer straight, hold your kayak upright.

You can now steer away from the paddle (use the blade on the left side to steer right) by extending your top arm a little more, until it is straight at shoulder height, which engages the face of the blade and, while keeping your other elbow against your hip, by raising your rear hand until your forearm slopes upward to your hand. Your blade should now be positioned with the neck of the blade farther from the kayak than the tip, and with the upper edge closer to the kayak than the lower edge. Edge your kayak down toward your paddle.

When crossing from an eddy, the main current hitting the bow should turn the kayak to the right, as in the image. A stern rudder on the downstream side (the right) is used to prevent that turn, angling the kayak into a ferry glide across the current instead. Blade position: The top-hand shoulder should be high; the top arm extended over the water, and the face of the blade should be lightly engaged. The kayak is edged toward paddle, away from current. Note the torso-rotated position.

Note: if you keep your top arm fully extended in this position, but gently lower it toward the water, the blade angle should change toward neutral. Starting in neutral with your arm low, you should be able to increasingly engage the blade face as you raise your straightened arm. It is useful to practice this, because when the face of the blade is engaged, it is all too easy to relax by dropping and bending your top arm. The effect is to drop into neutral, and once past neutral to engage the back of the blade, which steers you in the opposite direction. When this happens the solution is to lift the top arm again to shoulder height and straighten it, pushing out perpendicular from the kayak. The lower hand can then fine-tune the blade angle if necessary.

To deliberately steer in the opposite direction, drop your top hand to your lap and lift your on-side elbow from your hip to engage the back of the blade. The neck of the blade should now be closer to the kayak than the tip, and the upper blade edge should be farther from the kayak than the lower edge. As you turn toward the paddle, edge away from it.

To familiarize yourself with what happens to the blade during a stern rudder, walk along a dock trailing your paddle in the water parallel to the dock in the neutral position. For the blade to track straight, your front hand must be as far from the side of the dock as your blade. By holding the shaft with the front hand only, and loosening your grip, the blade will naturally find this neutral position when the blade is completely on edge.

Now rotate the shaft slightly until the upper edge of the blade is slightly farther from the dock than the lower edge. As you walk forward the blade will swing toward the dock.

If you trail the paddle with the upper edge of the blade closer to the dock than the lower edge, the blade will swing from the dock. When you hold the paddle in both hands to prevent any sideways movement of the blade as you walk, you will feel the sideways pull.

You see the same effect if you trail your blade across sand or grass, but you will need to mark out a straight line to follow.

With a stern rudder, these sideways forces pull or push your stern sideways depending on whether you angle the top edge of the blade a few degrees from or toward your kayak.

A kayaker "steers" a paddle across grass.

Which Version of Stern Rudder Should I Use?

Both the low- and high-angle stern rudders work well, although the high version offers more powerful correction and the most stability. I tend to use the low version when riding waves downwind. I trail the blade in neutral on one side of the kayak as soon as I catch a wave, and in this relaxed position I can steer without switching sides.

I use the higher version to counter weather-cocking when tracking straight across the wind, using it on the upwind side to gain the greatest stability. I use the high position in combination with other strokes for maneuvering.

But the positions are interchangeable. If you have difficulty getting into the high position to steer away from the paddle, maybe for reasons of torso flexibility or arm length, no matter; use the low version instead.

Instructors often encourage stern rudder positions that engage the blade face rather than the back, because when using the back of the blade

STEERING MAIN POINTS FOR AN ALTERNATE STYLE

- Trail the blade in neutral, on edge. Face toward the hull, kayak upright; your paddle acts as a skeg, and the kayak tracks straight.
- Keep both hands low over the water in neutral position.
- Moving your front hand to your lap engages the back of the blade; the kayak turns toward the paddle.
- Lifting your front hand to shoulder height and pushing out over the water perpendicular to the kayak engages the blade face; the kayak turns from the paddle.
- Edge the kayak away from each turn.

there is a tendency to use a reverse sweep at the stern to straighten up, instead of using a stern rudder. There is a big difference. Each reverse sweep will slow you quite a lot, while a stern rudder slows you very little. Think of it in this way: If you make ten stern sweep corrections, you will probably be ten paddle strokes behind where you would be if you had used a stern rudder instead.

Steering Using a Rudder

The usual way to use a rudder with foot pedal control is to press with the right foot to turn right, and press with the left foot to turn left. A control bar running from side to side of the kayak, with a pivot point in the center, is controlled with the feet. A T-bar rudder has a control stick that extends between your feet. Swing the tiller stick of the T bar left to turn left.

Reversing with a rudder is easiest when the rudder is in its center position; steer using your paddle at the bow.

Your kayak will naturally swing a little from side to side even when steering with a rudder, especially when there are waves. It is okay to let it do this. Loosen up and you'll find steering more relaxing. When you do nothing to correct this natural movement, your kayak will swing back again. Minimize the amount you need to correct, and your rudder blade will create less drag. After a while you will sense when you need to correct and when you don't.

Timing and good technique are essential when launching and landing through dumping waves, Brighton, England

Flat Water
Skills 2

Working on balance on a modular sit-on-top kayak, Shanghai, China.

From balance to edged turns and moving sideways.

Balance

Balance in a kayak improves the more you push the boundaries. The following exercises can be used to gradually improve balance over time. You may not see huge improvements immediately, but if you keep practicing, you will improve.

Start on flat water. Sit on your back deck and paddle forward with your feet in the water. If you feel sufficiently balanced, try lifting your feet to the surface, and then eventually out of the water altogether. Then try paddling with your feet on your seat.

To improve balance, try paddling while sitting on your back deck with your feet in the water.

Try standing in your kayak. Begin by sitting on your rear deck with your feet on your seat. Lean forward to grasp the front of the cockpit, roll your weight forward over your feet, and stand, letting go of the cockpit. Keep your eyes on the horizon and stretch your arms out to either side. Sit down by gradually, bending your knees until you sit on the back deck, and lift your feet into the water.

The One-Arm Outrigger Position

You can use your paddle for assistance when standing in your kayak. Rest the paddle shaft across one elbow with the blade behind you and

Use your paddle to aid balance while standing in your kayak.

your hand gripping the shaft. Extend your paddle to that side until the blade behind you is almost at your elbow. Roll your elbow until the hand gripping the shaft is in a downward pushing position,

Try standing on your rear deck.

WOBBLING AND BALANCE CONTROL

When first trying to balance in your kayak, you may wobble a lot. Wobbling is caused by a *feedback loop:* You feel the kayak tip to one side, and respond by overcompensating toward the other side. As soon as you feel the kayak tipping to that side, you overcompensate in the other direction, and the cycle repeats. The movement is quick and automatic, so you feel out of control because you are not consciously making any balance adjustments.

Although the unconscious process is quick, it does take time for a message that you are tipping to travel the neural pathways to the brain, where the information is processed, before a message is sent back to the muscles to react. The slower the messages travel, and the slower the information is processed, the more dramatic the wobbling becomes.

Your brain learns by trial and error. It sends out a message to the muscles to react, and then monitors the result. If the result was not right, it sends another message, and the loop repeats. The more you use the same neural pathways, the quicker the messages travel, the quicker your brain responds, and the smaller the adjustments needed to keep balance. This means the more often you challenge your stability and balance, the more stable and balanced you become.

It takes even more time to feel stable sitting on the back deck. Your improvement will show only after you push the boundaries. Paddling in choppy water, for example, will challenge your balance, but by paddling regularly in choppy water, your balance will improve. After successfully sitting on your back deck, you will feel that much steadier when you sit down in your kayak.

When you are challenged by a change in conditions and your kayak starts wobbling from side to side, it is useful to break the feedback circuit by deliberately taking one knee out of contact with the deck, and pressing only with the other. This reduces your body's ability to make big compensations, because your knees cause the biggest wobbling feedback loops. When standing in your kayak or on a paddle board, the equivalent solution would be to rest most of your weight on one leg.

rather than in a downward pulling position. With a spoon, wing, or flat curve blade, turn the extended blade so the back contacts the water. With a dihedral paddle, use the face. If you are not sure what type of paddle you have, see the section in Equipment Detailed on the paddle (page 270). Gently scull backward and forward across the surface for support, keeping the leading edge slightly raised. Once you can maintain the movement while standing up, this sculling action will help you balance.

More challenging: Once standing on your seat, turn around to face the stern, and then turn again to face forward. More gymnastic individuals can try a handstand on a kayak.

All of these exercises require more skill when there are waves. Be careful standing in wind. If you fall, your kayak will blow away from you. It is best

Falling in the water offers the opportunity to practice rescues or self-rescues.

Try standing in your kayak with the help of others.

to practice near shore with an onshore wind, so you can follow your kayak to shore.

The object of these exercises is to improve your balance in normal kayaking. The exercises should be fun, and as they encourage you to fall into the water, they offer an opportunity to practice solo or assisted rescues. They also improve your agility, confidence, and balance. Check the water for hazards before you start. Practice in deep water, without rocks or other hazards.

Edging

Edging is heeling the kayak (holding one gunwale higher than the other) within the body balance you can maintain without your paddle. Leaning is heeling beyond that point of balance. Edge by lifting one hip and curving your upper body toward that hip: If you lean beyond the balance point you will tip.

Kayakers frequently use edging as a way to change the handling characteristics of the hull. For example, it is usually easier to turn a sea kayak or a touring kayak when it is held on edge, rather than when upright. Leaning is used less often for the same purpose. There are several ways to hold an edge.

For this exercise, lightly hold or touch a dock or another kayak as a safety precaution—only to prevent capsizing, not to maintain balance.

Begin by sitting upright, with the top of your head directly above your tailbone. To edge your kayak, shift your weight onto one hip and lift the

SOME BALANCE EXERCISES

- Start on flat water. Sit on the deck with your feet in the water.
- Sit on the deck with your feet out of the water.
- Stand in your kayak.
- Use your extended paddle for balance assistance.
- Paddle forward in each position.
- Progress to choppy water.

Edging is holding one side of the kayak higher than the other. You do not have to edge far to make a difference to how a kayak handles.

other hip. Your head should now be centered above your low-side hip, instead of above your tailbone.

Edge until you lose balance, and right yourself by pressing down on the dock or kayak you are using for help. Identify the final balance point—the farthest you can edge without tipping. Note where the water reaches on the side of your kayak for a visual reference, or use your fingers to find where the water reaches. Practice finding a happy medium, edging approximately halfway between upright and maximum edge.

To help hold your kayak on edge, compare the effect of using these three leg positions in turn, each with your feet firmly in contact with the foot braces.

- Keep both knees bent up to lock into the knee braces or against the deck.
- Keep one knee pressed up against the deck (the one on the higher side of the kayak), and the other leg pressed down against the hull.
- Keep both knees out of contact with the deck.

You should find one of these positions more comfortable, or more effective, for holding the kayak steady. Compare the effectiveness of each leg position with the kayak fully edged—the farthest you can hold steady without wobbling.

All three leg positions are valid and common ways to help control balance with a kayak on edge, so use whichever offers the best control. Your favorite may vary with the kayak used and with the situation.

Fine-Tune Your Edge Control

Analyze your edge control to figure out exactly what you need to do with your knee, foot, leg, hip, and body. While edged, compare the effect of tucking your chin into one shoulder, and then tucking it into the other. Try pressing the leg on the lower side of the kayak down against the hull, and compare to when the leg is close to or touching the deck and passive (not engaged).

Try engaging and then completely disengaging the knee on the lower side of the kayak. Try pulling upward more assertively with the knee on the higher side of the kayak, and rotating your torso so that knee pulls up toward your sternum and your torso pulls down toward your knee. These nuances can accentuate your balance control.

Vary How You Edge

Many of the moves described in this book work best when the kayak is edged. Most only need the halfway-edged position. When trying these moves, experiment to find the leg and body positions that give you the most control, comfort, and confidence. You may favor a certain leg position for a particular maneuver.

Be aware that your choice is personal, and that someone else may find a different position works best in a certain situation. We are all different shapes and sizes, and we use different kayaks, seats, and paddles with different levels of confidence, so it would be surprising if this were

---

BASIC POINTS FOR EDGING

- To edge, shift your weight onto one hip and lift the other.
- Assist with your legs. For example, straighten the low one and push it down, or bend the other and push the knee up.
- Bend your upper body inboard to maintain balance while your kayak sits on edge.
- Rotate your torso and pull your sternum toward your upside knee.

not the case. Get used to making your own value judgments, and reevaluate and fine-tune them as your skills develop. If you are hesitant to edge your kayak, then edge it just a little. A nominal degree of edge when you practice maneuvers will get you used to the body position, and in time you'll gain confidence. It is more important to hold a steady edge than to edge a lot.

Braces, Support Strokes, and Recovery Strokes

Here are ways to use your paddle to help you keep in balance, maintain a position that is out of balance, or recover lost balance.

Braces

Using your paddle in a static position to help you maintain balance is called a *brace*. When edging, to improve a turn moving forward or in reverse, kayakers often rest the back of the blade on the water to help in balance. This is called a low brace. If, instead, the face of the blade is against the water, it is called a high brace. If the paddle were to

The back of the blade on the water is used to stabilize an edged kayak. This is a low brace.

disappear while bracing, the kayak would still be in balance. Braces help maintain balance, rather than recover balance.

Support Strokes

You can support yourself above or in the water with your paddle, even if you lean beyond the tipping point. In this situation, the paddle is all that keeps you in position; if it were to disappear, you would overturn. The technique is called a *support stroke*. Because it is difficult to push down on the back of the blade when you are off balance, a support stroke is almost always a pulling-down position, using the blade face against the water.

The blade must also move in relation to the water—otherwise it will sink, and you will follow. If your kayak is not moving, you will need to scull the blade across the surface to create the necessary lift.

If your kayak is moving forward, you can hold your paddle still and brace with the blade skimming the surface.

You can also change a brace to a support stroke when your kayak is being pushed sideways by a broken surf wave and your body is off balance; the blade moves shoulder-first across the water surface, providing lift to keep you from capsizing. But if the wave stops pushing you sideways, you will

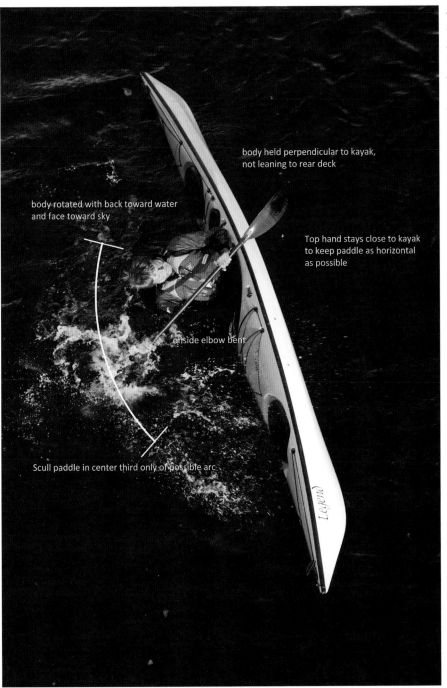

Sculling back and forth across the water surface with the face of the blade can hold the body; this is sculling for support. A recovery stroke must be used to regain balance. joelrogers.com

body held perpendicular to kayak, not leaning to rear deck

body rotated with back toward water and face toward sky

Top hand stays close to kayak to keep paddle as horizontal as possible

onside elbow bent

Scull paddle in center third only of possible arc

This static brace is really a support stroke, not a brace, unless the paddle is unnecessary.

find yourself unsupported, off balance, and likely to fall in. It is better to use an in-balance high or low brace while being pushed sideways.

The so-called *static brace,* in which the flotation of the paddle plus the flotation of the paddler's upper body combine to support the paddler at the water's surface, is technically a support stroke, not a brace, unless the paddler can maintain that position without the support of the paddle.

SUMMARY POINTS FOR SUPPORT STROKES

- **In a support stroke the paddler is held beyond the balance point by the paddle.**
- **Make sure your arms are in a pulling position.**
- **Use the face of the blade.**

Recovery Strokes

If you are using a support stroke, you will need to recover your balance eventually by using a *recovery stroke.*

Recovery strokes have two parts: what you do with your paddle, and what you do with your body. If you edge until you just lose balance, you can push the back of your paddle blade against the water to bring yourself upright again. This is called a *low recovery.*

But if you lean over until your body is just above the water, you must turn the blade face down, bring your elbow beneath the paddle shaft, and pull down to bring your body upright. Pulling down on the face of the blade to recover balance is called a *high recovery.*

With both the low and high recovery, the best position for the paddle is as low and flat to the water surface as possible.

Low Recovery

If you edge until you are just out of balance and simply rest your weight on your paddle, the paddle will sink and you will fall in. You need to bring yourself back into balance before the blade sinks. Do this by turning your head and torso to face the paddle, and lean your head down. Bring the hip, thigh, and knee on the low side of your kayak up toward your head and push down with your offside hip. This brings your kayak sideways and under you. You can practice this movement in slow motion sitting on the floor at home, but it is typically a quick movement.

High Recovery with Sideways Tuck

The body movement to recover from lying on the water has another stage. As you fall onto the water, twist so your back hits the water, with your body perpendicular to your kayak. This offers the most resistance, slowing the capsize, if not stopping it. You can add to that resistance by bringing your paddle blade face-down and flat onto the water, with your paddle perpendicular to your kayak and

SUMMARY POINTS FOR THE HIGH RECOVERY WITH SIDEWAYS TUCK

- Start with your back flat on water, looking up.
- Your body should be perpendicular to the kayak.
- The blade face should be down on the surface.
- Your arm should be in pull-down position.
- Paddle as horizontally as possible. Paddle perpendicular to the kayak.
- Your offside hand should be against the kayak by the offside thigh.
- Pull down on the paddle.
- Roll your head and shoulder forward from face up to face down.
- Pull your onside thigh toward your head and push the offside thigh away.
- Pull the paddle blade closer.
- Finish, then turn blade over into a low brace to keep balance.

as horizontal as possible. The elbow of your onside arm should be bent and underneath your paddle so you can pull down. Your offside hand should be touching the cockpit near your upper thigh, and it should stay in contact throughout the recovery. Your torso should rest on the water chest up, perpendicular to your kayak, not leaning back.

The moment you have stopped your fall, pull down on the paddle to start your recovery. Immediately begin rolling your offside shoulder forward, together with your head. Your head should roll along the surface from face up to face down, and your shoulders from chest up to chest down, while you raise your onside thigh and hip toward your head. Push away with your offside hip.

Because your kayak will roll sideways, away from your paddle, pull your onside elbow toward your hip as you raise your hip and thigh toward your face, keeping your paddle blade close to you. This will prevent overextending your arm. As a benefit, the blade movement adds lift.

Finally, turn the blade on its back into the low brace position to help keep you in balance until you are ready to continue paddling.

The Laying-Forward Body Finish

This variation starts as described above, but instead of bringing your head beside your thigh, bring it a little farther forward, to exit the water closer to your knee. Your chest will be lying on your spray deck and your head on your foredeck.

This shows the forward finish body position.

High Recovery with a Lie-back

An alternative is the lie-back method. Start with your body lying perpendicular to your kayak, face down, with your paddle face down, also perpendicular to your kayak. Pull down on your paddle and roll your head and shoulders face up. Push up against the deck with your onside hip, compressing your torso. Push away with your offside hip, extending your torso on your offside. As the kayak turns deck up, arch your back over the rear deck, and swing your body back into alignment with your hips. The back of your head should leave the water last, sliding sideways over the rear deck.

Tip: Try not to lie-back before you rotate your kayak upright. Your body can exert more twist

SUMMARY POINTS: HIGH RECOVERY WITH LIE-BACK

- Start face down on the water, with both shoulders to the water.
- Paddle perpendicular to the kayak.
- Position your offside hand against the kayak by the offside thigh.
- Your blade should be face down at the surface.
- Your arm should be in pull-down position, and your body perpendicular to the kayak.
- Pull down on the blade.
- Roll your head and shoulders from face down to face up.
- Pull up against the deck with your onside hip.
- Push away with your offside hip.
- When the deck is up, swing your body back over the rear deck.
- Pull the blade closer.
- Bring your head over the deck last, face up, with an arched back.
- Finish by sitting up, and turn your blade over into a low brace.
- Scull for support using the back of the blade.

when it is perpendicular to the kayak than when it is lying along the kayak.

Finishing a roll in the lie-back position tends to impact your back against the back of the cockpit. As it is always the same part of your back that hits, you risk impact injury. Arching your back to lift yourself from your seat during a roll can mitigate this, and custom fitting a shaped foam block behind the seat can help by spreading the load. Otherwise, the sure way to avoid this kind of injury is to avoid the lie-back option.

Sculling for Support Using the Back of the Blade
You can use the low brace to maintain balance when making turns on the move by skimming the back of the blade across the water. The blade moving across the water offers a lot more support than it would if it were not moving. When your kayak is not moving, you can create the same lift by skimming the blade forward and back across the water. This is called sculling for support.

The blade movement should create minimal water disturbance. You can demonstrate the effectiveness of slightly different blade angles if you lightly hold the end of one blade and skim the other in a wide arc across the water. The blade will stall if the angle is too steep, and depending on blade design, it may dive if the angle is too shallow. With a good angle the blade should skim freely.

Sculling for support with the back of the blade is typically used when the kayak is more or less upright, so you can keep your elbow higher than the paddle with the blade on or near the surface. Racing kayakers in tippy kayaks scull gently with the back of the blade to ensure stability when at standstill. Sea kayakers make use of the technique when at a standstill on unsettled water.

Use the blade in the middle third of the possible arc from bow to stern. This keeps the blade farther from the kayak, offering the greatest leverage. Keep your onside elbow bent and higher than the paddle so you can press down when you need to, and keep your offside hand as low as possible, near your belly button.

Sculling for Support Using the Face of the Blade
Sculling for support with the face of the blade, with your elbow below your paddle in a pulling position, is used to recover balance when a high recovery is not sufficient. It is often the basis of a roll.

With your body face up on the water and perpendicular to your kayak, scull the paddle blade in just the central third of the possible arc from bow to stern. With a light downward pull on the paddle, roll from your back to face down while bringing your kayak upright. Keep your onside elbow close to your torso and your offside hand low to your spray deck. Regain balance looking down into the water close to your cockpit and just in front of your arm. Flip your paddle face up into a low brace to finish in balance.

SUMMARY: SCULLING FOR SUPPORT

- **With your blade almost flat on the surface, skim in an arc forward and back. The leading edge of the blade should be lifted slightly higher than trailing edge in each direction.**
- **The back of the blade is in contact, typically, for maintaining balance.**
- **The face of the blade is in contact, typically, for recovering balance.**
- **Keep your offside hand by the offside thigh.**

SECTION SUMMARY FOR BRACES, SUPPORT STROKES, AND RECOVERY STROKES

- **A brace uses a static paddle position against the water to aid balance.**
- **A low brace uses the back of the blade.**
- **A high brace uses the blade face.**
- **Support strokes use a moving blade to hold you beyond the balance point without capsize.**
- **Recovery strokes bring you back into balance.**
- **Sculling can be used to keep the blade at the surface even under load.**
- **All the techniques described in this section benefit from a loose handgrip for greater sensitivity to blade alignment.**

Turning

It is most logical to start with the sweep stroke, although there are many ways to turn a kayak. Acquiring a wide repertoire is worthwhile, so you can match the best method to each situation. I divide turns into two sections: those you can perform when your kayak is stopped, and those to use when you are moving forward or in reverse.

Turning While Stopped

You can use three different types of turn to maneuver your kayak when it is stopped. The first, the sweep stroke, is the most widely used and its component parts have many applications. It is also the easiest to learn.

For the second, the draw stroke, you will need to first master the draw stroke as described in the

Moving Sideways section (page 76) before applying it to turning.

The third, spinning on the spot using a "stirring" stroke, is the most complex, but it is a wonderful skill that offers fine control particularly in a variety of rough water situations. As with all control skills, it pays to practice plenty on flat water.

Sweep Stroke

The sweep stroke is the best known for turning. The forward sweep uses the face of the blade in an arc from the front to back of your kayak. It pulls the kayak forward, hence "forward" sweep.

The reverse sweep uses the back of the blade in an arc from the back to the front of your kayak. It pushes the kayak into reverse, thus reverse sweep. You can turn on the spot, pivoting around the midpoint of your kayak, by alternating between a forward sweep on one side of the kayak and a reverse sweep on the other.

From where you sit in the kayak it seems as though the blade moves in an arc, but it is the kayak that needs to move.

The Forward Sweep

Edge your kayak and perform the forward sweep on the low side of the kayak.

Start with your blade flat against the hull near the bow, blade face outward, and finish with the blade lying flat against the hull behind you, with the blade face inward. Through the midpoint of the sweep keep your paddle low and wide, with your offside hand near your belly button.

Push with your onside foot against the foot brace.

Rotate your torso through the stroke.

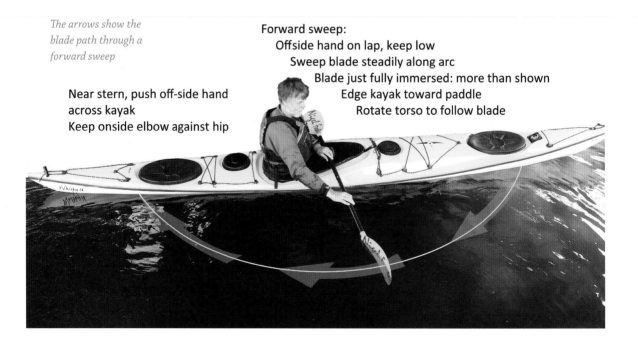

The arrows show the blade path through a forward sweep

Forward sweep:
Offside hand on lap, keep low
Sweep blade steadily along arc
Blade just fully immersed: more than shown
Edge kayak toward paddle
Rotate torso to follow blade

Near stern, push off-side hand across kayak
Keep onside elbow against hip

KEY POINTS FOR THE FORWARD SWEEP

- Edge your kayak toward the stroke.
- The blade face grabs water throughout.
- Start with the back of the blade flat against the bow and the offside hand low.
- Push with the onside foot.
- Rotate your torso.
- The offside hand stays near your belly button to midstroke.
- From midstroke, move your onside elbow to the hip, and your top hand pushes across the kayak. The top hand finishes extended over the water, perpendicular to kayak.
- Finish with the blade face toward the kayak near the stern.
- Skim the blade forward face up to repeat the sweep as needed.
- To fine-tune the turn, eliminate turbulence.
- Aim to move the kayak rather than the paddle.
- Sweep wide; the closer to the kayak the blade sweeps, the less turn you'll get.
- Alternate a forward sweep on one side with a reverse sweep on the other to turn on the spot.

Skim your blade forward into position for next sweep
Use blade to maintain balance while you hold your edge

Use the back of the blade for balance while repositioning for the next forward sweep.

Through the last third of the arc, keep your onside elbow at your hip, but not behind it, and push your top hand across your kayak. Your hand should finish above the water on the onside.

Pay attention to how hard you pull on the paddle. Your blade should be steady in the water, just below the borderline of turbulence or noise, moving as little as possible while you pull against it. It feels as if you pull the paddle in a semicircle.

Lift your blade out edge-first when it nears the side of the hull behind you.

If you need more than one sweep to complete your turn, either follow the forward sweep with a reverse sweep on the opposite side, which keeps your kayak turning more or less on the spot, or repeat the forward sweep, which propels your kayak forward while it turns.

To repeat the forward sweep, lift the blade partly from the water at the end of your sweep and push forward with a loose handgrip. The blade will trip onto its back. Fine-tune the planing angle of the blade so it skims smoothly across the water, retracing the semicircle of the sweep. Keep your elbow higher than your paddle shaft so you can press down as necessary to keep in balance. If you maintain your edge, your kayak will continue to turn between sweeps.

When your blade reaches the bow, grab the water again to start your next sweep.

The Reverse Sweep

Rotate, bringing your whole paddle low over the water parallel to your kayak. Place the back of the blade in the water, face to the hull, near the stern.

To reverse sweep use the back of the blade to push steadily out from the stern in a semicircle to the bow.

KEY POINTS FOR THE REVERSE SWEEP

- **Start with the blade face to the side of kayak behind you and the top hand extended over the water perpendicular to the kayak.**
- **Edge your kayak toward the stroke. The back of the blade pushes.**
- **Push with your offside foot.**
- **Push out in semicircle, shallow and wide.**
- **Your offside hand is at your belly button midstroke.**
- **The blade finishes close to the side of the kayak near the bow. The back of the blade is toward the kayak.**
- **Skim the blade backward, face down, to repeat the sweep as needed.**
- **To fine-tune, eliminate turbulence.**
- **The kayak moves, not the paddle.**
- **Sweep wide and shallow.**

Edge toward your paddle and push the blade out in a semicircle to the front. At the midpoint your offside hand should be in front of your belly button. Push with your offside foot.

If you repeat the reverse sweep to turn on the spot, turn your blade face down at the bow and skim it back to the stern, at a planing angle in a high brace position. Keep your onside elbow lower than the paddle so you can pull down if needed to maintain good balance. Keep a loose grip on the paddle so you can better feel the water pressure against the blade to fine-tune the planing angle. At the midpoint of the skim, your offside hand should be low, near your belly button.

Fine-Tune Your Edge

Edging toward the active side in both forward and reverse sweeps is the optimal way to make repeated sweeps on the same side. The kayak will start moving, and the trailing end will be edged appropriately to allow skidding. When switching sides with each sweep to turn on the spot, you will get a more effective turn if you edge away from the first part of a forward sweep, and then edge toward the last part of a forward sweep, switching edges mid-sweep. Likewise, you will get the most effective turn when you edge from the first part of a reverse sweep and toward the last part. This allows each end, in turn, to skid freely.

The difference between holding a single edge throughout a whole sweep, and switching edge mid-sweep while turning on the spot is most noticeable in a straight-tracking kayak, while in a flat-hulled, maneuverable kayak you will see very little difference.

Refinements to the Sweep Stroke

The full sweep may be divided into three sections, the front, middle, and back, each taking a third of the full arc. It is useful to work on each part in isolation because single parts are used for certain applications.

Bow Section of a Forward Sweep

In the first section, pull the blade sideways from the hull to move the bow sideways. The effect should be like a bow thruster on a ship, where a propeller in the bow aims sideways to push the bow sideways to or from a dock. To perfect this part of the sweep, repeat the first twelve inches of the sweep, lifting the blade out immediately to reposition for the next. Start each short sweep with the blade flat against the hull and pull it away

KEY POINTS FOR THE BOW SECTION OF THE FORWARD SWEEP

- Start with the back of the blade flat against the bow.
- Pull the blade sideways from the hull, not back.
- Make this a short movement only, and then repeat.
- Keep your offside hand close to your body.
- To fine-tune, experiment to find the best edging solution.

sideways, rather than back toward you. Your off-side hand should be close against your body.

The point is to push the bow sideways without much effect on the stern, so try this with someone immobilizing your stern while you move the bow.

You can use this part of the sweep to your advantage if you want to turn the bow into the wind. It will work even when you have no forward speed. It anchors the bow, while the wind continues to blow the stern. Several short strokes at the bow are more effective for this purpose than a full sweep stroke. In this case edge your kayak toward the paddle side, which unlocks your stern and allows the wind to blow it more freely.

Midsection of a Forward Sweep

A midsection sweep stroke works on both the bow and stern. It is a powerful part of the arc and one in which the paddler feels balanced. This is the part of the sweep you might use to initiate a turn when moving forward.

The Stern Section of Forward Sweep (Modified Version)

The last third of a sweep is a crucial maneuver, and is used to keep a kayak on track in quartering seas and tailwinds. It is used a lot for steering when the kayak is moving forward.

The stern section of a standard forward sweep requires more torso flexibility than many paddlers can achieve. It is also difficult to complete if you have contact with a full back support. Without full torso rotation, there is a tendency to either bring your onside elbow behind your hip, which puts your shoulder in a vulnerable position, or to lift your elbow, which flattens the blade so it ceases to grab water through the last third of the sweep. Both result in an ineffective stroke at the stern.

I prefer to modify the final part of a sweep stroke into something closer to a draw stroke. At the midpart of the sweep, your onside elbow should be level with your hip, and your offside hand near your belly button. Bring your onside elbow in to touch your hip. It will stay in contact here until the end of the stroke. As you continue to sweep, work simultaneously on three movements:

1. Push your offside hand out over the water, climbing steadily to reach shoulder height, with your arm fully extended and perpendicular to the kayak by the end of the sweep.

2. Straighten your onside leg and bend your off-side knee to aid torso rotation.

3. Incline your onside forearm above the height of your elbow, and swing it back as far as possible, keeping your elbow on your hip.

Your blade angle in the water should lift from low to high, finishing behind you and about a foot from the side of your kayak, with the upper blade edge slightly closer to the hull than the lower

For the modified finish to a forward sweep, push your top hand up to end at shoulder height out over the water perpendicular to the kayak. The active blade should now have the face engaged, in a high angle stern rudder position.

In comparison, the standard finish to a forward sweep stroke ends with both hands low to the water and torso fully rotated.

KEY POINTS TO THE MODIFIED STERN PORTION OF A FORWARD SWEEP

- The start position is midway along the kayak, out from its side.
- Keep a low shaft angle.
- The blade faces back.
- Your offside hand is at your belly button; your onside elbow is in, against your hip.
- To sweep, the offside hand pushes out over the water with a steady climb to shoulder height.
- Your torso rotates from neutral to fully rotated.
- Your onside elbow stays against your hip; your hand steadily pivots back and lifts.
- Straighten your onside leg and raise your offside knee.
- Edge toward the stroke.
- In the finish position, your torso is fully rotated.
- Your top arm is extended, straight, and perpendicular to the kayak.
- Your onside elbow is still at your hip.
- Your onside hand is higher than, and behind, your hip.
- The blade should be slightly open toward the bow. The trailing edge should be slightly closer to the kayak, the leading edge slightly out.
- The stroke finishes 1 foot from the side of the kayak. The finish position is the same as a stern rudder, with the face of the blade engaged.
- To refine the stroke, open your hands.
- At the end of the stroke, if the stern of the kayak skids toward the blade, drop into low brace position to avoid tripping.

edge. In other words, the blade is slightly open, face engaged, angled slightly down to the water. The blade face is visible from the bow, with the back hidden. Keep your kayak edged toward your sweep.

This end position is the same as in the high-angle stern rudder (page 31), with the face rather than the back of the blade engaged. This means that when you use the final third of a modified forward sweep to correct your direction in wind, you can hold your final position a moment or two longer for greater effect: This mode of the stern rudder steers your kayak in the same direction as the sweep.

Finally, fine-tune the effectiveness of the ending blade position. If the blade is too far forward, you will get reduced rudder effect, in which case you should move it farther toward the stern. Open or close the blade using the fingertips of your low hand until you find the optimum angle. Your blade should be slightly open: think 10 degrees to start. Even when you use the sweep on the move to aid tracking and hold the position, gradually opening your blade, your final blade angle should still be less than 45 degrees.

If you need a second sweep on the same side, lift both elbows and drop your hands to flatten the back of the blade to the water, and skim forward for your next sweep.

Turning with a Draw Stroke

For a draw stroke the blade enters the water upright at arm's reach, and you pull the kayak sideways toward the paddle. Start with the blade vertical in the water, away from the side of the kayak, and more or less level with your hip. The blade face should be toward the kayak, against the direction of the pull. You can find a more detailed explanation of the draw stroke on page 76.

To turn your kayak using a draw stroke, all you need to do is change the direction of pull and the blade alignment. Align your blade face toward your feet and pull the blade in that direction. The front end of your kayak should move toward your paddle. Recover the blade by turning the face toward you until it is edge-on to the starting position, and slice it back to repeat the draw stroke. This is a bow draw. Your bow swings around while your stern remains more or less in the same place.

In a similar way you can draw the blade in a line toward your rear deck. When recovering your blade, turn the face toward you. Drawing to the stern leaves your bow more or less stationary while your kayak swings around it. This is a stern draw.

You can achieve similar results using a sculling draw to the bow or to the stern.

Spin Stroke

It is possible to turn your kayak through 360 degrees using one blade only, keeping the blade in the water throughout the maneuver. Essentially, the stroke is a sequence of forward and reverse sweeps, but when the blade reaches the side of the kayak, instead of passing over, it passes underneath.

Begin with a bow draw. Pull the blade toward your feet. Then push your top hand across your kayak and out over the water on the onside, until it is farther from the kayak than your bottom hand. This should let you sweep your blade under the hull in a curve, taking it beyond the keel line of the kayak to the offside. This section of the stroke essentially completes the front half of a forward sweep on what is the offside, although the paddle shaft slopes beneath the hull, not over it.

At the midpoint, and at the pivot point of the kayak, where the paddle reaches across beneath your seat, rotate the paddle by rolling the palm of your top hand downward until you engage the back of the blade. Continue to sweep with the back of the blade toward the stern, until the blade emerges from beneath the hull in position to begin a reverse sweep on the onside.

Perform the first half of a reverse sweep on the onside. Once level with your hip again, drop your onside elbow, rotating the blade until the face is forward, and continue to sweep toward the bow to complete the second half of the reverse sweep (perhaps better described as a bow draw). This is where you started.

KEY POINTS FOR TURNING WITH A DRAW STROKE

- The start position is as for a standard draw stroke.
- Angle the blade toward a point forward or behind the typical draw stroke finish point.
- Draw the blade directly to that point.
- Recover, with the blade face toward the paddler.
- Repeat as needed.

KEY POINTS FOR THE SPIN STROKE

- The blade describes a circle relative to the kayak, with the center of circle as close to where you sit as possible.
- Engage the blade face when the blade is in front of you.
- Engage the back of the blade when the blade is behind you.
- Edge or not, depending on whether it improves your turn.
- Lean forward when the blade is back; lean back when the blade is forward.

Repeat the circle until you have turned your kayak through 360 degrees.

Experiment with your edging. By edging toward the bow-rudder section and from the reverse sweep section you may turn faster, but that will depend on your kayak. Some kayaks respond better when not edged.

Try leaning your body back when the blade is in front of you, and forward when your blade is behind. It helps to lighten the end you are trying to move, and anchor down the other. This is known as trim.

You can modify this maneuver to extend the effect of a bow rudder when turning on the move. Begin edging from a bow rudder. Power the blade into a sweep under your hull, reversing the blade under your seat and finishing the turn with the reverse sweep. Hold your kayak on the same edge throughout the turn. You should be able to achieve a 180-degree turn, which is as far as you would ordinarily need in either direction. It's a very fluent, effective controlled turn.

This is a useful stroke for solo canoe, where it originated.

Turning on the Move

We most often need to turn when we are already moving, either forward or in reverse. In this section the basics of turns on the move are described, as well as ways to secure your balance, to maximize your turn, and to refine your precision.

Edging from a Turn

Paddle forward four or five strokes to get your kayak moving, edge to halfway, then make a low forward sweep stroke on the low side of the kayak. The sweep needs be no more than a third of the possible sweep. Your active blade should grab the water to turn the kayak, but should be quiet in the water. Pull hard enough to bring the blade to the verge of creating turbulence. At the middle third of the possible arc, lift your paddle from the water and hold your edge. Your kayak should continue to turn until you run out of speed, so relax and wait.

Edging into a Turn

Make your sweep stroke on the high side of your kayak. The low side of the kayak is toward the inside of the turn.

Compare the effect of turning toward the low side of your kayak with turning toward the high side, using the same degree of edging in each case. Depending on your kayak, you may find one is more effective, or you may find them similar. Remember which proved more effective, but continue to practice both ways. A loaded kayak will respond differently than an empty one, and different kayaks will respond differently.

Shift Your Weight Forward

Once you can turn confidently on edge, start a turn and lean your weight forward. It is uncomfortable to lean a long way forward while also holding a kayak on edge. Prioritize keeping the edge, and lean forward only as far as is comfortable, even if this is only a little. Any shift of weight forward lightens your stern, and this affects how easily your stern skids. The higher in the water your stern floats the more easily it will skid, and the quicker you will turn. Adjusting trim by shifting your weight forward or back to lighten one end of the kayak is a useful addition to turns on flat water, but it also improves turns in wind, catching waves, and maneuvering on waves.

How Edging in a Turn Works

When you paddle forward, you create pressure against the bow and turbulence around the stern. This means the bow resists sideways movement against the pressure, but the stern moves sideways readily into the turbulence. Thus, when you are moving forward, a forward sweep has little effect on your bow and a lot of effect on your stern.

For the same reasons, it is difficult to stop the turn when moving forward by using correction strokes near the front of your kayak, but easy using correction strokes near the stern. This is also why rudders are installed at the back of a boat rather than at the front.

If you try to turn on the move when your kayak is fully upright, your maximum keel length is in the water, and the "V" shape of the stern resists most sideways movement. When you edge, you lift the bow and stern, shortening your effective keel. Your kayak will turn more easily with this shorter keel.

When you edge away from a turn, the stern shape is angled to slide across the water like a knife spreading butter: The stern skids. You can hear the water churning under the stern, and see the

smeared effect on the water surface behind the skid.

When you edge into a turn your stern section bites the water like a chisel biting into wood, countering a skid. Your kayak carves the turn. The water flows along the hull past the stern quietly, without smearing of the water surface. A carved turn (on the inside edge) will skid minimally compared to the skid on an outside edge.

How Kayak Design Affects Edged Turns on the Move

A narrow kayak with horizontal keel line, and its bow and stern sitting deep in the water, will show a marked difference in the radius of a carved turn and skid turn. The stern will clearly bite or slide depending on which way it is angled.

In contrast, a wide kayak with a highly rockered keel line will display exactly the same turning characteristic. When the kayak is edged, the flotation in the center section of the kayak will lift the stern from the water so it cannot bite. You will get a full skid turn whichever way you edge.

A low-profile Greenland kayak may turn more quickly when edged into, rather than from, a turn. This is because, when edged from a turn, the low back deck locks against the water, opposing the turn. The same will happen if a kayak with higher profile is loaded sufficiently to bring the level of the back deck close to the water surface, even if that kayak may turn faster edged from a turn when empty.

Turning While on the Move in Reverse

Try the same exercises—edging from a turn and edging into a turn—but this time reversing. Use the back of the blade rather than the face, and initiate each turn with a reverse sweep in the midsection, using the back of the blade.

KEY POINTS FOR TURNING ON THE MOVE

- To set up, generate forward speed.
- Edge.
- Sweep on the low side for a skid turn. Sweep on the high side for a carved turn.
- The action only requires part of the full sweep. Hold the edge.
- Refine by keeping your sweep powerful but quiet.
- Lean your weight forward.
- Compare turning with no edge, an outside edge, and inside edge, going both forward and backward. The effect depends on the kayak's design.

When edging from the turn, you will be able to see your bow skidding. Edging into the turn you should see the bow in its most locked position.

In reverse you should benefit from leaning back a little, which lightens the bow and frees up the turn.

Bracing for Balance While Turning on the Move

Holding an edge and waiting while your kayak turns on the move is a good balance exercise that helps demonstrate how far you can turn using just the middle of a single sweep stroke. But it is not easy to balance on choppy water—nor is it necessary, for you can use your paddle as an outrigger for extra security. The low brace is ideal for this. By using the back of the blade you can keep in balance while you are edged, even when you come to a standstill. You can use a high brace if you prefer.

Outside-Edge Turn with a Low Brace

Moving forward, edge your kayak away from the direction you wish to turn. Initiate a turn with a forward sweep on the low side. Use the middle third of the sweep only. This provides enough sweep to start the turn, and by avoiding the last third of the sweep you can make an easier next transition to a low brace.

At the end of the sweep, lift the blade halfway out of the water, and with a loose handgrip guide it gently forward. The paddle should rotate in your hand as the blade is tripped face up by the water.

KEY POINTS FOR OUTSIDE-EDGE TURN WITH A LOW BRACE

- Initiate a turn with forward speed, edge, and a forward sweep on low side, using only the middle third of the full sweep.
- Position the brace from the end of the sweep.
- Lift the blade half out of the water.
- Push gently forward.
- Allow the blade to fall face up, flat on water.
- Adjust for a climbing angle. Slide the blade forward until perpendicular to the kayak.
- From the brace, position the blade perpendicular to the kayak at the cockpit.
- Your offside hand is at your belly button; your onside hand is in push-down position.
- Use a fingertip grip to keep the blade at a skimming angle.
- Your body weight is forward. Maintain the edge.
- Smile.

Initiate your turn with forward speed, edge, and a sweep stroke on the low side. Use a low brace on the low side of your kayak for balance while the kayak continues to turn. Tomas Öhman

Adjust the leading edge of the blade slightly higher than the trailing edge for a climbing angle. Skim the blade forward until it is perpendicular to your kayak, level with the cockpit. The blade should brush the water like a feather. Maintain only just enough pressure on the blade for you to feel the water surface, but no more: Too much pressure will stop the kayak from turning, or even make you turn toward the paddle. Keep your offside hand low to the deck to keep the paddle as horizontal as possible. Keep your offside hand close to your belly button as well, so that your elbow stays bent at an appropriate angle for pressing down if needed.

The purpose of the brace is to help you maintain balance, rather than to recover lost balance, and you can adjust by pressing down lightly on the paddle as necessary.

Note: When you skim the blade across the water, keep a loose grip on the paddle with your fingers. You need fingertip sensitivity to feel the angle of the blade as you direct your attention to where you are turning, rather than watching what your blade is doing.

Inside-Edge Turn with a Low Brace

Make your forward sweep stroke on the high side, then brace on your low side in the same way as with an outside-edge turn, only this time you turn toward the paddle rather than away from the paddle.

You can vary the radius of this turn by changing the pitch of the paddle blade on the water. Increase the angle by a few degrees and you increase the drag, sharpening the turn. But if you increase the blade angle too much, you'll create enough drag to stop your kayak with less turn. Try to find the compromise to maximize the turn while keeping momentum.

Initiate the turn with forward speed, edge, and a sweep stroke on the high side of the kayak. Use a low brace on the low side. Tomas Öhman

Maintain an almost neutral (flat), slightly climbing blade angle. Tomas Öhman

Lean more onto the paddle and/or raise the leading edge of the blade for greater turning effect. Tomas Öhman

KEY POINTS FOR INSIDE-EDGE TURN WITH A LOW BRACE

- Initiate the turn with forward speed, edge, and a sweep on high side, using the middle third of a full sweep.
- Brace on low side, with the blade perpendicular to the kayak at the cockpit, your offside hand at your belly button, and your onside hand in push-down position.
- Use a fingertip grip to keep the blade at a skimming angle.
- Your body weight should be forward; maintain the edge.
- To refine, know that skimming pressure on the blade only offers one radius of turn.
- Engage the blade more to shorten the radius of the turn.
- Lean on the blade to heel the kayak farther, also shortening the radius of the turn.

Because you gain a lot of support on the back of the blade, you can heel your kayak until you are leaning on the blade. When you do this, keep your offside hand on your spray deck, close to your belly button. When you lose speed your blade will stall and sink under your weight, so bring your body back into balance or you will fall in.

Outside-Edge Turn with a Low Brace on the Inside

When your blade is positioned perpendicular to your kayak at the cockpit, hold your edge and slide the paddle across your kayak to touch the water with the other blade on the inside of the turn. Skim your blade lightly, like a feather, on the water.

Shifting your blade to the inside of the turn means any drag on the blade helps, rather than hinders, your turn. In addition, the position of your arms acts as a counterbalance, adding to your stability. Your optimum position is straight arms holding your paddle perpendicular to the kayak at the cockpit, with the blade as far from the kayak as possible.

You can fine-tune this turn by leaning your weight forward to help the tail skid, and also by adjusting the pitch of the blade. A slight change in angle, from say 5 degrees raised at the leading edge to 15 degrees, together with a light downward pressure on the blade, will help your kayak turn more quickly. It will also help you edge farther, which also speeds up the turn. If you raise the leading edge of the blade a lot, you will turn abruptly, but quickly kill your speed.

KEY POINTS FOR OUTSIDE-EDGE TURN WITH A LOW BRACE ON THE INSIDE

- Set up the turn with forward speed, edge, and a sweep on the low side.
- Skim the blade forward until perpendicular to the side of the kayak.
- Extend the other blade out to touch water on high side of kayak.
- Make light, skimming contact with the water surface.
- To refine, lean forward. Change the pitch of the blade by a few degrees to increase drag. Push down lightly against water.

Begin with forward speed. Edge your kayak, and then sweep on the low side to start your turn.

Brace lightly on the high side of your kayak, with the blade almost neutral/flat.

Straighten your onside arm perpendicular to your kayak to maximize the counterbalance effect.

Lean forward to lighten the stern.

Raise the leading edge of your blade slightly, and press down lightly to sharpen your turn as you lose speed.

Your kayak will continue to turn until you run out of speed. If you need to turn more, hold your edge and make a sweep stroke on the low side.

In practice, use this turn for precise maneuvering, adjusting the blade pitch and the degree of kayak edge to steer.

Reversing Turns

To use these turns in reverse, use the back of the blade to reverse sweep, and the face of the blade to brace. Lean your weight back to accentuate the turn.

Bow Rudder

The bow rudder is an effective way to turn your bow to the wind and a precise way to make a rapid turn on the move, depending on the position of the blade relative to the kayak. I will describe two extremes of blade position, first with bow rudder close to the bow, and then the bow rudder with a vertical paddle position, although a bow rudder can be performed with the blade between these positions, or moved about within the range to change the radius of turn.

Bow Rudder Close to the Bow

This is the bow rudder position that works best for turning to the wind. To begin, imagine you are weight lifting with your paddle. Hold it with your elbows tucked down below your hands and both elbows tucked against your torso. Bring the face of one blade to the side of your kayak in front of you, then reach the blade forward as far as you can. The face of a curved blade will cradle around the curve of the side of the kayak. Touching it against the kayak will set it at the angle, close to the neutral, you should aim for when you immerse the blade.

Lift the blade sideways about 8 inches away from the hull and lower just the tip into the water. This allows you to adjust the angle to neutral if you do not have it right. Lean forward to immerse

the whole blade. Once the blade is fully immersed, angle the leading edge slightly away from the side of the kayak, maybe 5 degrees, so the face is slightly open to the bow. Edge your kayak away from the paddle so your bow rudder is on the high side of your kayak.

Your offside hand should remain in front of your offside shoulder, with your elbow comfortably bent open, not tightly closed. Open the fingers of both hands to maintain a loose, controlling grip.

When using a wing blade, you may find it better to immerse only one third of the blade. Use a Greenland paddle in the extended position for greater effect: Slide your offside hand close to the

---

KEY POINTS FOR THE BOW RUDDER CLOSE TO THE BOW

- Set up your turn with forward speed, edge, and a short sweep on the low side.
- To position for the bow rudder, reach toward the bow on the high side.
- Position the blade face toward hull, about 8 inches from hull. Start in neutral.
- Lean forward to partially immerse the blade to check, then fully immerse the blade in neutral.
- Open the blade a few degrees to engage the face.
- Hold your position as the kayak turns.
- To refine, open your fingers to maintain sensitivity and greater reach. Keep the offside hand in front of the offside shoulder, elbow comfortably bent.
- To finish, power the blade around into a forward stroke and sit the kayak upright.

Start your turn with forward speed. Edge your kayak, sweep on the low side to start your turn, then place your bow rudder on the high side far forward, with close-to-neutral blade position, face lightly engaged. Hold this position while you turn.

Keep your low arm straight.

Keep your top arm bent at a comfortable angle in front of you.

Keep your offside blade in a position where you can easily drop it to brace if needed.

Lean forward to lighten the stern.

When you run out of speed or have completed your turn, draw your blade forward away from the side, and scoop it around to start a forward stroke.

All: Roland Johansson

offside blade tip, and reposition your onside hand to your usual hand spacing. This brings the active blade closer to your bow, and into a lower angle to the water.

Performing the Bow Rudder Close to the Bow
You must be moving forward. Edge, then sweep on the low side of your kayak to initiate a turn. You only need to use part of a sweep stroke, perhaps the middle third of the possible arc. You can choose to edge before starting your sweep, or start your sweep before edging.

Position your blade and feel the water with the tip to make sure it is in neutral. Lean forward to immerse the whole blade. Finally open the blade a little to engage the face, and hold the position while the kayak turns. Your blade should grip the water throughout.

Toward the end of your turn, you may find it useful to open your blade wider to keep the water pressure against it.

Finish by slicing the blade diagonally forward away from your kayak, and then curve it around into the position you use for the catch of a forward stroke, set your kayak upright, and continue with a forward stroke. This will accelerate you in your new direction.

If you watch your blade alignment in relation to a fixed object throughout the finish, you should see the blade holds the same alignment while your kayak pivots around it. (One way to visualize the path of your blade is to sit still in your kayak, then guide a small object like a ball around the curve with the face of the blade.)

Rudder in Reverse
When moving in reverse, position your blade to steer from the back of your kayak. Edge, and then reverse sweep on the low side of your kayak, using

> ### KEY POINTS FOR RUDDER IN REVERSE
> - To set up, build speed. Edge, then initiate a reverse sweep on the low side of the kayak.
> - To position the rudder, rotate your torso toward the high side.
> - Place the rudder on the high side at the stern.
> - Turn the blade face toward the hull, about 8 inches from the hull.
> - Immerse blade in neutral, or close-to-neutral.
> - Open the blade face toward the stern to increase power in the turn.
> - To refine, lean your weight back to free the bow.

the middle third of the possible arc. When you lift your blade from the water on the low side, it will be about two-thirds of the way forward, so your other blade will be about two-thirds of the way back—more or less where you want it. Hold your edge and lower the other blade into the water on the high side of the kayak, holding it in position relative to the kayak. You will pivot around the blade with your bow skidding. Lean your weight back for greater effect.

Keep your offside forearm on your lap while you experiment with how far out from the kayak to hold your onside blade. Farther out there will be a lot of pressure on the blade, and an immediate grabbing action. Closer to the side of the kayak, you get a smoother reaction and a slower immediate response, but your turn may continue farther and longer. Try starting your turn with the blade close, and then gradually widen the gap.

Edge your kayak, and make a reverse sweep on the low side to start your turn. Place your blade to steer on the high side, angled out from the stern, blade on edge and face engaged.

Lean back to lighten the bow.

Keep your blade close to the kayak for a gentle turn, or a little farther from the side for a sharper turn.

From where you sit you should be able to watch your bow skid.

All: Roland Johansson

Bow Rudder with a Vertical Paddle

This is the bow rudder position that works best for precise rapid turns on the move. Hold your paddle upright in the water a few inches from your hull, close to the front of your cockpit, with both hands above the water. Start with the blade in neutral position, blade face toward and parallel to your kayak. Straighten both arms. Edge your kayak away from your paddle so your paddle is on the high side of your kayak. Open the fingers of your top hand to set it in a good pushing position. Your bottom hand is in pulling mode. This is the starting position for the bow rudder. You will engage your blade by opening the face toward the bow by a few degrees.

The more upright your blade when viewed from the front of the kayak, the more effective your bow rudder will be, but it is challenging to accurately self-assess how upright your paddle is. What initially feels upright is usually sloping by as much as 45 degrees, so it may be useful to ask someone to give you feedback.

Another useful way to familiarize yourself with the correct position is to sit on the floor alongside a wall, four or five inches away from it, with half of a paddle in your hands. Hold the paddle against the wall near your knee, blade uppermost. Keep one hand near the end of the shaft, touching the floor, the other near the blade. Then, edge your body away from the wall. Both arms should straighten completely when you do this, creating a very strong frame. Both ends of the paddle should stay in contact with the wall. This simulates the position you aim for in your kayak.

There are several ways to get into position. You can begin with a bow rudder as far toward the bow as possible, bringing the blade closer and more upright. Or you can slice the blade edge first into the water alongside your hip, and curve it through the water into position. Or you can slide it edge first into the water behind you, slicing it down and forward, in neutral and in a straight line, into position. Which you use will depend on your situation, so learn all three and modify them as necessary.

For the first option, start in the bow rudder position as far forward as you can reach, but with the blade in neutral. Edge your kayak so your rudder is on the high side. Keeping your onside arm straight, bring the blade back until it is roughly level with the front of your cockpit, at the same time straightening your offside arm to bring your offside hand above your onside hand. You should finish with your paddle

The bow rudder with vertical paddle.

KEY POINTS FOR BOW RUDDER WITH A VERTICAL PADDLE

- **To set up, establish forward speed, then edge your kayak.**
- **Make a partial sweep on low side. The rudder is on the high side.**
- **Both arms are straight for the forward reach.**
- **Lean forward.**
- **The blade face is toward hull in neutral, and a few inches from the side of the kayak. The blade roughly level with knee.**
- **Engage the blade face by opening it toward bow.**
- **To refine, keep the blade angle small; gradually increase through the turn if needed.**
- **Try different entry paths for the paddle, from behind or from the side.**

upright, though it may slope forward to the water. Engage the blade by angling the leading edge away from the kayak by about 5 degrees. You can gradually increase this angle, but you get the best control by keeping it small.

For the second option, initiate your turn with part of a sweep stroke on the low side of the kayak. By the end of this sweep stroke, your other blade will be above the water on the high side of your kayak, about as far forward as you need a bow rudder. But your paddle shaft will be near horizontal. Slice the lower/back edge of the blade into the water using your onside hand to steer it in a curve down, back, and around, as if carving a downward spiral with your blade tip. At the same time rapidly push your top hand up across your body. Finish

with your paddle positioned as if against a wall parallel to your kayak. If necessary, quickly adjust your blade angle to neutral, then gradually open it 5 degrees or so, with the leading edge away from the kayak to bring pressure against the face.

For the third option, set up for your bow rudder with part of a sweep stroke on the offside, then lift your paddle across your deck to the onside until it is parallel to and a few inches from your kayak. Slice the blade behind you edge-first down into the water, and then forward into position for the bow rudder, while lifting your front hand into position. Once in position, angle the leading edge from the kayak by about 5 degrees.

Uses for the Bow Rudder

In wind: The bow rudder with the blade as far forward as possible is useful when turning your bow to the wind. The anchoring point should be as far forward as possible; the wind pushes the stern. In the same situation a more central position of bow rudder works poorly because there is more of the bow forward of the anchor point for the wind to catch, so the kayak balances side-to-wind rather than bow-to-wind.

Tight maneuvering: The bow rudder is great for precise maneuvering. The upright-blade position closer to the cockpit permits more confident edging, and the turn is sharper than with the blade positioned closer to the bow. You can adjust the radius of the turn by changing the blade pitch.

Transitioning: You can also transition from a gentle turn to a sharper one by moving the blade from the bow position to a closer one during a turn. This is useful to accurately reach a target while turning.

KEY POINTS FOR RUDDER IN REVERSE (VERTICAL PADDLE)

- Set up with reverse speed, edge, and a reverse sweep on the low side of the kayak.
- Rotate your torso toward the high side.
- Hold the paddle parallel to the kayak over the high side.
- Keep both hands low, both arms straight.
- Slice the blade down, in neutral, to bring your onside elbow to your hip and raise your offside arm to shoulder height, arm straight.
- Open the blade angle toward the stern to engage the face.
- Lean your weight back to free the bow.
- To refine, position the blade forward or back a little, and/or adjust the blade angle more or less, for an optimum turn.
- Keep your fingers open for greater sensitivity.
- Watch where you go.

Rudder in Reverse (Vertical Paddle)

In reverse, once you have started your edged turn, slip the blade into the water behind you on the high side of the kayak, both hands low, only just engaging the blade face. Raise your offside hand to shoulder height and straighten your arm. Bring your onside elbow to your hip. This should bring your blade to within a foot or so of your cockpit. Control the pitch of the blade, and the turn, using your onside hand to reduce or increase the pressure on the face. Your kayak will pivot around your blade.

The Cross-Bow Rudder

The cross-bow rudder uses the offside blade on the onside of the kayak. The sequence makes use of the same blade to make the sweep to initiate the turn, and then to rudder.

With forward hull speed, edge, then sweep on the low side of the kayak to initiate a turn, and then swing the active blade across your bow to position it in the water in the bow rudder position on the high side of the kayak. The blade face will be toward the kayak. You will need to rotate your torso and reach out with a straight front arm to make a space between the hull and the blade.

As with the standard bow rudder, you can position the blade well toward the bow or closer to your cockpit. Your back hand determines the position. The higher you lift your back hand, the farther back the rudder moves. As with the standard bow rudder, the more upright position, closer to the cockpit, offers a tighter turn.

The cross-bow rudder offers a good stretch across your shoulder, which can be pleasing at the end of a day on the water.

For a cross-bow rudder, start with forward speed, edge, and a sweep on the low side. Cross the blade over the bow to the high side to steer. Roland Johansson

Other Turns on the Move

Multiple sweep strokes to turn a kayak: If you run out of speed during an outside edge turn while using a low brace, you can skim the blade toward the bow to start another sweep, or sequence several full sweep strokes, skimming the blade forward between strokes to maintain your balance on edge. You can also use this technique when you start a turn from standstill.

Turning full circle using just one sweep stroke: When you have forward momentum, edge and then sweep on the low side of the kayak, your kayak should continue to turn until it comes to a standstill, unless something stops it from doing this. By holding your edge and paddling forward to keep the kayak moving, you should turn full circle. Start your turn, then accelerate using your normal forward stroke on both sides. Because your forward stroke ends before the blade reaches the turbulence around the stern, even if you only paddle on the inside of the circle, you should continue to turn in the same direction. The first third of a forward sweep stroke should not stop the turn either.

If you decide to stop the turn, sit your kayak upright and make a minimal correction stroke at the stern.

Turning full circle with one sweep is a useful way to compare the effectiveness of inside and outside edge turns. Make a full circle with each. The more effective way will result in a smaller circle. Keep in mind that different kayaks reveal different results.

You can try the same exercise in reverse, circling while edging from the turn and also while edging into the turn. When you compare effectiveness, the results will not necessarily be consistent with the results you found when paddling forward. When you reverse the results will depend on the

shape of your bow in the water. Moving forward, the results depend on the shape of your stern.

Moving Sideways

Moving sideways is useful for maneuvering to a landing, to another kayak, or for maintaining position against the push of wind or current. There are several ways to move sideways. Here are three versions; the sculling draw, the draw stroke, and the overside draw.

Sculling Draw

The sculling draw is a stable way to move sideways when the water is deep because there is a continuous pulling or holding pressure against the paddle blade, which helps you keep balance. The more upright your paddle as viewed from the front of the kayak, the more stable your position.

Hold your paddle horizontally above the water to one side of your kayak. Open your fingers for a relaxed handgrip. Raise your front hand to shoulder height and extend it straight out, perpendicular to the kayak. Rotate your torso toward the paddle to make this possible. Straighten your onside leg and bend your offside knee to help; turning your head toward your sideways direction

TIPS FOR TURNING FULL CIRCLE (USING JUST ONE SWEEP STROKE)
- Set up by paddling forward, edge, and sweep.
- Hold the edge and resume paddling forward.
- Lean forward.
- To refine, compare edging into and edging from the turn. Alternate a bow rudder on the inside and a sweep on the outside.

This sequence shows a sculling draw stroke. Left: neutral blade angle, pendulum parallel to dock, toward and from camera. Center: sculling angle to engage face, move blade parallel to dock toward camera. Right: sculling angle to engage face, move blade parallel to dock from camera.

Changing the Blade Angle

Once you are comfortable with the movement in neutral, angle the leading edge of the blade a few degrees away from the kayak and swing it forward. At the front end of the swing, pause for a moment, bring the blade to neutral, and then set the new leading edge at an angle a few degrees away from the kayak for the return swing. Pause again when the blade reaches the back end of the swing to bring the blade angle through neutral to open a few degrees toward the bow again. The water pressure in both directions of the swing will be against the face of the blade, pulling the kayak toward the paddle. Keep the pendulum swing at constant distance from the side of the kayak.

Try angling the blade so the leading edge in each direction is slightly closer than the trailing edge. This will put pressure on the back of the blade, and will push the kayak away from the paddle. This is often called a sculling pry.

By using these positions for a few strokes in turn—leading edge out, neutral, and leading edge in—you should be able to pull the kayak sideways, slip into neutral, and then push the kayak sideways.

Fine-Tuning the Blade Angle

The greater the angle at which you set your blade, the more you will push your kayak forward or pull it back with each swing. Experiment with blade angles to find the optimum for the greatest sideways movement with the least movement forward and backward.

Using all three positions is valuable in rough water and in rock gardens, when you need to hold position between rocks while the water surges around you.

Most commonly you will follow your paddle when you pull your kayak sideways. But when in

of travel will help. You should see the face of the blade, not the back.

Pendulum

Slice the blade behind you, down and forward, in neutral. There should be no pressure against the face or back of the blade. At the midpoint your top hand should be immediately above your lower hand, which will touch or almost touch the water. If, at this point, you were to let go with your bottom hand, your paddle should hang straight down. Continue to swing the blade forward until it reaches the surface, and then slice it back till it almost surfaces behind you.

Use this pendulum motion for the sculling draw. With your blade in neutral, your kayak should not move sideways yet.

The sequence below shows a sculling draw in the water.

The blade is at center, face open toward the stern, with the blade moving back.

The blade is stopped at the stern, ready to rotate.

The blade is stopped; rotate until it is open to the bow.

The blade is at center, open to the bow and moving toward the bow.

The blade is at the bow, stopped and ready to rotate.

The blade is stopped at bow, and rotated open to the stern.

The blade is open to the stern and moving toward the stern.

final approach to a dock or another kayak, it is more useful to push your kayak sideways so your paddle does not get trapped.

Steering While Sculling Sideways

It is easy to wander off track when trying to go directly sideways. This is sometimes due to wind or current, but often is caused by the blade having a higher climbing angle in one direction compared to the other. The remedy is to set a higher climbing angle on the swing toward the end of the kayak that you want to move faster, and a lesser angle toward the end of the kayak you want to move more slowly. For example, the angle set for the front half of your kayak will be either greater or smaller than the angle used behind your hip, which means changing the blade angle each time the blade passes your hip.

Edging While Sculling Sideways

Whether you edge or not, and which way you edge, will depend on your kayak and how it is loaded. A narrow kayak with a deep bow and stern, and a prominent keel, may benefit from edging down toward your direction of travel. In a kayak with a low back deck, edge from the direction of travel. A kayak with high rocker, a flattish hull, and a shallow footprint may move sideways most rapidly when held upright. Try all three positions to find out which works best with your kayak, as well as when you paddle a different kayak, and when your kayak is loaded differently.

Draw Stroke

An alternative, easy-to-conceptualize way to go sideways is known as the draw stroke. The blade enters the water upright at arm's reach, and you pull the kayak toward the paddle.

TIPS FOR SCULLING DRAW

- **Start with the blade upright in the water.**
- **Rotate your body toward the paddle.**
- **Fully extend your top arm in "pushing" position, perpendicular to the kayak and shoulder high.**
- **Guide the blade with your bottom hand as it pendulums forward and back.**
- **The blade pitch should be open slightly to the direction of swing.**
- **To refine, find which edging option works best.**
- **Brace with your legs to help with torso rotation and edging.**
- **Steer by varying the pitch from behind the cockpit to that used in front of the cockpit.**
- **Try the blade in three modes: pulling, pushing, and in neutral.**
- **Watch where you are going.**

There are some details worth paying attention to. If your paddle is static in the water, you will trip over it if you do not move it out of the way. The easiest way to avoid tripping is to turn the blade edge-on to your direction of travel, with the face toward the stern, before the kayak makes contact. Then you can slide the blade edge-first away from the kayak into position, or lift it and replace it for your next draw stroke. An alternative is to slice the blade out of the water edge first behind you when the blade comes close to the hull, and then reach for your next draw stroke.

To make the draw, rotate your torso toward your direction of travel. Straighten your onside leg and lift your offside knee to make torso rotation

The sequence below illustrates a draw stroke.

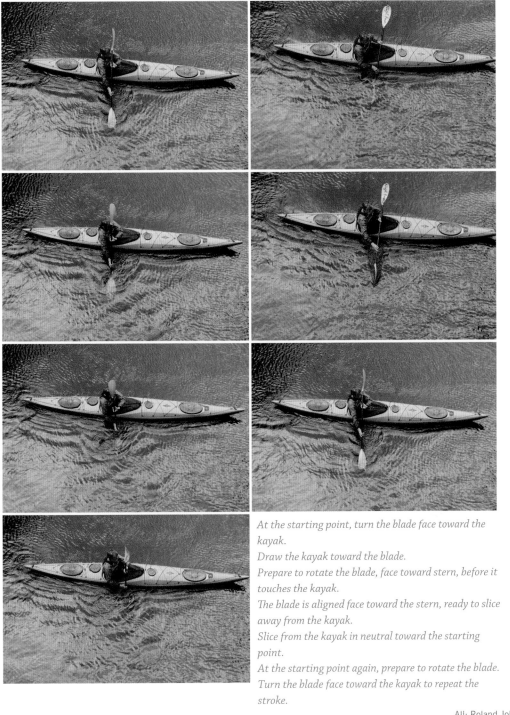

At the starting point, turn the blade face toward the kayak.

Draw the kayak toward the blade.

Prepare to rotate the blade, face toward stern, before it touches the kayak.

The blade is aligned face toward the stern, ready to slice away from the kayak.

Slice from the kayak in neutral toward the starting point.

At the starting point again, prepare to rotate the blade.

Turn the blade face toward the kayak to repeat the stroke.

easier, but you may need to modify this position to both rotate and edge away from your travel.

Your top arm can remain straight, reaching out perpendicular to the kayak in pushing mode, fingers open, in which case the draw stroke and slice away is performed and controlled with the bottom hand only. Or you can bring your top hand inboard while your bottom hand slices the blade away from you, pushing your top hand outboard again when your bottom hand pulls. Both are valid ways to make this draw work.

As with the sculling draw, if you reverse this stroke to push against the back of the blade instead of pulling, the kayak moves from the paddle instead of toward it. This is a pry.

Steering Sideways

To move directly sideways, pull from a point perpendicular to your kayak and level with your hip. Pull directly to your hip, with the blade aligned parallel to your hull. Depending on your kayak you may need to start and finish a little forward or behind this line.

Steer by starting in the same place, but angling the blade to follow a line slightly forward or slightly back, keeping the blade perpendicular to its line of travel. For example, if you angle the blade to pull toward the front of your cockpit, you will pull the bow more than the stern, and so your kayak will turn as it moves sideways.

When slicing away, keep a loose handgrip and steer the blade in neutral with the face toward the back of your kayak. Use your bottom hand to guide the path of the blade. Any pressure on either side of the blade will cause you to turn, so it is important to keep it neutral.

You can choose to keep the blade in the water between strokes or lift it out each time, but you

KEY POINTS FOR THE DRAW STROKE

- During the draw, keep the blade upright, blade face toward the kayak.
- Turn your torso toward the paddle.
- Position your top hand perpendicular to the kayak at shoulder height.
- Be ready to turn blade to neutral before the kayak reaches the paddle.
- During blade recovery, slice the blade edge first, in neutral, back to the starting point.
- To refine, steer by pulling the blade from the start to a point in front of or behind where you sit. Return in neutral to the starting place.
- Upright paddle makes steering easier.

cannot use your blade to maintain balance during this recovery phase. For better balance control, use the sculling draw.

Overside Draw

Imagine paddling forward. Turn your body to face sideways, and make a forward stroke with each blade, in turn, over the same side. You can lower the stroke to the water or bring your top hand to shoulder height.

Often used as an exercise to develop balance and flexibility, this is a useful technique when you need to move sideways in shallow water, or in places with limited headroom such as in caves, mangrove channels, and beneath docks or low bridges.

This sequence shows an overside draw. Roland Johansson

The Sideslip in Reverse

When you sit still and perform a draw stroke, you pull the paddle blade directly along a line perpendicular to your kayak. This line crosses the bow-to-stern midline at the balance point of the kayak, or at the pivot point when your kayak is not moving forward or backward. You can spin your kayak with alternate forward and backward sweeps more or less around this point. Typically the pivot point is where you sit, but if your skeg is deployed the point moves farther back.

When you paddle your kayak forward, the pivot point moves back. When you paddle in reverse the pivot point moves forward, perhaps as far as the front of your cockpit.

To perform a smooth sideslip in reverse, begin by moving your kayak on a straight line in reverse. On the sideslip side, finish a reverse stroke by bringing the paddle completely upright and rotating the blade to face inward, parallel to your hull. Push out with your top hand as far as possible, straightening your arm to get the shaft as upright as possible. Your blade position will be somewhere near the front of your cockpit. Gradually open the blade to engage the face, with the blade edge nearest you slightly farther from your kayak than the

edge nearest the bow. Your kayak should begin to slide sideways.

If you simply hold your position, then as the kayak loses speed the pivot point will move gradually toward your hip. This will leave your blade in front of the pivot point, and it will draw your bow sideways faster than your stern, turning you. To maintain a parallel position, you need to balance the sideways draw at the bow and stern by moving your blade gradually back toward your hip.

Sideslip

This is sometimes called the hanging draw. It is used when moving forward to slide a kayak sideways without turning it.

Paddle forward in a straight line. Slip your blade into the water and slice it in neutral to a position a foot or two behind your hip.

The easiest blade entry is in a straight line from behind, in neutral, exactly as in the pendulum for the sculling draw. Start with your paddle horizontal over the water, parallel to your kayak, and slice the rear blade down into the water, pushing it into position while lifting the front hand. Rotate your torso and straighten your top arm out over the

KEY POINTS FOR THE SIDESLIP

- To set up, employ forward speed, with no edge.
- Hold the paddle horizontal beside the kayak. Both arms are straight and the torso is rotated toward paddle.
- The back blade is in neutral position, face toward the hull.
- Slice the back blade down and forward, in neutral.
- Swing the front blade up and away from the side of the kayak.
- Bring your top arm perpendicular to the kayak at shoulder height.
- Bring your onside elbow to your hip and swing your hand back.
- The blade should be 1 to 2 feet behind your hip. Open the blade slightly, face to bow, to engage.
- If the kayak turns toward the paddle, move the paddle back.
- If the kayak turns from the paddle, move the blade forward.
- Make sure your top arm is at shoulder height, at full reach.
- Your bottom hand adjusts the blade pitch with a fingertip touch.
- As the kayak slows, move the blade slowly forward to prevent turning.
- The blade should end beside your hip when kayak stops.

water at about shoulder height. Your blade face should be toward the hull.

Open the leading edge of the blade by about 10 degrees to engage the face. Your top arm should be straight and in a pushing mode. If you cannot straighten your elbow to bring your hand over the water, and to bring the paddle parallel to your kayak, you probably need to rotate your torso a little more. Ideally your paddle will be upright as viewed from the bow, which offers you the most stable blade position and the most effective sideslip.

As soon as your kayak begins to move sideways, watch your direction and straighten up if necessary. To adjust direction, move your blade a little forward to pull more on the bow, or back to draw sideways more at the stern.

As you slow down, the pivot point of your kayak will move forward. When you come to a standstill, the pivot point will be more or less where you sit. To keep the kayak from turning, move your blade gradually forward toward your hip as you slow down.

If you do not move your blade forward, the pivot point of your kayak will move ahead of your blade, leaving you in a stern rudder position, and your bow will increasingly aim to the offside.

S-Turn

You can use a bow rudder to make a turn in one direction, followed by a stern rudder on the same side of your kayak to turn straight again. You will finish with your kayak tracking parallel to, but to one side of, your original path, as with the sideslip. You will have completed an S turn of sorts.

Unlike the sideslip, the bow turns first, and it moves aside faster with the bow rudder than it does with the sideslip. This means you can avoid a

For a sideslip, the blade face is lightly engaged, positioned upright just behind the hip. The kayak slides sideways without turning as it moves forward.

Check that your torso is rotated toward your paddle. Your top arm is straight, extended over the water perpendicular to the kayak. The blade is upright.

As you lose speed, gradually move your blade forward toward your hip to prevent a turn.

All: Roland Johansson

collision more easily with an S turn than you can with a sideslip. Once the bow is clear move the stern aside too, otherwise you will hit the obstacle with your stern.

Start at slow speed in a straight line. Edge your kayak from a bow rudder. Once the kayak has turned through about 45 degrees, perform a stern rudder on the same side, edging now toward the rudder to straighten up your kayak. When complete, you will be moving in the original direction but a few feet to the side. Use a target in practice, to monitor the effect.

To link the bow rudder smoothly to the stern rudder using a forward stroke, at the end of the bow rudder scoop your active blade around to begin a forward stroke while bringing your kayak upright. Make your forward stroke with your kayak upright. To finish, scoop your blade as a draw stroke to your stern: Push your offside hand across your chest to extend that arm over the water at your side, and pull your onside elbow to your hip, hand raised higher than your forearm. At the end of this short draw your blade should be aligned with the neck farther from the kayak than the tip, and the upper edge closer to the kayak than the lower edge, in the high stern rudder position. Edge your kayak toward your paddle.

You need not apply much power to the forward stroke component. You will have time to make all the moves smoothly if you rely on your kayak's glide.

This fluent move offers precision control around rocks and other obstacles. Practice at very slow speeds so you have plenty of time to blend the moves, and to fine-tune the blade positions and angles. Your blade face should be engaged throughout the maneuver.

Cross-Bow Rudder to Stern Rudder

You can perform a similar move using a cross-bow rudder with one blade, followed by a stern rudder with the other on the same side. With both blades on the same side of the kayak, the back blade drops to the water as the front blade lifts. There is no in-water transition. Edging shifts with the change of blade.

Set up with forward speed, then edge the kayak and sweep on the low side to initiate the first turn. Reach the same blade over the deck from the low side to make the cross-bow rudder on the high side to continue the turn. Once the kayak has turned sufficiently, lower the back blade into the water as a stern rudder, and shift to the onside edge to straighten the kayak.

KEY POINTS S-TURN

- Set up by paddling forward in a straight line, kayak upright.
- Use a bow rudder; edge from the bow rudder.
- Maintain grab with the blade as you turn the blade and make a forward stroke.
- Sit the kayak upright for the forward stroke.
- At the end of the forward stroke, guide the blade toward the stern and away from the hull.
- Use a draw stroke toward the stern until in the stern rudder position.
- Edge toward the paddle through the draw and stern rudder.
- Continue to hold in high stern rudder position, the blade face lightly engaged until kayak is back on track.
- To finish, sit upright.

Flat Water

Skills 3

Kayakers watching manatees on the Weeki Wachee River, Florida.

Rolling and rescues.

Rolling

Rolling is the most convenient and rapid way to recover after overturning in a closed cockpit kayak. You can also roll a sit-on-top or ski kayak if you are strapped on, but it can be just as quick to cowboy reenter (see Rescues on page 91).

The roll can be divided into two basic parts: what you do with your paddle, and how you use your body. There are three easily distinguished body movements and two basic paddle modes.

The body movements are defined by the finishing position of your body once you have rolled up: tucked to the side, lying forward, or lying back. The paddle options are to brace or scull. Work on the paddle movements already described for sculling support, high recovery (page 49), and on the body movements already described for recovering balance (page 46).

You can use whichever combination of body and paddle movement you choose to complete a roll, so it is useful to look at the components separately.

Starting Position

There is usually enough time between when you realize you are falling in and the moment you hit the water to tuck into the starting position. If you should unexpectedly find yourself in some other position underwater, you can usually rearrange yourself into this position. For this reason, it is convenient to describe the start of a roll from here.

Start in a secure position, with your body tucked forward, face tucked to your onside shoulder, and the paddle secured against the deck along the capsize side. This is the "tuck" position.

After capsize, lean toward your paddle and push it past the side of your kayak and around the hull with both hands. This brings your whole paddle clear of the water. The flotation of your PFD should help you float toward the surface. This will save the effort of dragging your body through the water during the roll itself.

It helps to leave enough time for your body to float before you make your next move. You should be more or less at the surface looking up, with your body rotated onto your back and perpendicular to the kayak. Your roll, in essence, will either be the same as a high recovery, or you will scull yourself upright.

Roll Using a High Recovery

Use the face of the blade against the water, perpendicular to the kayak, with your arm in pulling position. Bring the blade into position by pushing your back blade—the one nearest the stern—across your hull (in the air) to a position under your seat, and your front hand away from the side of your kayak, straightening it up into the air. Your paddle should now be perpendicular to your kayak. Your face should be looking up at the water surface. Your chest should be rotated toward the surface.

From here, pull with your front hand to bring your body out of the water and upright, using whichever body movement you favor.

Once upright, turn your blade on its back and skim it forward into a low brace position. This will help you balance and stay upright.

Vertical Paddle Roll

You can roll using a vertical paddle, gaining support from a forward stroke or a draw stroke. Neither option offers as much leverage as the previous option in normal conditions, but the blade is positioned to brace against water at a distance below the surface and can work when aeration offers insufficient support for a surface brace.

When rolling, tuck your paddle against the side of your kayak and follow it into the water.

Underwater, lean toward your paddle to let your PFD help float you to the surface. Reach your offside (rear) blade under your seat and reach your active blade to the surface and pull down.

As you pull down on your paddle, roll your head face down . . .

. . . pulling your offside shoulder toward your onside knee.

Bring your kayak upright while pushing face down beside you.

Your elbow will still be below your paddle.

Finally, lift your elbow to turn your blade face up. Press down with the back of your blade to keep balance.

An alternative body movement is to lie back.

Rolling into the lie-back position is easiest with a low back deck.

Roll by Sculling

Start as with the high recovery roll to bring your blade clear of the water. Scull the blade backward and forward across the surface within the middle third of the possible sculling arc from bow to stern. You can surface gradually when sculling because the blade maintains lift, always climbing toward the surface, or staying at the surface. Use whichever body moment you prefer.

Alternatively, you can start the scull from the original setup position, sculling the blade back into the center sector. You may not need to reverse the direction of sculling to bring yourself upright, but it is good to practice for those occasions when you

might need an extra little support to complete a roll.

Because a sculling roll can be done slowly, practice sculling to the surface and then staying there until you have arranged your ideal body posture and are ready for the final part of the roll. You will be able to breathe and see. Taking the extra moment offers an opportunity to perfect your technique.

A sculling roll can be started from the back if you find yourself capsizing face-first with your head near the stern, and it can also be performed with the paddle vertical in the water, gaining leverage from a sculling draw. Experiment with these alternatives once you have a reliable roll.

Rolling in Conditions

Surf, current, and wind offer plenty of opportunities to capsize, and each requires a similar approach to rolling.

If the wind blows your kayak sideways with you hanging underneath, your body will trail toward the surface on the upwind side. This makes rolling easier on that side, and more difficult on the other. Likewise, if a broken wave throws you over and carries your kayak sideways, you will trail toward the surface on the up-wave side. Current does something similar, especially when you capsize crossing an eddy line. Your body will be carried faster in the current than your kayak.

In each of these situations, if you set up by tucking your paddle to the side you fall on, as described earlier, you will be set up to roll with the forces of wind, wave, or current helping you.

The greatest challenge arises when you capsize before your kayak is turned by wind, wave, or current. Now you have to sense the side of your kayak your body is trying to float on, and to roll up on that side. You may get it wrong, and struggle to

---

KEY POINTS: PRACTICING A ROLL

- Always lean your body toward the surface before you begin your roll.
- If your roll is not completely successful at first attempt, try to retrieve the situation by sculling up.
- If your roll starts getting worse rather than better, practice your body movement without the paddle, perhaps using the bow of another kayak. Ask someone to support your kayak so you can perfect your paddle movement.
- Rehearse your roll in your imagination whenever you have a quiet moment.
- Once you have a reliable roll, practice in as many different situations as possible. This will make you more adaptable, and will improve your confidence for those times when you accidentally find yourself upside down.
- Set yourself a goal, such as completing a roll every time you go paddling.

KEY POINTS: PRACTICING A ROLL IN WIND, WAVES, OR CURRENT

- **Switching sides:** Practice switching sides underwater. Set up for a full roll and allow yourself to float to the surface ready for a roll. From this position, bring your paddle across your body into position on the other side, tuck your body forward to your deck and bring it across to the new paddle side. Lean out to that side to allow your body to float up, and then roll. You may have difficulty getting your body from one side to the other. In this case, use your paddle to scull around into position.
- **In waves:** To familiarize yourself with the effect of breaking waves on your roll, find a place with small, broken waves rolling across a sandy beach with no rocks. Turn sideways to an approaching breaker, and capsize away from the wave. Set up for your roll, but wait until you feel the sideways push of the wave before you roll up. The wave will help you roll, so roll gradually rather than abruptly, or you may find yourself rolling up and over again.
- **In wind:** Turn sideways to the wind. Capsize away from the wind and complete a full roll.
- **In current:** When in current, practice your roll on the eddy line. Capsize upstream as you cross from the eddy into current, and complete a full roll.
- **Roll with it:** In wind, waves, or current, try rolling against the elements instead of with them. If you succeed, you will be aware of the difference. If you do not succeed, switch sides and roll up on the easier side.

reach the surface. In that case, you might need to duck underneath again to roll up on the other side.

Rolling for Fun

If you enjoy rolling, you can perfect a whole range of rolls with subtle variations: using a sweep in only one direction; pushing on the blade instead of pulling; performed while holding the paddle in unconventional ways or in awkward positions. These rolls make use of all the alternative body movements. You can use whatever type of paddle or kayak you like, although some are easier for rolling than others. Be sure to use a nose plug, ear protection, and adequately warm clothing if you practice a lot.

Also, just as you can paddle your kayak forward with your hands, it is also possible to roll your

kayak upright using your hands, pulling directly down on the water or sculling.

It is possible to power roll using a paddle to compensate for poor body movement. Rolling with no paddle eliminates that possibility. You must have good body movement to succeed with hands only. You may never need to hand roll after an accidental capsize, but by perfecting your hand roll you will make any roll with a paddle that much more reliable and efficient.

Greenland kayakers have made a sport of rolling. In fact, the origin of rolling is often attributed to the people of Greenland, even though kayaking itself is not. Competitors show their ability to roll up with the paddle held in many specified ways, finishing with their bodies in different positions. They also roll without paddles, holding heavy objects, or while being dragged. If you enjoy being

KEY POINTS: ROLLING

- To set up, adopt the "tuck" position as you capsize, or as soon as possible afterward.
- Lean toward your paddle so your body drifts toward the surface.
- Bring your paddle perpendicular to the kayak, blade at the surface.
- Position the blade flat on the water, face down.
- Place your offside hand in the air against the hull under (more accurately, above) your seat.
- Pull down or scull to initiate the roll.
- Tuck forward onto the deck, tuck sideways, or lay back.
- To refine, take your time. Practice in slow motion.
- Finish by stabilizing in a low brace.
- Keep a loose handgrip to better feel and adjust the blade angle against the surface.
- To discover your blade angle, if you cannot initially tell, lift the blade above the water, then pat the surface or scull.

underwater, but perhaps not enough to take up diving, then this could be the sport for you! You do not need much water.

Some Greenland kayaks are specifically designed to make rolling easier. Greenland paddles are also commonly touted as being great for rolling. Tongue-in-cheek, you might suggest this is because the kayaks do not make it easy to stay upright. Broader blades never got a reputation for being great for rolling because they more readily

prevent capsize. But you can try your hand at the Greenland competition rolls with whatever type of kayak or paddle you usually use.

Rolling a Tandem

Rolling a tandem takes coordination. Make sure you agree with your partner on which side to roll up. After accidental capsize, this is usually following the direction of capsize to roll completely, and up the other side. One partner can roll a tandem unaided if the other tucks forward to hug the deck, so neither need exit.

Rescues

Think of a rescue in terms of a motoring breakdown. You are stopped unless you deal with the situation. You may be able to get back on the move by fixing the problem yourself, but it might be easier with help. Maybe you need a tow.

A capsize and wet exit is the most common reason for a rescue. But a kayak may get lodged on a rock by a wave; a kayaker may be unable to make progress against the wind or tide; perhaps a tired swimmer or someone incapacitated by fatigue and cold needs rescue.

Here are some simple ways to help someone who has exited a kayak, an explanation of how to deal with towing and, finally, what to do if all else fails.

Self-Rescue

It is safer to paddle with other people than to paddle alone. If you tip and exit your kayak, an assisted rescue can be quick and efficient if well-rehearsed. But it is reassuring to know how to deal with such a situation by yourself, if you need to. And you do not need to be alone to perform a self-rescue: Sometimes it is the quickest and easiest alternative.

The ultimate self-rescue after capsize in a sit-in kayak is to remain in the kayak and roll up (see page 84). If you are wearing a spray deck, you should get very little water in your kayak and you will not need to pump out. The cowboy straddle and sidesaddle reentry methods can be as fast as a roll for sit-on-top kayaks and surf skis.

Cowboy Reentry

A cowboy reentry, straddle, or cowgirl, if you prefer, is a quick way to reenter your kayak without a paddle float. Flip your kayak upright and then launch yourself face-down across the cockpit, or close to the cockpit over the rear deck, until you reach the balance point. Swivel with your head toward the bow and spread your legs across either side of your stern. Your legs now act as stabilizers. This is the straddle position.

Shuffle forward if necessary, until you are in position to drop into your seat.

Hold your paddle in the one-arm outrigger position, with the back of the blade on the water to balance (see page 39). Push your legs down and forward in the water, push your body upright, and drop into your seat. Brace with your paddle while you lift each leg into the cockpit, and then bail.

This is a standard way to board a sit-on-top kayak or ski from the water, but then you do not need to bail or secure a spray deck.

Reach face-down across to the center of the kayak and kick your legs to the surface behind you.

Launch across your kayak to a balance point.

Third, pivot to bring your legs up.

Aboard and in balance, now reseat yourself.

KEY POINTS: COWBOY REENTRY

- Flip the kayak upright. Enter from upwind, and enter horizontally.
- Launch your body across the cockpit to the balance point.
- Pivot your head toward the bow face down. Your legs straddle the stern.
- Drop into your seat, then bring your legs inside.

A second way to board a ski from the water is sidesaddle. Grab the nearside footrest and your paddle with one hand, and the far side of the ski with the other. Swivel toward the front as you lift yourself aboard. You will be facing a little sideways (hence "sidesaddle"), with both feet together in the water offering a little stability. Use your paddle for balance while you center yourself in the seat and bring your feet aboard.

Tip: You will find it easier to get out of the water when you slide out horizontally rather than vertically. Hold the kayak and kick your legs up to the surface behind you as you slide from the water.

Tip: In wind, it is easiest to reenter from the windy side of the kayak, so the kayak is not blown up against you as you attempt to surface.

Tip: It is better to point your craft into waves before reentering, to avoid having waves hit from the side once you are in. It is difficult and potentially dangerous to reenter from down-wave.

The next options require a pump to empty the kayak.

Paddle Float-as-Outrigger Rescue

The paddle float is an accessory that has been widely promoted as a rescue aid, and is often carried along with a stirrup pump. To use, hold your kayak with your feet while you slip the float over one blade of your paddle, and secure. If the float is made of mini-cell foam, then you are ready for the next stage. If the float is inflatable, then inflate. Some floats have two air bladders.

There are many variations on the theme of a paddle float rescue. For this one, flip your kayak upright, and either strap your paddle at the blade end to the rear deck, so the end with the float extends as an outrigger to one side, or pinion the paddle behind the cockpit coaming with both hands, so it is secure in the same way.

Grasp the back of the cockpit and paddle with both hands, facing the back of your kayak.

Lift the foot that is nearest the paddle float over the paddle near the float, and launch yourself horizontally, face down, across the back of your cockpit to the point of balance.

Shift your body as needed to feed your free leg into the cockpit.

Your legs will now be astride, one supported by the paddle float and the other in the cockpit. You will be face down across your kayak, slightly pivoted toward the stern, still holding the paddle to the back of the cockpit with both hands. By now

Lie face-down across the kayak using the float for balance and then bring one leg into the cockpit.

With both legs in the cockpit, switch your hand positions and pivot into your cockpit, favoring balance toward your float.

you will likely have your chest or abdomen over your hands.

Bias your weight slightly toward the paddle float and move your second leg into the cockpit.

Now carefully switch hand positions, bringing your offside hand behind your back to the paddle, closer to the float, and moving the other across the cockpit to the original offside hand position. You will need to pivot your body a little to do this. Continue to pivot in the same direction, favoring your balance toward the float until you are seated.

At this point you will be holding the paddle in both hands, but it will be behind your back. If the paddle is strapped in position, you can let it go, and pump your kayak dry. Otherwise, using the float as an aid to balance, feed the paddle away so you can bring it in front of you. Pin it in position close against your body under your PFD, and hold it in position with your elbows while you pump dry. Hold a stirrup pump in place between your legs while you pump. Balance by slightly favoring the float side.

Once your kayak is empty, your next challenge is to replace your spray deck and remove and stow your paddle float. For speed and ease, you might

clip an inflated float to your kayak rather than deflating it.

Variations in the float rescue include either starting behind the cockpit with the paddle between you and the bow, or in front of the cockpit, either facing down while feeding the first leg into the cockpit, or facing up to use a heel-hook exit from the water, and either pivoting away from the float or toward the float as you seat yourself.

Likewise, there are several solutions to pumping and to stowing your float. These variations come down to personal preference, and all that matters in the end is that you do what is easiest for you.

To discover the easiest method for you, practice and experiment. Remember that you will most

KEY POINTS FOR A PADDLE FLOAT RESCUE

- Required equipment: paddle float, pump.
- Hold the kayak, attach the float on the paddle, and inflate if necessary.
- Extend the paddle perpendicular to the kayak, with the float as an outrigger.
- Pin the paddle behind the cockpit with straps or your hands.
- Support one foot near the paddle float.
- Launch your body from the water to balance across the kayak.
- Feed your other foot into the cockpit.
- Readjust your hand positions to pivot into the seat.
- Use the float as an outrigger to support behind (if strapped) or in front (if not strapped) while you are bailing.
- Replace your spray deck, and remove and stow the float bag.

likely need the float when the conditions are rough enough to tip you in. The most awkward stages are typically sliding into your seat without overbalancing, and disassembling your outrigger. Then the conditions that tipped you over in the first place may conspire to repeat the process.

To make this rescue effective, practice in choppy conditions in a safe location until it becomes second nature. If you are nimble and practiced, you might succeed when you really need to. Simply carrying a float is not enough.

Reentry and Roll with Paddle Float

If you exit your kayak, you can reenter and use your paddle float to help roll the kayak upright.

Keep hold of your kayak while you attach the float to your paddle and inflate. Right your kayak. Face the bow and lay the paddle across your kayak, pinning the shaft near the blade neck to the front of your cockpit with your closest hand, so the paddle extends in front of you like an outrigger. Using your other hand to assist, turn your kayak slightly onto its side. Feed your feet into the cockpit and begin to slide into your seat. Take a breath, pull yourself fully into your seat and grip with your knees. During the final stage your head will sink underwater.

Take your paddle in both hands and gently bring yourself to the surface. Now you can breathe again and look around. With the paddle float for assistance, you can take your time to float your body into the position you want for the next step. Finally pull down gently on the paddle and roll the kayak upright using the high recovery with sideways tuck or with lie-back (pages 46 and 47).

It is very easy to roll with the aid of a paddle float if your body movement is remotely reasonable. You do not need to already be a successful kayak roller.

KEY POINTS: REENTRY AND ROLL WITH A PADDLE FLOAT

- Required equipment: paddle float, pump. Hold your kayak, attach the float onto the paddle, and inflate the float if necessary.
- Flip the kayak upright.
- Face the bow and hold the front of the cockpit, with the paddle, using the closest hand.
- Extend the float as an outrigger in front of you, perpendicular to the kayak.
- Turn the kayak slightly on its side to feed your feet into the cockpit.
- Hold your breath, and then seat yourself securely.
- Grasp the paddle in both hands, and roll up slowly using the float.
- Use the paddle and float as a stabilizing outrigger while bailing.
- Secure your spray deck and stow the paddle float.

Your kayak will be swamped, so you will need to bail, secure your spray deck, stow your float.

Tip: This will be much easier from the windy side of the kayak. You will remain closer to the surface throughout and the wind will help your roll.

Sponsons

Sponsons are an underrated rescue aid. They have been around for more than a century for canoe use, but seem to have hovered below the radar as an option for kayakers.

As with the paddle float, sponsons may be inflatable or made of rigid foam.

Right your kayak, and strap the sponsons to the hull either side. Inflate if necessary. Perform a cowboy reentry, bail, and secure your spray deck. The sponsons add stability, making every stage of a cowboy reentry easier. Once your rescue is complete you can continue with the sponsons in place. The drag will slow you slightly, but you will be much more stable, reducing the likelihood of another capsize.

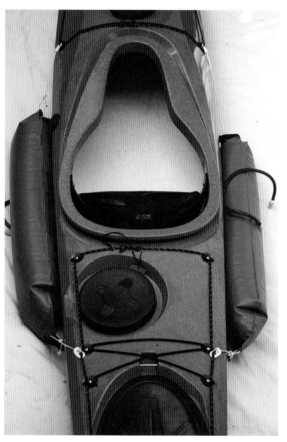

Sponsons add considerable stability.

Self-Rescue in Summary

Self-rescue devices have, for a long time, inspired inventors. I have encountered rigs with extendable swinging arms and floating buckets that fill with water to offer considerable stability. I have seen inflatable platforms that serve as temporary docks, and tubes fitted through the hull to hold spare paddles underneath as stabilizers. In the end, the challenge still comes down to you. Do you know if you can successfully perform a self-rescue in the type of conditions where you might need to, using whatever equipment you carry?

In all likelihood, you will rarely need a self-rescue on flat water, or when you paddle in a group that is practiced and skilled in assisted rescues. But conditions often turn out to be a little rougher than expected. If you are not sure whether you can perform a self-rescue in rough conditions, do not paddle alone. Self-rescue devices are only helpful if you are able to use them, so try them out. Experiment in a safe place, in conditions that challenge you.

Assisted Rescues

An assisted rescue means someone assists someone else. Both parties need to do their part in the rescue. It is possible for a rescuer to do much of the work, but the person in difficulty must be prepared to play a part too. For simplicity, I call the two parties the swimmer and the rescuer.

Single Kayaks: The Swimmer's Role

Retain your kayak and paddle. Hold on as you exit. You will need both, so keep hold.

Attract attention. If necessary shout to your companions, wave, bang your hand on the hull, or blow a whistle. In rougher water you may need to signal with your paddle in the air.

Take hold of your bow. You don't need to move to get to the bow; simply float your kayak past you into position, keeping in contact all the way. If your kayak has a skeg or rudder, it is easy to tell the stern: Take the other end. It is important to pass the bow to the rescuer so he or she can drain the cockpit. You will then be in position to hold that kayak.

Look around. Assess your situation and respond to any potential dangers around you. For example, if you are in danger of being carried onto an uninviting shore, then swim your kayak into safer water, where you can accept the help of a companion. On the other hand, perhaps your quickest or safest rescue solution will be to swim your kayak to a nearby safe shore.

Be proactive. When someone is coming to your aid, be prepared to help by swimming your kayak toward the rescuer as necessary. For example, if a rescuer is having difficulty maneuvering to reach you, you may be able to move your kayak more easily to him or her.

Heed instructions. Take heed of the instructions of the rescuer. If possible and practical, go along with the plan the rescuer is comfortable with. If the rescuer has little experience, you may be able to direct the rescue effectively from the water.

The Rescuer's Role

Approach quickly but carefully.

Get organized: Direct the swimmer to hold your front deck. Hold the bow of the swimmer's kayak in your hands, with the kayak perpendicular to yours.

Approach the swimmer. As you approach, check that the swimmer is holding the bow of his or her kayak. If not, direct the swimmer to do so. Aim to be in position so the swimmer can take

hold of your kayak a little in front of the cockpit. (2 to 3 feet in front of you is about right). A deck line will make a convenient and secure hand hold for the swimmer. Point and say where you want the swimmer to hold your kayak. Without letting go, the swimmer will now be able to pass to you the bow of the kayak, and there will be enough space between you to empty the kayak without the swimmer letting go or moving. Be confident when directing.

Deal with the paddles. Choose whether to hold both paddles, or leave one in the hands of the swimmer. It is essential that both paddles are retained throughout the rescue. I prefer to keep control of my own paddle at all times, and never pass it to the swimmer. I am less likely to let it drift, and I have more options available if I have a paddle. I tuck my paddle, and sometimes the swimmer's also, across my lap, leaning back to make a gap, then leaning forward to pin it (or them) under my PFD. Some prefer to use a paddle leash, or do both.

Maneuver the swimmer's kayak into position and upturn. Once you have a hold of the swimmer's kayak, don't let go! You can use it for stability. Reach across your kayak to grasp the end grab with your offside hand. Reach farther along the keel with your other hand, but keep your elbow bent. With both hands in position, twist until the two kayaks are perpendicular, and then pull your hands apart to roll the kayak upright.

Drain the kayak. With the swimmer's kayak upright, float it as far as you can across your deck. Kayaks with a raked bow will likely reach at least as far as your onside hip when upright. You will be more stable lifting a load in front of you than trying to lift while reaching over the side.

When you have floated the kayak as far as possible across your deck, roll it onto its side to bring

Roll the kayak upright to float, bow across your deck. The swimmer keeps hold of the rescue kayak.

it farther. Roll it so you can see the deck, deck lines, and cockpit. With the kayak on its side and the side of the bow on your deck, you should see water draining from the cockpit. You seldom need to bring the bow of the swimmer's kayak farther across your deck than a point at which you can still reach the bow with your offside hand.

Roll the kayak toward you, onto its side, to see the water drain. Then invert the kayak completely to drain any remaining water.

Roll the kayak upside down and lift a little higher to finish draining. Rocking it gently from side to side may release any water trapped behind the cockpit.

Roll the kayak upright and float back onto the water.

Maneuver the kayak alongside. The stern of the swimmers kayak needs to go toward your bow, so float the bow past your hip and draw the kayaks together by working hand over hand along the deck lines until you can grasp the cockpit.

The swimmer meanwhile should still be holding on in exactly the same position as before, but now he or she will be between the two kayaks.

Prepare for the reentry. There are several ways to bring a swimmer into a kayak, but all require you to stabilize the kayak so it cannot tip and fill with water as the swimmer gets in.

Take both paddles and position them across both kayaks so they rest close against your body. Reach your arms over the paddles to grip the front of the swimmer's cockpit firmly with both hands, one at each side. You may find a deck line provides a better grasp for one hand.

Reentry. Direct the swimmer to face you. The swimmer should hold the far back corner of the cockpit with one hand, reaching the other onto your front deck at a point level with the first hand. From this position the swimmer can lean backward into the water, lifting his or her feet up between the kayaks and into the cockpit. Then, by arching the back and pulling the two kayaks together, the swimmer can drop straight into the seat.

Keep hold. Keep a secure hold on the swimmer's kayak. Inevitably, the swimmer will need to wriggle into position to find the foot braces, and maybe to retrieve the spray deck. Usually some water drains from the swimmer into the kayak: If the time is right, sponge out before securing the

This shows a reentry from between kayaks.

spray deck. Finally, make sure the swimmer has the paddle correctly aligned, and that he or she is ready and confident to continue before you relax your hold.

Notes: This method of reentry requires the swimmer to pull the two kayaks together when getting in. Pushing instead of pulling sends the kayaks apart, almost always resulting in failure, as it becomes impossible for the rescuer to keep the kayaks close together.

It is important that the swimmer starts reentry close to the cockpit, holding the back of the cockpit rather than a point farther back. Starting farther back makes it more difficult to keep the kayaks together, and requires a lot of wriggling forward to reach the cockpit, rather than dropping straight in.

In rough water, both kayaks tend to move as one, rather than acting as an anvil and hammer. The swimmer is able to hold securely in place while preparing to reenter.

Alternative Reentry Methods

The plan described above is likely the most secure rescue technique because the swimmer keeps hold of the rescuers kayak in the same place throughout the rescue. There is no moving around, so little

opportunity to be separated by wind and waves. All other alternatives require some hand-over-hand movement, so they are intrinsically less secure. Also, in the plan above, the wind direction, or direction of drift, is irrelevant. All others are easiest when the swimmer enters from the upwind side.

However, different reentry styles work best for different people, so practice them all both as a rescuer and as a swimmer so you understand the advantages and challenges. Your kayak, your body shape, and your agility play an important part in your choice of reentry method.

The remaining options involve entering from the outer side of the swimmer's kayak, or by first crossing the rescuer's kayak.

Reentry over the Rescuer's Kayak

This involves sliding from the water almost horizontally over the rescuer's deck, face down. First grasp the deck with both hands and kick your feet to the surface. This is difficult to do from the downwind side, so turn the rescue if needed. Pull yourself forward, pushing down on the deck until the rescue kayak is under your abdomen. Pull far enough across to reach a point of balance, from which you can swivel, reposition, and drop into your cockpit.

The front deck of a kayak is typically higher from the water than a rear deck; this is one reason reentry over the swimmer's back deck is usually preferable.

Reentry over the Swimmer's Back Deck

Method one: Float face up on the water alongside your kayak, on the upwind side. Lift the foot farthest from the kayak into the far side of the cockpit and grip. Reach your farthest hand across the back deck to grip the deck line of the rescue kayak,

Float face up in the water with your head toward the stern. Hook your offside foot into your cockpit and reach to grasp the rescuer's kayak.

Pull to roll face down onto kayak.

Feed your free leg into the cockpit.

Pivot into seat.

Once comfortably seated, bail as necessary.

and your near hand onto the nearside deck line of your kayak. At this point you are almost hugging your kayak.

Pull up against the deck with the foot in the cockpit, and pull with both hands to roll face down onto your back deck (the swimmer's kayak). Feed the free leg into the cockpit and swivel toward the rescuer to corkscrew into the cockpit.

The rescuer can make this easier by letting your kayak tip slightly toward you before you start, and helping to right it as you exit the water, but tipping it too much will swamp the cockpit.

Method two: From the upwind side, and face down, hold the cockpit with both hands and kick your feet to the surface, so you float perpendicular to your kayak. Launch yourself horizontally across your kayak to a point of balance, and then swivel face down so your head is toward the stern. Feed your feet into the cockpit and twist toward the rescuer into your seat.

Method three (stirrup): A stirrup can be simply arranged with a 10- to 12-feet length of nonfloating line tied as a loop. Pass the loop around the cockpit and drop the excess into the water toward the swimmer.

The swimmer keeps hold of the kayak, places the foot closest the stern into the loop and stands, turning to face the stern. Feed the free leg first into the cockpit, then the leg from the loop. Swivel toward the rescuer to corkscrew into the seat. The loop will still be around the cockpit, so lift that free, or untie and pull it free.

The advantage of the stirrup is that it is typically much easier to use leg muscles to stand than to use arms to pull upright. The stirrup is often the last thing that works when exhaustion and lack of coordination set in. It is a good option for bulky paddlers and paddlers in bulky clothing, who might find other techniques challenging.

The length of a stirrup varies, both with the size of cockpit and the length of the leg. A short paddler in a Greenland kayak with an ocean cockpit might only need a 7-foot length of line, while a tall paddler with a long cockpit could need double that. The trick is to make the loop easy for the swimmer to stand up in, with a standing height suitable for easily entering the cockpit. Experiment with different loops until you find the length that works for you.

If you like the technique, carry a loop for personal use in your pocket. To assist other paddlers, you should carry a length of line long enough to create a loop for a tall paddler with a long cockpit. Tie a loop in one end, and adjust the length to what you need when the occasion arises. In the meantime, you will probably use the line for many things, from hanging gear to dry to tethering kayaks together.

Note: I recommend nonfloating line. If the line floats it is difficult to get your foot into it. The downside is that if dropped, the line will sink, so attach a small float where it will not be a hindrance. Choose a diameter of line that fits easily under the cockpit, thick enough to avoid causing discomfort to the swimmer's foot. Brightly colored line should be easiest to see in the water.

Method four (scoop): The scoop is a way to help a partially incapacitated kayaker from the water into the kayak. The rescuer holds the kayak on its side so the swimmer can float and wriggle his or her legs into the cockpit. Once positioned well enough to grip firmly in the seat, the rescuer helps right the kayak, typically gripping the swimmer's PFD while simultaneously rotating the kayak upright. This assistance may be useful for a swimmer who is chilled to the point of reduced coordination, or injured in some way, as with a dislocated shoulder. With practice and the help of an extra paddler, it is possible to feed the swimmer's legs into the cockpit and right the kayak without the help of the swimmer, but it is not easy.

I prefer to use the stirrup method in most such scenarios, because the kayak may be drained before reentry rather than bailed afterward. However, the scoop can work if the stirrup fails or is not an option.

Reminder: Keep hold. Whichever reentry method used, once the rescued swimmer is seated, keep hold and help stabilize the kayak. Help fasten the swimmer's spray deck, and ensure the paddle is correctly aligned and in hand. Check that the paddler is OK: warm enough, confident to continue paddling (either back or onward), and stable enough to continue if released. If not, then you will need to take further action. But if all is OK, then gently release.

Note: In awkward conditions, such as when the wind is blowing strongly toward an unfavorable shore, a third paddler can anchor the rescue using a towline (see page 105).

How Long Should a Rescue Take?

A rescue shouldn't take very long. A paddler can be back in the seat thirty seconds after a capsize and wet exit in easy conditions, if the rescuer is right on hand and both are practiced in what they need to do. I have seen very quick rescues performed in unfavorable conditions by people who know what they are doing. Nothing is a good substitute for practice, but the best results come from people who practice together.

Should You Talk?

One point often overlooked in a rescue situation is the tension that can build. If you are well practiced in rescues together, then that should be less of a big deal, but otherwise it's worth remembering

that the swimmer is probably uncomfortable, embarrassed, and maybe scared. The more you can make the swimmer feel at ease, the better you will be able to communicate and do what is needed efficiently.

Some people respond well to barked orders, but would that make you perform better? Often it is more effective to treat a rescue as routine. Be matter-of-fact, give calm clear instructions, smile, and check that the swimmer is OK. If needed, give reassurance and let the swimmer know that he or she will soon be back in the kayak. If you, too, are a little anxious, hide it. Smile: Be calm, courteous, concise, businesslike, and methodical. Things will work more smoothly.

Loosen up

Rescues take a toll on a paddler's energy, whether you are being rescued or rescuing. Partly it is the exertion. Partly it is the anxiety. If you find yourself swimming time after time because the conditions are too much for you, you are likely to be tense, both because of cold and anxiety. Your tension is likely to contribute toward your next capsize. It will also make your rescuer apprehensive. There are ways to defuse this.

How do you hold yourself in your kayak? Locking in with both knees makes you feel secure, but when you are stressed and the kayak rocks, you

---

KEY POINTS: SWIMMER

- **Retain your kayak and paddle.**
- **Go to the bow.**
- **Attract attention.**
- **Be active in rescuing yourself, or to move to the rescuer.**
- **Follow instructions.**

KEY POINTS: RESCUER

- **Head quickly to the swimmer. Ensure the swimmer retains the kayak and paddle.**
- **Have the swimmer hold your deck lines and stay there through the rescue.**
- **Have the swimmer pass you the bow of his or her kayak (if given the stern, you need to get to other end).**
- **Flip the kayak upright if necessary.**
- **Push the kayak perpendicular to yours, and float the bow over your cockpit.**
- **Turn the kayak on its side toward you. Pass the kayak across your deck until water begins draining.**
- **Invert and fully drain the kayak. Then right and refloat.**
- **Bring the kayaks alongside each other, swimmer's bow to your stern.**
- **The swimmer reenters from between the kayaks, or over the side.**
- **Fasten the spray deck, ensure the paddle is in the swimmer's hands, and check that everything is OK.**
- **Release.**

end up trying to balance by tensing with first one knee and then the other. This can set the kayak wobbling, while you struggle to control the wobble. If, instead, you hold with one knee, freeing the other completely, your kayak will move within reasonable limits but you will have eliminated the tension. You will no longer be gripping. Your kayak probably works better on the water than you do.

Next, your paddle: A tight handgrip limits the feedback you get from the water. You are far more likely to put weight on your blade when it is at the wrong angle when you grip tightly. You can feel the water better when you have a looser grip. Loosening your handgrip for better performance will also be better for your wrists.

Finally, smile. When your facial muscles relax, you relax, your companions feel more relaxed, the situation is defused, and you all perform better.

If someone in your group is clearly capsizing more often than anyone likes, maybe the conditions are not appropriate for that paddler. What are your options? Is this a good time to head to shore, turn back, or raft and tow?

Assisted Rescues from Tandems

Debatably, all tandem rescues could be described as assisted rescues, as the two paddlers help each other. I describe that type of rescue as a self-rescue. Others require help from another kayaker.

A tandem rescue may be approached in the same way as a single kayak. The longer length of a tandem, and the position of the rear cockpit closer to the stern, sometimes combine to make the back cockpit difficult to drain, in which case you will need to bail more. But you can usually drain at least some of the water out. The swimmers can support themselves using the deck of the rescue kayak while they lift the bow of their own kayak, each holding one side of the bow and lifting together.

The easiest reentry for the swimmers is over the side farthest from the rescuer while the rescuer stabilizes the kayak. With both swimmers back in the kayak, bail any excess water. The cockpit of a tandem can hold a lot of water, so you will need a high-volume bailer or pump. A sponge will not suffice.

Loaded Tandem Rescues

Lifting a fully laden tandem kayak that is also swamped is more than most paddlers wish to attempt. A standard assisted rescue is possible, but it may be simpler and safer to right the kayak, and then pump it dry once the swimmers are reseated. If the kayak has a center compartment between the two cockpits, which is usually about the widest part of the kayak, holding the kayak on its side will allow flotation to lift the kayak, allowing at least some water from both cockpits to drain and making subsequent bailing easier.

Tandem cockpits usually hold more water than singles, so pumping takes longer. Use a high-volume pump. It is especially useful to reduce the cockpit volume as much as possible before setting out with loaded kayaks. For example, fill empty cockpit space beyond the foot braces and behind the seat with shaped blocks of closed cell foam, securing them so they cannot float free.

Self-Rescue of a Tandem Kayak

This is the simplest self-rescue if the kayak has at least one bulkhead (preferably two) between the paddlers, and a sealed compartment in each end.

Following capsize, right the kayak. One swimmer should stabilize the kayak while the other climbs aboard from the opposite side. The seated kayaker then stabilizes the kayak with a paddle brace while the second swimmer reenters. Carry stirrups to make both steadying the kayak and reentering easier if the higher deck of a tandem makes other reentry methods difficult.

Once both paddlers are aboard, pump both cockpits dry. If necessary, take turns to stabilize while the other bails. If you have a lot of water to bail, consider whether it is appropriate to head for shore, with one kayaker paddling and the other stabilizing, or to raft against another kayak for stability and assistance while pumping.

As a precaution, test how stable your kayak is when swamped with two paddlers aboard. Securing lightweight foam blocks along each side, behind the seat and between your feet and the bulkhead, will reduce the available space for water, making a self-rescue much simpler.

Towing

A tired swimmer can hold the end grab of your kayak while you tow them to shore, and you can also push a kayaker who holds your kayak's end grab. But in many ways it is easier to use a towline to help a tired paddler, to reassure an anxious paddler, to anchor a rescue in one spot against the wind or current, or to bring an injured or incapacitated person back to safety. You can also use the towline to retrieve a drifting kayak. At its simplest it is a length of line, but it is remarkably versatile.

Transporting a Swimmer

A swimmer expends more energy staying afloat than a kayaker in the water wearing a PFD. Swimmers do occasionally get into difficulties and drown. A kayak offers an easy way to help a tired swimmer, but be cautious when approaching someone who is clearly panicking. You do not want a capsize to complicate the situation.

Reassure and direct the swimmer as you approach. The easiest place for the swimmer to hold your kayak, so you can see what is going on, is at the bow. The swimmer holds the bow with his or her head safely beside it, legs trailing under the hull, or with legs wrapped around the kayak, feet on deck. Take care not to hit the swimmer with your paddle as you push to safety.

This works well in calm conditions, but your kayak will weathercock a lot in crosswinds, and it is challenging downwind. Especially if moving downwind, better have the swimmer hold at the stern and trail behind.

The exercise pictured here was for fun. In practice, it is usually easier to carry a passenger onboard a sit-on-top kayak.

Towing a swimmer like this is like dragging an anchor. If you can carry the swimmer on deck, there will be less resistance, and it will be warmer for the swimmer too, if that is a factor to consider.

Carrying is easiest on the rear deck. The swimmer slides across the deck and pivots face-down, head toward the cockpit, holding either the paddler's waist, the back of the cockpit, or onto a suitable deck line. Even with the swimmer lying flat, the weight high up will reduce your stability, so the swimmer should spread his or her legs on the water surface as outriggers.

It is possible to carry a swimmer wrapped around the front deck, where you can see the person, but that is a little less stable as the deck is usually higher. It is also more awkward to paddle.

You can carry a child sitting upright and hugging you from behind. You can compare the effectiveness of different methods when you practice kayak rescues.

It is, unfortunately, quite common to see a kayak blown away from a kayaker following capsize in wind, and is often impossible for someone to swim fast enough to catch a kayak drifting in wind. That is why it is essential to always retain hold of your kayak throughout capsizing and wet exit. A realistic rehearsal is to practice carrying a kayaker while someone else practices emptying and towing a kayak.

If the water is cold, the swimmer will soon conclude that being carried on deck is much preferable to being in the water. There is a real risk from cold not only in a real situation, but when you practice too. Safeguard against a real emergency by practicing near where you can immediately warm up again on land as soon as needed.

Towline

This is basically a length of line or webbing, but you will find it gentler to use if there is a shock-absorbing feature to prevent jarring shocks when the line pulls tight. Usually a length of shock cord or flat elastic is tied to or sewn in running alongside a section of the line or webbing. To prevent damage to the elastic, the line takes the strain before the elastic is overstretched.

There is an active end, with the person towing, and a passive end, with the person being towed. The active end can be attached to the kayak by means of a quick-release cleat, or to a quick-release waist belt around the person towing. For long-distance towing, I recommend attachment to the kayak because a body tow becomes punishing over time. For short distances and for quick deployment, a body tow is often the most practical.

Attachment to a Kayak Being Towed

The attachment to the kayak being towed can be a simple knot around the end grab, but a carabiner or clip is quicker to deploy and release. To offer release control to the paddler being towed, the end of the line may be passed through the end grab and to the deck line at the cockpit, and tied there with a quick-release knot.

However, attaching to or through the end grab of the towed kayak is not the best option when the end grab is the highest point of the kayak. In waves when the line comes taut, the pull will often be down or down to one side. This holds the bow down in the water, which causes the kayak to veer off course, makes it unstable, and sometimes capsizes it. A simple "twin-tow" harness clipped to the deck line on either side of the bow can remedy this. Position the harness far enough back to allow the attachment point at the midpoint of the twin-tow to rest under the foot of the bow, at the start of the keel. Fasten the towline to this attachment point.

A towline pulling under the keel lifts the bow, angling the stern down. As a result, the kayak tracks straighter and becomes more stable. I prefer using a twin-tow when I need to tow for some distance. But it is not as quick to deploy, so for rapid, short duration, and emergency tows, I usually clip to an end grab or deck line at the bow.

Attachment to the Towing Kayak

At the active end of the line, tow from a point near the center of your kayak, close behind you. Your kayak must be free to turn and steer, pivoting from the center independently of the line, so do not pass the line through your end grab.

A cleat on your back deck may be positioned to one side, close to the cockpit so you can reach it easily for quick release. A fairlead (a ring that keeps the line captive) is also necessary to prevent the lifting and falling action in waves from lifting the line free of the cleat. Thread the end of the line from the towed kayak through the fairlead and then cleat it, so on release from the cleat the loose end runs through the fairlead to freedom. Do not knot or daisy-chain the line on the upside of the fairlead, or it will prevent quick release. If you need to daisy-chain the line to make it shorter, do so on the section between the two kayaks.

Towing from one side of the kayak is okay, but you can add a second fairlead in the center of the kayak, and feed the line through that to center the pull. Remember to position the fairlead near the cockpit to leave you free to turn when towing, and not at the stern.

Towing from a Waist Belt

When towing from a waist belt, the waist belt should be broad and, if possible, padded, to spread the load for comfort. It must have an easily located quick-release feature.

Float

Your towline should float in case you drop it. Whether the line releases with the belt attached, or the line releases from the belt, make sure you cannot lose any part through sinking.

Length

For towing in simple conditions, allow about one kayak length between the towing stern and the towed bow. For an 18-foot-long towing kayak, this means about 18 feet, plus the length of the back deck (add another 9 feet), plus any overlap at the bow of the other kayak. Expect about 30 feet.

For following seas, when the kayak being towed could end up surfing into the towing kayak, a longer line is advisable—perhaps 60 feet. The extra length may be carried separately and clipped to the end of the first length, or a longer line may

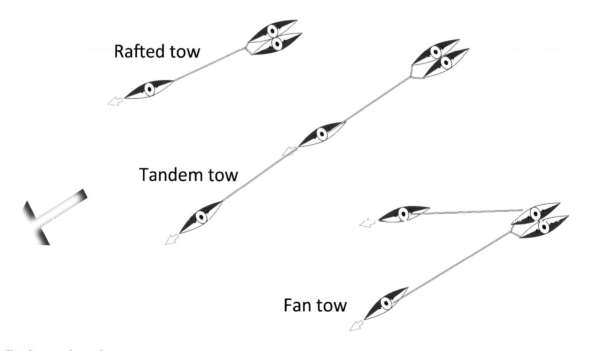

This diagram shows alternative towing arrangements.

be daisy-chained to keep it shorter until more length is required.

Stowing

Your towline should stow so it is not an entanglement hazard, and is quick and easy to redeploy. Typically, with a waist-tow system, the line packs into a pouch closed against accidental escape. Sometimes the line stows directly into a pocket of the PFD. Deck-tow systems sometimes stow into a pouch, and sometimes daisy-chain and store under bungees. If you are wearing a waist-tow system for emergency use, you might carry an additional deck-mount system in the day hatch, in case you need to set up for a longer-duration tow.

After releasing from emergency tow, you can simply stuff the line inside your PFD until you find a more suitable time and place to stow it properly.

Note: Think of a towline as a practical piece of everyday equipment to help with the safety and enjoyment of a group on the water. Use it to help a paddler experiencing difficulty with directional control, or who is tired. Raft two kayaks together for stability to prevent capsize in rough conditions, to reassure a paddler who is feeling insecure, or to tow the two kayaks together. Another paddler may attach a line to pull the towing kayak if more help seems appropriate. This is known as a tandem tow. A tandem tow, or an even longer line of kayaks, can make steering easier as well as adding power.

A full towline should have:

- A way to attach to the kayak being towed
- A way to attach to the towing kayak or kayaker
- A quick release from the front end
- Possibly a quick release at the back end
- A shock absorber
- Flotation

The towline should also be quick to deploy, easy to stow, and should have at least 30 feet of line or strap; double for following seas.

Anchored Rescue

In awkward situations where there is a danger of the rescue coming to harm, such as a rescue close upwind of rocks, then a towline can be employed to tether the rescue stationary until the swimmer is secure, at which point both rescuer and rescued may be towed from danger before being released. The skill here is to anchor, rather than move, while the rescue is completed because it is tricky performing a rescue while moving. With the rescued kayaker seated, towing is appropriate while the spray deck is being replaced and any pumping is completed.

Fan Tow

A fan tow is arranged with several kayaks towing, each clipped to the kayak or raft of kayaks being towed. The outer, towing kayaks can clip to the sides of kayaks in the raft near the cockpit to control the sideways position of the raft as it is being towed.

When the towing kayaks spread (fan out) to avoid getting in each other's way, they will experience extra rope drag in the water. This usually makes a fan tow less practical than a tandem tow. But a modification—a line attached closer to the stern of the towed kayak from a kayak paddling to the windward side—can be used to prevent a tandem or a raft of kayaks from weathercocking under tow, speeding up the tow.

An extra kayak attached by line behind to steer a towed raft of kayaks around rocks or to prevent it surfing forward is also occasionally useful.

Contact Tow

One kayaker can push another forward for a short distance without any lines. The two kayakers face one another. The one to be pushed holds the front of the pushing kayak with hands far enough apart to lever his or her bow against the side of the pushing kayak. This keeps the kayaks tracking fairly straight, and leaves enough room to use a paddle.

The kayaker being pushed can steer by changing the angle of his or her kayak, which is achieved by levering against the bow of the other kayak.

In a similar way, one kayaker can pull another, facing in the same direction, with the second holding the stern of the first. With hands spread sufficiently, the person being towed can hold his or her bow tightly against the side of the kayak to keep it out of the way of the paddle. As in the first example, the person being towed can steer by changing the angle between the two kayaks a little.

A short tether at the appropriate place between the bow of the kayak being towed and the side of the towing kayak may also be used. The tether position will vary depending on the length of the kayak being towed and the length of the stern of

Here a short tether is used to help push another kayak.

the towing kayak. It should be positioned to allow the kayaker being towed to comfortably hold the stern of the other kayak. Alternatively, the towing kayak may be positioned to push the towed kayak, with the stern of the pushed kayak attached close to the cockpit of the pushing kayak, and the bow of the pushing kayak attached near the cockpit of the pushed kayak. This offers the pushing kayaker a better view of the other kayak, and makes it easier to give directions.

A contact tow is a useful way to offer stability and security to another paddler when there are only two paddlers, and for quick action to move someone from a danger zone. For longer distances, use a rafted tow or sponsons to aid stability.

Caution: A contact tow is awkward in choppy conditions, when the bow of the towed kayak can lift to impact under the arm of the person towing. Exercise caution.

Other considerations: Take a glance at the kayaks in your paddling group. How would you attach your towline to each one? Would you choose the same attachment point in each case? What are the chances, when using a particular attachment point, of causing damage to a kayak, and what would be the professional repair cost of any damage you might become liable for? For example, what if you attach to an end toggle or deck line, and the line breaks? What if you attach to a deck line and the deck attachment point breaks? What if you attach to a deck line and the attachment point pulls a hole through the deck? I've seen each happen more than once, but the consequences and cost of repairs are greater for some more than others. Ask the person you intend to tow if he or she is happy with your choice of attachment point, and respect that preference, even in practice sessions.

If you tow when attached to a deck line, it is possible to exert a powerful outward and upward jolt on a single deck fitting, causing it to fail. You might expect that deck fitting to withstand the kind of jolt it could take if you were hanging onto the kayak in surf, or expect that diameter of line to support a weight your hand would be comfortable holding, but in a towing situation in rough conditions, you will likely far exceed those forces. If a deck line appears your best option, consider using a twin-tow system, where any pull is downward and close to the kayak. Try not to exacerbate a simple towing situation by pulling a hole through the deck.

When towed, a kayak will usually swing from side to side, causing drag from the tow line. When towed across the wind it will tend to weathercock, again creating water resistance on the tow line. Reduce line drag by dropping the skeg on a kayak before towing it, using a twin tow as described earlier, or by the towed paddler steering directly toward your stern using paddle or rudder.

When All Else Fails

You should aim, as a kayaker, to be as self-sufficient as possible. As a member of a group you should contribute to make the group as self-sufficient as possible. There are more ways for a group to deal with an awkward situation than for a solo kayaker.

However, even with the best planning and decision-making, there may be a time when you need outside help. A medical emergency may require immediate evacuation. Conditions might have changed, making it evident that the group cannot make it back safely.

At this point you will need to attract attention and communicate your problems and needs. There are several ways to attract attention.

A marine VHF radio is the standard way for a boat to transmit an SOS call. When your call goes out, it may be picked up by any receiver within range. If you fail to get a direct connection, your signal can be relayed to the regional coast guard and to rescue services. With direct connection you can explain your position and situation, and find out what to expect.

There will likely be a significant delay between first contact and rescue, so you may be better off staying active, perhaps paddling toward shore, or away from danger. If so, state your plans. From then on, keep your radio switched on, with volume turned high enough to hear. It is a good idea to learn how to operate a VHF radio, even if you do not have one of your own.

Here the VHF radio is secured for easy hearing.

Nowadays, cell phones can get reception along many, but by no means all, coastlines. Dial for emergency services, specifying that you need the coast guard. For an expedition in a remote area, a satellite phone offers a better option for communication than radio or a cell phone.

Flares are less certain. Firing a rocket parachute flare emits a ball of red fire for the time it

Check with the harbormaster about active shipping before passing a busy port.

takes to float down from an altitude of up to 1,000 feet, and in that time someone must see the signal, identify it as a flare and not a firework, and alert the authorities to its location and time. It is unlikely you will know whether the signal has been spotted unless, or until, rescuers appear, and that may be an hour or more away.

Handheld flares have less chance of being noticed. Orange smoke flares in certain conditions may have a greater chance of being spotted in daylight than a burning flare.

Flares have limited shelf life, diminishing in reliability and intensity as they age. For this reason they show an expiry date, beyond which they should be replaced. Flares must be kept watertight. If they get damp in storage they will almost certainly fail.

Laser flares and mirrors can be used to attract attention visually. Over short distances, waving paddles in the air can also attract attention.

Flares and handheld signals can be useful to draw attention when you spot rescuers within range searching for you. Smoke flares are useful to indicate the wind direction when a helicopter is coming to your aid. Expect a helicopter to approach from downwind. Let the lineman create an electrical ground with the water before reaching you, and follow instructions implicitly.

Given that attracting attention and eliciting help is not necessarily going to be successful, you must have an alternative plan of action. Even if rescue eventually arrives, you might already have succeeded with Plan B.

An orange smoke flare is in action during a coast guard-approved practice session.

Handheld pinpoint flares often drip burning plastic, so allow for wind and hold well away.

From a planning angle, it makes any rescue easier when the rescuers know what they are looking for, in which area, and whether the group has any particular means to signal. If a helicopter knows it is looking for a group of three red kayaks, it will save time by bypassing a group with four yellow ones, but would check if it spotted two red ones. Before you set out, leave appropriate information with someone reliable on land. Contact that person when you are safely ashore, or beforehand if your plans change.

What information should you leave? Here are some suggestions that would be overkill for a two-hour trip on a fine summer day on a small lake, but insufficient for an extended, multiday expedition in a remote area.

- Total number of people
- Leader name: The name of a designated leader in event of emergency, not necessarily the trip organizer
- List of kayakers' names with phone numbers of home contacts or next of kin
- Ability level or group experience
- Number of kayaks
- Color of hull and deck of each kayak
- Type of kayaks (sea kayaks, recreational kayaks, sit-on-tops, whitewater kayaks, etc.)
- Color of clothing if appropriate (e.g., color of PFDs)
- Level of equipment (e.g., all wearing dry suits, all wearing shorts and T-shirts)
- Means of attracting attention: VHF radios/cell phones; number and type of flares
- Lights (in case of darkness)
- Launch place and time
- Proposed finish place and time
- Any potential alternative finish places
- What to do if the land contact has not heard from the group leader by a certain time/date

Your land contact should be someone reliable and responsible, who is prepared to talk with the coast guard or rescue services if he or she has heard nothing by the cutoff time (e.g., "If I have not called you by this time to say we have returned safely, then please contact the coast guard"). Of course make sure that person will be in a position to receive your "I am home safely" call, and remember to make that call when you return, before the rescue services are alerted!

Expedition kayaks beached for a sheltered break on the Åland Islands

Dry Skills Foundation
for Trip Planning

Planning a route using a book of sea charts on the island Tåsinge, Denmark

Kayaking involves on-water time, but many of the questions that arise when we paddle can be best answered ashore. I see the weather change and wonder what to expect. I can read a road map but I want to understand a sea chart. I would like to plan a day trip to take advantage of the tides and the weather. I see marker buoys and don't know what they mean. Am I in a dangerous place? This chapter offers an overview of charts, tides, buoy identification, basic trip planning and other such aspects of kayaking you can study away from the water. Satisfy your curiosity here to enrich your experience afloat.

Charts

Sea charts offer a wealth of information not typically displayed on land maps, such as the direction and strength of tidal streams, the location of tidal rapids, the depth of the water, the position of dangerous rocks, and the extent of mud flats that become exposed at low water. A sea chart may look a little intimidating if you have never used one before, so here (see next page) is a simplified chart on which you can reference the details that follow. This should help you find your way and locate some of the detail useful to a kayaker, but I recommend you look at a real chart, where there is more detail and a lot of extra information.

You may find a key to symbols on a topographic map, but there is no key to symbols on a chart. Instead you will find everything identified in the booklet: *Chart No.1 United States of America Nautical Chart Symbols Abbreviations and Terms*, and in the British Admiralty equivalent booklet "Symbols and Abbreviations" published as Chart 5011," These are usually referred to simply as "Chart number 1" and "Chart 5011." All other member nations of the International Hydrographic Organization also

adhere to this common format in such publications. I will highlight only a few symbols.

There is at least one phone app that covers the same marine information as paper sea charts. At the time of writing, this app was available across Western Europe and North America from seapilot .com. The app helps you plan routes, and can incorporate wind and current. However, you still need to be familiar with how a chart looks, and how to read it. Whether you intend to use paper or an app, the following introduction should help.

What the Colors Mean

For many years, charts were printed on white paper in black and magenta. Most recent charts are also printed on white paper, but use black, yellow, green, blue and magenta. Charts from around the world are gradually moving to color, but there are plenty of places served only by the older style. Several manufacturers of recreational charts use different color schemes, but modern international charts use the following format:

Yellow represents dry land.

White and blue are used for areas always covered by water. White is the general color for deep water. A highlighting band of blue is used to visually accentuate the shallower side of a submarine contour, while solid blue adjoins the coast between a depth contour and the shore. These areas of blue shading serve to easily identify at a glance the areas of shallow water offshore, and also the gradient rising to the shore.

Green, when used, is applied to the foreshore; that area along the shore covered and uncovered by the tide.

Magenta is used to indicate special notices, submarine cables, outlines of more detailed charts, lights on lighthouses and buoys, and traffic lanes

Chart Title

Read the information given under
the chart title first
when you refer to a chart.

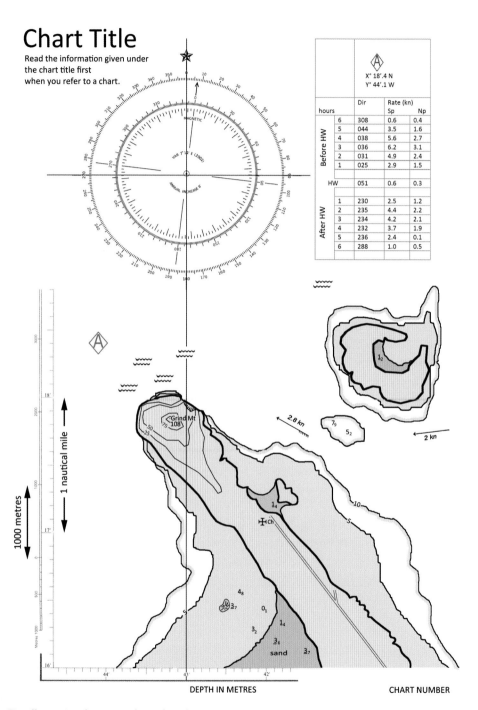

hours		Dir	Rate (kn)	
			Sp	Np
Before HW	6	308	0.6	0.4
	5	044	3.5	1.6
	4	038	5.6	2.7
	3	036	6.2	3.1
	2	031	4.9	2.4
	1	025	2.9	1.5
HW		051	0.6	0.3
After HW	1	230	2.5	1.2
	2	235	4.4	2.2
	3	234	4.2	2.1
	4	232	3.7	1.9
	5	236	2.4	0.1
	6	288	1.0	0.5

X° 18'.4 N
Y° 44'.1 W

DEPTH IN METRES

CHART NUMBER

This illustration shows some basic chart features.

for shipping. The general direction of buoyage and tidal diamonds are also shown in magenta.

Chart Border and Margin

The border and margin of a chart are good starting places for study before you explore the main chart itself.

A black border surrounds the chart. In the margin outside this border, you'll see a statement indicating whether the soundings (depths) on the chart are in meters or in fathoms. A fathom is 6 feet. A meter is 3 feet, 3.375 inches.

Also on the margin you can read where the chart was published, the chart number, and when it was printed.

Title

The title of the chart will be somewhere in the main body, in large print together with a block of text. This is typically displayed in a place of low significance to navigation—perhaps inland—so its position on the page will vary from chart to chart. In the title and text, you can discover how the map was projected, its scale, the datum line from which soundings are taken, and the datum line above which the heights are measured. Other important and useful information for each particular chart will be displayed here. Read through it on every chart you use so you don't miss anything, even if some details are not of interest to you as a kayaker. The approximate scale is displayed here.

Scale

Inside the outer margin of the chart, you will see the markings for degrees and minutes of latitude and longitude. The latitude is shown on the sides of the chart, the longitude along the top and bottom. Because the lines of longitude converge toward the poles, a degree of longitude will

represent a shorter distance closer to the poles than at the equator. Lines of latitude are spaced evenly.

To make a representation of the curved surface of the earth on flat paper, there is inevitably some distortion. This is often revealed when you compare the spacing along the side of the chart between lines of latitude closer to the top with those closer to the bottom. The general scale on a chart is often marked at specific latitude: the only latitude at which it is accurate, so use the latitude spacing near the bottom of the chart when you measure distances near the bottom, and near the top of the chart when you measure in that area.

One degree of latitude (60 minutes of latitude) measures 60 nautical miles. One degree is displayed as 1°. Every minute of latitude is one nautical mile. One minute is displayed as 1'. As an example, a latitude of 20 degrees, 32 minutes will be displayed as 20° 32'.

With the measurement of the globe divided simply into degrees of latitude, it is easy to measure speed on the water in nautical miles per hour (knots). A speed of 1 nautical mile in one hour is 1 knot. You may also see a scale in meters along the side of the chart, in case you prefer to work in metric. 1 nautical mile = 1.852 km = 1.151 statute miles. 1 knot = 1.151 mph.

Depths and Heights

Depths: These are indicated at specific spots by a number, or by a number followed by a fraction in smaller numerals (subscript), such as 5_3. On a metric chart the depth would be in meters and tenths of a meter (5_3 = 5.3 meters). On a fathom chart it would represent the depth in fathoms and feet (5_3 = 5 fathoms, 3 feet, or 33 feet). In each case the depth is measured from chart datum: the name

Low tide can reveal long expanses of sand, mud, or rocks. Britta Johansson

given to that base level. The level commonly used for chart datum is approximately the level of the *lowest astronomical tide,* but refer to the data area of the chart under its main title to check, because it varies from chart to chart. Astronomical tide levels are predicted only from the effect of the moon, sun, and planets, and do not take into consideration atmospheric conditions, high or low pressure weather systems, or the effect of wind.

In areas well served with depth soundings you will often find various submarine contours shown as black lines, which may be solid or broken, perhaps shaded with blue.

Foreshore heights; drying heights: Foreshore is the land covered and uncovered by tide. On the foreshore, which is often shown as green, any numbers (except the subscript) will be underlined, such as $\underline{4}_2$. These represent drying heights. Drying heights are normally measured up from chart datum, but you can confirm this in the text below the chart title. When the tide falls to chart datum, the drying height represents the height of the land above water. At mean high water springs, (MHWS; the average spring tide, high tide level, when sea level rises to the sea level contour on the map) all foreshore will be covered. With smaller tidal ranges, some of the foreshore will remain uncovered at high water (HW; high tide), and some will remain covered at low water (LW; low tide). A $\underline{4}_2$ on a metric chart will represent a drying height of 4.2 meters. On a fathom chart it would represent a drying height of 4.2 feet unless otherwise indicated.

The Grey Area

The sea level line separating land (yellow on the chart) and foreshore (green)—sometimes covered by water—is usually MHWS. That means whenever a tide exceeds the average high water spring level, water will spread onto what is marked on the chart as yellow. Low-lying sand shores and marshes, for example, may be inundated, changing the expected shape of land as seen on the chart. Be aware: This could affect a proposed camping spot.

Charted levels are also for mean atmospheric pressure. Tides will rise higher whenever there is low pressure. A higher-than-average spring tide together with low pressure can cause extensive flooding across coastlines.

Land heights: Shown as numbers on land (yellow), land heights are usually measured not from chart datum but from MHWS. Land contours are shown only where it will help you recognize the shape of land as seen from sea.

Land features: Features recognizable from the water that could be an aid to navigation are shown, with a few roads and centers of population. You will see prominent hills, recognizable cliffs, towers and aerials, chimneys and buildings. If a feature is not visible from the water it is unlikely to be shown on a chart, with the exception of a few roads and rail lines. For better information about land, refer to a land map.

Compass Rose

Charts are drawn with reference to lines of longitude that show the direction of true north and true south rather than magnetic north and magnetic south. A compass rose displays 360 degrees around a circle, making it simple to mark a direction with a rule and slide it parallel to the rose to read off the angle. You can also measure your bearing from the marked lines of longitude, which show true north.

When you paddle you need your bearing to be relative to magnetic north if you intend to use it with a compass. The compass rose may have a magnetic rose within the larger true north rose. If the variation of the magnetic rose is correct, you can simply transfer the direction on the chart across to the magnetic rose and read off the bearing. But that depends on the date marked within the rose. The date at which the variation was recorded and the rate at which the variation is changing with the movement of the magnetic North Pole should allow you to calculate what the current variation will be.

You will need to add or subtract the variation from your true bearing to find the magnetic bearing you will use with your compass.

If north on the inner magnetic rose (after correcting for changes in variation) is showing to the west of true north, then add the difference. If it shows to the east, then subtract the difference. At the time of writing the Mississippi River is roughly zero variation, so you would add the difference if you are east of the Mississippi (US East Coast, Europe), and subtract if you are to the west (US West Coast, Australia, China). There is another changeover line in the region of India (for countries east of India, subtract; west of India, add).

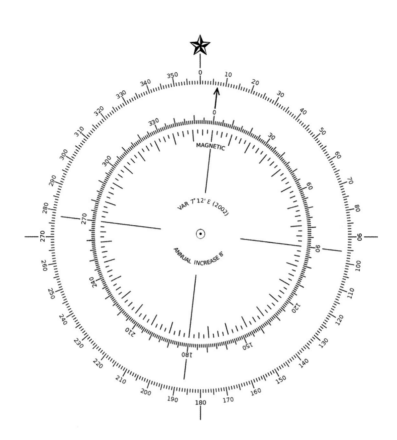

On this compass rose, the outer rose shows true north; the inner, magnetic north. Magnetic, in this case, is indicated to the east of true, so add the variation to true to find magnetic. The variation is shown in the center.

For convenience, there is often more than one compass rose on a chart. Check to see if they all display the same magnetic variation, and when they do not, use the one closest to the area you are working on the chart.

Water Flow
Charts display available information about tidal flow in several ways.

Tidal diamonds
Reference any magenta-colored diamonds to the tables you find displayed in a less-used part of the chart. During the lunar cycle the tide range increases to a maximum, known as a spring tide, occurring after each full and new moon, and decreases to a minimum, a neap tide, after each half moon. The bigger the tidal range the faster any associated currents. Some spring tides and some neaps are bigger than others, so for simplicity, mean tidal stream rates are displayed. Each table shows the direction, mean neap rate, and mean spring rate of the tidal stream at the location of the diamond, referred to as high water at a specified location. You can usually obtain tide tables that refer to that location, or find the tidal constant

		Dir	Rate (kn)	
			Sp	Np
hours				
Before HW	6	308	0.6	0.4
	5	044	3.5	1.6
	4	038	5.6	2.7
	3	036	6.2	3.1
	2	031	4.9	2.4
	1	025	2.9	1.5
HW		051	0.6	0.3
After HW	1	230	2.5	1.2
	2	235	4.4	2.2
	3	234	4.2	2.1
	4	232	3.7	1.9
	5	236	2.4	0.1
	6	288	1.0	0.5

The diamond symbol above the table is labeled:

X° 18'.4 N
Y° 44'.1 W

A magenta tidal diamond positioned on the chart refers to tidal information displayed as a table like this one. The latitude and longitude on this table will help you locate the tidal diamond on the chart. Expect to experience rates in excess of those shown whenever the tidal range is greater than mean. Likewise, when the tidal range is less than mean, expect lower-than-shown rates.

necessary to calculate times from a table from another location.

Tidal Arrows

You may find an arrow, usually with a rate in knots (kn) for spring and neap rates. If the arrow shows no flight feathers, it represents the direction of the ebb stream. With flight feathers on only one side, the arrow represents the direction of the flood stream. When there are flight feathers on both sides, the arrow points the direction of the current in restricted waters, such as a river. Ocean currents are shown as wavy-line arrows.

Eddies and Tide Races

Whirlpool or spiral shapes indicate areas with eddies, and wave shapes indicate the presence of tide races or overfalls.

SOME REMINDERS FOR USING A CHART

- Remember to check the *Title* area to find what applies to that chart.
- There are many chart symbols used, more than you may feel inclined to remember, but they are all identified in the US booklet "Chart No. 1" and the UK booklet "Chart 5011."
- The symbols most commonly referenced by kayakers are for: rocks, cliffs, and hills, tidal arrows; tidal diamonds, indicating the position of tabulated tidal information; dangers (overfalls, tide rips, races, eddies); the nature of the ground in intertidal areas; compass rose.

Sound Signals

Some lights and lighthouses are fitted with signals that sound warnings in fog. The type and frequency of a signal is shown on a chart, to make it possible to identify one specific sound signal from several in the fog. If you hear a sound signal in fog, it might be a fixed signal, or it could be a ship.

Ships Also Have Sound Signals

Here are some of the common sound signals used by ships, which are worth memorizing so you can anticipate a vessel's action.

- One short blast lasting about one second = Vessel is altering course to starboard
- Two short blasts each about one second = Vessel is altering course to port
- Three short blasts, each about one second = Vessel is reversing (operating astern propulsion)
- At least five short, rapid blasts means "Wake up!" The intention of the other vessel is unclear.
- In areas of restricted visibility, vessels should sound one prolonged blast at intervals of not more than two minutes.

As a kayaker you are not expected to make these sound signals. But you are expected to keep out of the way of vessels to avoid collision, so it is valuable to understand what the signals mean, and to correctly differentiate between the sound signal of a lighthouse and that of a ship.

Transits or Ranges

A transit, or range, is when two separate objects and the observer are in line. It is useful to line up landmarks ahead while kayaking, sighting a close object against a distant one to paddle a straight line. Likewise, a transit to one side quickly shows whether you are moving forward or not, and helps you gauge your speed.

This is the parallax effect. To understand, close one eye, and line up a finger held in front of your face with the spine of this book. When you close that eye and open the other, your finger will appear to move. If your viewpoint moves from left eye to right eye, the background will appear to move to the right in relation to your finger. Your finger appears to move to the left.

On the water, when your fixed background appears to be moving to the right relative to a closer fixed landmark, your kayak must be moving to the right. The bigger the distance between the closer and more distant landmark, the greater the visual effect, and the easier it becomes to see the movement.

Harbors often use markers, such as triangles one higher and at a different distance than the other, with the lower one pointed up and the upper pointed down, to indicate a line of safe approach. This is known as a **leading line.** When lights are used to the same effect, they are known as **leading lights.**

You can draw transit lines between easily visible features onto the chart to use when you paddle. You can then pinpoint, for example, the line you are on when an island disappears from sight behind a cliff. You can pinpoint exactly the place where a second line intersects the first, or use two or more lines as boundaries for a particular sector of water, such as one encumbered by rocks that might cause boomers. (A boomer is a wave that breaks occasionally over a submerged rock, but only when a larger wave arrives. Otherwise, the water appears calm because there is enough depth

In this photo showing two transit lines, the yellow boards with red stripes line up, and the two white triangles also line up.

for smaller waves to cross over the rock without reaction.)

Lighthouses often display sectors of different color you can use at night. You know exactly the line you are on when you are on the boundary between a red and green, for example, and you know which area of sea you are in when you see only one color. Any transit lines you draw on your chart can serve the same purpose when you have sufficient visibility to use them.

Buoys

Buoys are markers that display information, such as the position of areas of danger, areas of special interest, and to show safe traffic routes for boats. Just as with road signs, the color and markings indicate the purpose of buoys, so the meaning is recognizable internationally.

As with driving, there are rules of the road for the water too. As far as buoyage is concerned, the lateral marks designate the roads, and within these roads you should keep to the right. When crossing a channel, do so at right angles to the channel, crossing in the shortest possible distance and time.

Unfortunately, two different systems are operated by the International Association of Lighthouse Authorities (IALA). The difference is only the colors of the lateral buoys and their lights, so there is little extra to remember.

System A, introduced in 1977, is used all over the world, with the exception of those areas later grouped under System B in 1980. These exceptions include the Americas, Japan, the Republic of Korea, and the Philippines.

Since 2010, there have been a few additions to the Maritime Buoyage System (MBS). These include a new, blue-and-yellow, "New Dangers" emergency wreck-marking buoy, descriptions of other aids to navigation such as lighthouses and sector lights that were previously excluded from the MBS, and the integration of electronic marks using radio transmission.

Each marker buoy may be identified by color and shape. Many may also be identified by their top mark, and at night by the color and flashing sequence of lights.

The buoys come in these categories:

1. Lateral marks

2. Isolated danger marks

3. Cardinal marks

4. Special marks

5. Safe water marks (fairway and midchannel)

6. New danger marks

Lateral Buoys

Lateral buoys mark the position of traffic routes on the water—in effect, roadways. Red markers are used along one side of the road and green on the other. Where a route divides, a buoy with both red and green colors indicates a preferred route by its pattern of color and its shape. For example, if the preferred route is to port, then a starboard shape buoy will be used, but the color will be both red and green. A ship need not follow the preferred route indicated.

Because every set of lateral buoys is used by vessels moving in opposite directions, there is a convention for the way they are laid out. For rivers, estuaries, and other waterways, the direction of buoyage is from sea to land. In coastal waters, check the chart for the magenta-colored arrows. (In general, these follow the direction of rising tide along the coast.)

This chart symbol shows the direction of buoyage, port mark to the left, starboard to the right.

Port and starboard describe the left and right sides of a boat respectively when you are on board facing forward. These terms come from the tradition of boats having a steering oar hung over right side of the boat at the stern when facing forward, presumably to the advantage of right-handed helmsmen. To enable steering and protect the steering oar when coming alongside the dock in port, the other side (the left side when facing forward) was the port side. The "away from port" side was the "steer-board," or starboard side. If you imagine coming into port, you keep the port-side lateral marks to your port side until you berth. In System A, it then becomes easy to confirm you are lined up correctly. The port side of your boat and the port-side buoys are both red, as is port wine. With this alignment you are heading home! That is: port to port (in) to port . . . perhaps for a glass of (red) port.

Lateral marks differ in color between the IALA Systems A and B. The colors red and green are swapped over. This is only in buoyage, not on the boats. If you are paddling into harbor, or port, with System A you keep the red markers to your left; with System B you keep the green markers to your left.

A way to remember how to navigate in the region covered by System B is "red right returns (you to port)."

You just have to remember where you use each system. If in doubt, do as those colorblind to red and green must do: Ignore the colors and go by the shapes. Port marks are can-shaped, and starboard marks are cone-shaped in both systems. When top marks are displayed, these are the same shape as the buoys themselves. Lights, when shown, are the same color as the buoy they are mounted on.

Where there is a choice of channel, **the preferred route** is indicated by a lateral buoy with

A can-shaped (flat-topped) red buoy: This must be in System A.

The color and shape combinations of these lateral marks indicate they belong to IALA System B. (The green buoy is can-shaped, not cone-shaped.) With System B, the direction of buoyage, for example typically sailing toward harbor, would be between the buoys from the right of the picture toward the left. (Against the current you see around the green buoy.)

a contrasting horizontal band of green or red. To follow the preferred channel in both System A and B, interpret the buoy as a lateral mark of the shape and color (and top mark if applicable) without the contrasting band.

Isolated Danger Marks

These buoys are positioned at a danger, where there is navigable water all around. The danger might, for example, be a rock in a channel. If the rock is at the surface, then a spar might be mounted directly on the rock. Otherwise, a spar or a pillar-shaped buoy will be chained to the rock. The color is black with one broad, horizontal red band. The top mark consists of two black spheres, one above the other. The light, when fitted, is white, group flashing (2).

This isolated danger mark has red and black bands, with two black balls, one above the other, as a top mark. In this case the buoy marks a shoal that has collected a wreck.

Cardinal Marks

Cardinal marks are positioned to the north, south, east, or west of an area of danger. A north cardinal will be placed north of an area of danger. A single

A westerly cardinal mark is positioned to the west of danger.

An easterly cardinal spar is positioned to the east of danger.

A northern cardinal buoy is positioned to the north of danger.

Cardinal marks are placed around an area of danger.

When the yellow color of a Special Mark is unclear, identify by the diagonal cross top mark.

buoy may be all that is necessary to mark an area, but multiple buoys may be used, especially in busy areas, or to mark larger areas. Shaped as a pillar or spar, these buoys are colored yellow and black in broad horizontal bands, with a different sequence for each cardinal. Top marks are two cones, one above the other. The alignment of the cones alone can be used to identify the cardinal. White, quick-flashing or very quick-flashing lights also are sequenced to identify each cardinal.

Special Mark

Special marks are not primarily navigation marks, although they can fulfill a dual role. They are used to mark special features such as firing ranges, sunken moorings, and sewerage outfalls, so they are of relevance to sea kayakers. Sometimes pictographs are painted on the buoys to show the nature of the special interest, but otherwise you will find an explanation on the relevant chart. Shapes vary, but the color is yellow, as are the optional light and X-shaped top mark.

Safe Water Marks

Safe water marks have navigable water all around. They are used as landfall, or fairway markers, at the start of a sequence of lateral marks, and as midchannel markers to separate traffic. Safe water marks are spherical, or a pillar or spar, and have red and white vertical stripes. The top mark, if any, is a single red sphere. The light, when fitted, is a white isophase (alternating equal periods of light and dark), occulting (dark periods shorter than light ones), or one long flash every ten seconds.

New Danger Marks

New danger marks are used to identify newly discovered dangers such as a wreck, until its location is more commonly known, and a permanent, standard buoy is installed. New danger marks are shaped like a pillar or spar, and have vertical stripes in yellow and blue. Any top mark is a vertical yellow cross, and the lights are alternating yellow and blue.

Buoys in the Tideway

Anything tethered in a current can create a potential hazard. Buoys will swing from side to side, so they do not present a fixed target. Moored boats are the same. Allow for your drift and aim to pass downstream of a buoy or mooring, especially if you are not certain of the strength of the current.

This is a mooring buoy. Keep well clear in current.

Ships in marked channels move sideways a lot as they turn, so it is safest to wait on the inside of a bend for a ship to pass. Given sufficient depth of water, boats are free to travel outside the marked channel. Keep a good watch for all traffic, and try to anticipate its movement. Ships cannot stop easily, or quickly, and they travel deceptively fast, so leave them plenty of space and wait to cross a channel rather than taking a risk.

Tides

Tides are water movements caused by the gravitational pull of the moon, and to a lesser extent by the more distant sun. The effect of the moon's gravity is not to pull the water up at the closest point on Earth, but to pull it along where it is free to move. Imagine grasping a tethered balloon in both hands, and pulling it gently away from that tether. You feel the skin of the balloon move. The end of the balloon is equivalent to the point on Earth closest to the moon, and the skin stretch is equivalent to the water movement resulting from the pull of the moon's gravity.

But the analogy is not quite complete. When the moon's gravity moves the water from the part of the globe it influences most, it does so in two directions, toward and away from itself. It is as if you were to hold the balloon around the middle and gently squeeze. The balloon would start to bulge at both ends.

As the earth spins, so the two bulges of water move around the globe. There would be a constant movement of water around the world as the levels rise and fall, but where land masses block the way, the water flows into dead-ends, then stops and changes direction. We end up with a complex pattern of tidal water movement.

When the sun, earth, and moon are in a straight line, the total gravitational pull of the sun and moon are greater than when they are out of alignment. They are aligned when the light of the sun completely covers the face of the moon, at full moon, and when the face of the moon is completely hidden, at new moon. When the moon, sun and earth make a 90-degree angle, the gravitational pull is at its least. That is when we see a half-moon.

In practice, the tides peak about two days later than the phase of the moon might indicate. The biggest tides, known as spring tides, occur two days after each full or new moon, which is roughly twice a month. Tides with the least range, known as neap tides, occur two days after a half-moon.

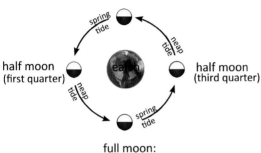

sun

new moon:
we see only the dark side

spring tide

neap tide

half moon
(first quarter)

earth

half moon
(third quarter)

neap tide

spring tide

full moon:
(second quarter)
we see only the bright side

The range of the tides depends most on the cycle of the moon.

The moon's orbit is not circular. It comes closer to earth at times, creating even bigger tides. Sometimes the alignment of sun and moon are so perfect we see an eclipse, and also get bigger tides.

We can easily predict whether the tide will have a big or small range by the state of the moon. But it is more difficult to predict whether it will be an exceptional tide.

That is where tide tables are valuable. Tides can be predicted accurately with reference to all the relevant astronomical data. Tide tables show the times of high water and low water through each tidal cycle at a given location. Sometimes they also show the level of the tide by means of a graph, although you can calculate this information for yourself using the "rule of twelfths," described below.

The Effect of Atmospheric Pressure on Sea Level

When the air pressure is high, then sea level will be pushed lower than usual. You might routinely kayak through a channel at certain tides, but find it too shallow during times of high pressure. Or you might plan to lunch on a ledge or bank when it becomes exposed at low tide, but find it remains covered because of low atmospheric pressure: With low air pressure the level of the sea will be higher than marked on tide tables.

The differences in level caused by air pressure does not influence the range of the tide, but it will affect the nature of tidal rapids by exposing or covering obstacles in a way you might not have anticipated, which may also affect the speed of the current.

The Effect of Wind on Sea Level

The effect of wind drift, a wind-induced current, is one way that weather can affect a tidal stream, making the resulting flow start earlier or later than predicted, and affecting the speed in each direction. Strong wind can also affect the level, pushing the sea level higher with an onshore wind or by funneling into a narrowing waterway. Strong offshore winds have the opposite effect.

Given all the variables, predicting the time of high water or the change of direction of a tide stream is only a guideline, not a guarantee. As a kayaker you need to temper any predictions with your own observation.

Rule of Twelfths

The hourly rate of rise or fall of the tide through a tidal cycle can be roughly calculated by applying this simple rule. From high water, the level will fall by one twelfth of its total range in the first hour,

Rule of twelfths

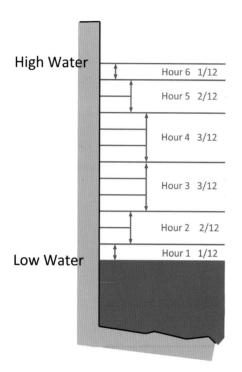

High Water

Hour 6	1/12
Hour 5	2/12
Hour 4	3/12
Hour 3	3/12
Hour 2	2/12
Hour 1	1/12

Low Water

This image shows the rule of twelfths, showing the proportional hour-by-hour change of tide through six hours.

two twelfths in the second hour, three twelfths in each of the third and fourth hours, two twelfths in the fifth hour, and one twelfth in the last hour, ending at low water. The rising water follows the same pattern.

Processing this information in a different way, you see half of the total rise or fall in the middle two hours of the tide. If the tidal range is 40 feet, on average the tide will rise 2 inches per minute through the middle two hours of the tide. That is 5 feet in half an hour. You'll find tides of this order in the English Channel Islands, northern France, the Hudson Strait, and the Bay of Fundy.

With a 20-foot range you'll get 1 inch per minute of rise or fall through this period. This rise or fall translates into how fast a beach covers or drains. With a big tidal range, a fairly level beach will cover very fast during these midtide hours. There are notable places around the world where beaches are inundated, anecdotally, at speeds faster than a galloping horse, and people drown because they cannot escape the rising water. Morecambe Bay in England is a classic example, with a tidal range of 34 feet and rising tides rushing across the flats at up to 9 knots.

Take into consideration the tidal range and the rule of twelfths when you plan launching and landing times and locations, when scoping out places to play in the surf, and when exploring cliff coastline with rock-hopping. Landing at high water or during the early part of a falling tide will, for example, offer an easier landing opportunity, with more time to get organized, than landing at midtide on a rising tide.

Tidal Streams

The tidal rise and fall in water level is usually accompanied by a flow of water along the shore in one direction, which periodically stops and then reverses direction.

You can see the big picture in a world atlas showing the general direction of flood (rising) and ebb (falling) tides along a continental coast. For example, the tide floods in a northerly direction along the European coast, and ebbs back south.

That generalization offers a starting point on which to add detail. For example, the tide rises through the English Channel from west to east, but also floods around the north of Scotland to flow south into the North Sea. There is a meeting point for water entering the North Sea from the English Channel, and water approaching in the opposite direction from Scotland.

You will find more detail about tidal streams presented as hour-by-hour charts in books such as *Reeds Nautical Almanac*: Different volumes cover Europe, the North American East Coast, the North American West Coast, and specific areas of United Kingdom. Individual tidal stream atlases are produced for about ten areas around Britain, and others for elsewhere, such as the Faroe Islands. The atlases are typically for areas with complicated patterns of water movement, but also significant ship traffic.

At the next level of detail, study the features along a section of coast and imagine where the water will flow when it passes prominent headlands and crosses bays. Its behavior will be similar to the patterns seen on a smaller scale on a river or stream. The flow will accelerate past a headland, and an eddy will form behind the headland. The flow will cross a bay, but may set up an eddy on the near side and an accelerating flow along the far side, where the water from the bay converges on the current that crossed the bay. These more local tidal streams make sense when you consider the big picture, but may seem bewildering if you know, for example, that the tide floods east, your tide tables tell you the tide should be flooding, but the water you see in the bay appears to be flowing west.

The time at which a tidal stream reverses direction rarely coincides with the time of high or low water. In fact, it more commonly changes direction midtide. The change in rate of the stream varies from place to place, so consult a tidal stream atlas or a chart to predict what will happen. You may be able to devise a local rule of thumb for future reference.

Rule of Thirds

One such rule of thumb is the "rule of thirds." This indicates how far the tide might carry you from a given spot during each hour of a tidal cycle, and it is easy to apply. First, take the figure for the maximum rate, which is how far the tide should carry you in one hour. If the maximum rate is 6 knots, it would carry you 6 miles in one hour. Applying a rule of thirds, maximum represents three-thirds (3/3), which applies to the hour before and the hour after the time of maximum rate. The rates, which reflect how far you would be carried each hour, change according to the following formula:

Rule of Thirds
Hour 1 = 1/3
Hour 2 = 2/3
Hour 3 = 3/3
Hour 4 = 3/3
Hour 5 = 2/3
Hour 6 = 1/3

This becomes useful when your chart shows a single tidal arrow with a number for spring tide, and another for neap. These numbers are for the maximum rate at mean springs and mean neaps respectively, in the direction of the arrow. The rule of thirds can be used to generate the approximate rates for the remainder of the tidal cycle for that direction of arrow.

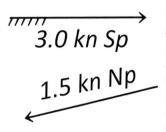

These tidal arrows on a chart represent the maximum rates at mean spring (3 knots) and mean neap tides (1.5 knots) with the flood arrow showing feathers; the ebb without.

Interpreting the arrows in the diagram, the maximum rate of both flood and ebb will be 3 knots at springs, or 1.5 knots at neaps. At a mean spring tide, during the hour following the maximum rate, the tide would carry you 3 (nautical) miles in one hour. The following hour it would carry you two-thirds that distance: 2 miles. The hour after that it would only carry you one-third of the distance: 1 mile.

During a neap tide, in this example, the rate is half that of the spring rate. The arrows show the direction of flood and ebb. The rates show maximum flood and ebb rates for mean springs and mean neaps.

The rule is not completely accurate, but it does offer a quick way to gauge an approximate rate.

As noted, the tide will more commonly change direction midtide than at high or low water, so don't assume the "rule" will fit your location. Check the data for your location first, then see if you can adapt the rule in a useful way. But on a simple coastline, if you know slack water occurs at HW and LW, then you might assume the time of the maximum rate to be midway between.

Around island groups in midocean, tidal streams typically rotate gradually through 360 degrees with the tide cycle. Closer to the continental coast, they often have a much more complex pattern of flow.

Tidal Data

Tidal information is measured at specific places, and will only be accurate there. Usually you can extrapolate the figures to find values between one data position and the next. But this does not always work. At one location in North Wales, the tidal data from the closest chart tidal diamond shows slack water, when the tide a little more

than half-a-mile away can be running faster than a sprinting kayaker. Local knowledge is valuable. *Admiralty Pilot (Sailing Directions)* will offer detail not displayed on the chart; you can also learn from local paddlers and fishermen.

When what you expect is not what you find, trust your own observations rather than your researched data, and try to figure out why there is a difference. Predicted tide times are sometimes inaccurate for many reasons. Maybe you are not at the spot where the tide was measured initially. Perhaps the wind direction has set up a wind drift—a surface current running in the direction of the wind that will affect the speed or direction of the tidal stream. Look for fronds of kelp to see which direction they are streaming, or signs of water running past pot floats, water eddying behind rocks, or signs of wave action caused by wind against tide. The better you get at observing the natural signs, the easier it will be to make good use of water flow.

Watch kelp, and water running past pot buoys, for signs of the direction of current.

Tides at Redport -- 20XX

Greenwich Mean Time

moon	Day	Morning		Afternoon		Mean Range in feet	Mean Range in meters
		hr	min	hr	min		
0.5	1 F	03	48	16	19	11.5	3.5
	2 Sa	04	42	17	20	10.5	3.3
	3 Su	05	46	18	28	10.2	3.1
	4 M	06	53	19	34	**10.5**	**3.2**
	5 Tu	07	57	20	32	12.1	3.7
	6 W	08	51	21	24	14.4	4.4
	7 Th	09	41	22	13	16.0	4.9
1.0	8 Fri	10	28	22	59	17.7	5.4
	9 Sa	11	15	23	46	19.0	5.8
	10 Su	--	--	12	03	19.7	6.0
	11 M	00	32	12	50	20.0	6.1
	12 Tu	01	17	13	37	19.7	6.0
	13 W	02	04	14	26	19.0	5.8
	14 Th	03	50	15	15	17.4	5.3
0.5	15 Fr	04	39	16	10	15.7	4.8
	16 Sa	05	37	17	13	14.4	4.4
	17 Su	06	44	18	29	12.5	3.8
	18 M	07	03	19	51	11.8	3.6
	19 Tu	08	19	21	00	13.1	4.0
	20 W	09	22	21	52	14.1	4.3
	21 Th	10	13	22	34	15.7	4.8
0.0	22 Fr	10	55	23	12	16.7	5.1
	23 Sa	11	33	23	49	17.7	5.4
	24 Su	--	--	12	07	17.7	5.4
	25 M	00	21	12	38	17.7	5.4
	26 Tu	00	52	13	06	17.4	5.3
	27 W	01	21	13	34	16.7	5.1
	28 Th	01	49	14	04	15.7	4.8
0.5	29 Fr	02	20	14	37	14.8	4.5
	30 Sa	02	56	15	18	13.1	4.0
	31 Su	03	39	16	12	11.2	3.4

Tide tables typically offer times of low and high water, height of tide and/or range, and frequently the state of the moon for a particular location.

Working with Eddies

Sea kayaking can be more fun when you keep close to shore. You see more, and you can gauge your progress more easily. But it may affect your tidal planning. To take advantage of the main tidal stream, you typically need to keep away from shore. To explore close to shore along an indented coast, you might make better progress using eddies during an opposing tide.

Tidal Bores

A tidal bore is a body of water that rushes up a river with the incoming tide, flowing against the direction of the current in the river. It is caused by the tide rising into a funnel-shaped estuary. The narrowing channel pushes the level higher until it accelerates up the river, reaching high speed.

Because of this funneling effect, a wave at the front leads the higher water level, so there is an immediate and big increase in river depth with a bore. The tide rises extremely fast.

Bores normally only occur at spring tides, and when the tidal difference is at least 20 feet between low and high tide. They are known to occur on at least fifty rivers worldwide, so when you make a trip on an unfamiliar river, bores are something to check for.

The Qiantang River at Hangzhou China has a particularly spectacular tidal bore, which rushes upstream at 25 miles per hour led by a 30-foot-tall leading wave.

Currents

A current is defined as a steady flow of water in one direction, such as down a freshwater river, or as a constant flow of water in the ocean. Currents are nontidal movements of water, and the ones that concern kayakers are horizontal surface currents. Caused by differences in temperature, salinity, or pressure, some maintain an almost constant flow in the same direction, while others fluctuate seasonally. Some are relatively short-lived.

Ocean Currents

Well-known ocean currents include the Gulf Stream, which originates in the warm Gulf of Mexico, flows north, and then crosses the Atlantic northeast to Europe. The Kuroshio (Black) Current is its counterpart on the west side of the north Pacific. Another well-known example is the cold Labrador Current, which carries icebergs past Labrador and Newfoundland. It eventually runs into

---

NOT ALL WATER CHANGES ARE TIDAL

Small bodies of water do experience tides, but the effect is smaller. In Lake Michigan, for example, the tidal range is from 0.5 to 1.5 inches. That is not enough to affect a kayaker.

Other factors such as changes in atmospheric pressure and rainfall, will have greater influence. In the United Kingdom, a high pressure system may depress sea level as much as a foot, while a low pressure system may allow a rise of up to 3 feet. One millibar (mb) of pressure above or below mean atmospheric pressure (1,013 mb) will cause the level to fall or rise respectively by 1 centimeter. Severe weather conditions crossing a lake can cause the lake water to oscillate, known as a seiche (page 148). The water level at a location onshore may lower by several feet before rising several feet above its original level. This effect is much faster than a tide.

the Gulf Stream off the Grand Banks of Newfound-land, causing legendary fog banks. These currents do not reverse direction.

Some ocean currents vary in strength and direction depending on the season.

Wind Drift Currents

These are surface currents caused by winds blowing constantly in one direction. A 40 mile-per-hour wind blowing in a constant direction for a couple of days can generate a surface current of 1 knot. This type of current is short-lived; when the wind drops, the current stops.

When you paddle in a place with significant current, try to take advantage of it. A current will reduce the speed of any tidal stream that runs against it. A tidal stream running with the current will combine to give a faster flow, which will run in the same direction until the opposing tide has gained enough speed to overcome it. This makes the duration of flow in one direction—the direction of the current—longer than in the other.

Any moving water, whether current or a tidal stream, will be affected by wind. An opposing wind will make the sea state much rougher than expected, while current running with the wind will be calmer than expected for a given wind speed.

Weather

Weather affects us considerably as kayakers. Not only must we be prepared for changes in weather, from hot to cold, dry to wet, clear skies and fog, but we also need to learn how to control a kayak in wind, which is responsible for a variety of sea conditions.

Since a large part of learning to kayak is concerned with controlling the kayak in conditions created by weather, understanding more about weather makes a kayaker better equipped to make decisions about when to paddle, as well as making decisions while on the water.

World Weather Systems

The powerhouse of world weather is the sun heating the equatorial regions. The air heats up, becomes less dense, and rises, creating a region of low atmospheric pressure. Air moves in at the surface level from the tropics to replace that rising air.

The air that rises at the equator spreads north and south at altitude, moving around the tropics and around the poles to create high atmospheric pressure in these zones. Cooled surface air moves from the poles toward the tropics, and warm surface air from the tropics toward the poles, meeting along a zone known as the polar front. The turbulent boundary between these air masses at the polar front spawns the circulating low pressure weather systems that run across the Atlantic as storms.

As the surface air currents move around the world, they are influenced by the spin of the earth, resulting in circulations constant enough to be used to advantage by traders to cross oceans under sail. These are known as trade winds.

Warm Fronts and Cold Fronts

Warm fronts and cold fronts are parts of low pressure weather systems. Low pressure systems form in a similar way to whirlpools between a current and an eddy, but in the case of weather systems, the eddy forms between two air masses moving in different directions. In the Northern Hemisphere, this would be between cold air moving south out of the Arctic and warm air moving north from the tropics. The two meet at an angle along an edge called the polar front.

Just as whirlpools develop when two water currents meet, so vortices form when two air currents glance against one another. Viewed from above, the effect looks like a wave of warm air within the cold air. This wedge of warm air is called the warm sector. As the vortex develops, this wave creates a spiral, but because one air mass is warmer than the other, the leading edge of the less-dense warm sector rises above the cold air, and the leading edge of the denser cold air pushes under the back end of the warm sector.

Warm air can hold more moisture than cold air, so when warm air cools, the moisture held in it condenses into cloud, just as your breath condenses in cold air. The two weather fronts, the warm front, which is the front of the warm sector, and the cold front, which is the front of the cold air behind the warm sector, are places where warm air is cooled and condensation occurs. Clouds form at the warm front and cold front.

The warm front forms a gentler gradient than the cold front, so you can see the effect of condensation high in the sky long before the warm front arrives at sea level. The first signs are very high ice clouds called cirrus. Gradually, as the low pressure system crosses, you will see clouds at steadily lower altitudes until the cloud base is low enough and deep enough for rain to start. When the warm front passes at ground level you will feel the rise in temperature.

Associate a warm front with the appearance of cirrus high in the sky, forming a thin layer that gradually thickens and lowers, as well as

Low pressure systems, or depressions, are caused when the warm air mass from the tropic meets the cold air mass from the pole and creates a vortex. Where the moist warm air is cooled by the cold air, condensation causes cloud.

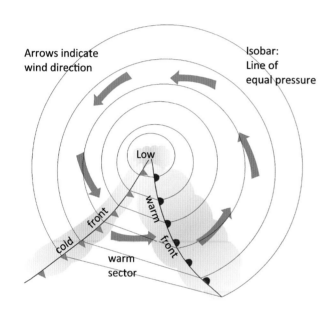

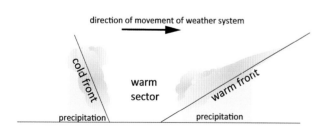

Low pressure weather system in the northern hemisphere

A warm front approaches, with a lowering cloud layer.

rain and rising temperatures. Expect the wind to increase and veer (shift in direction from south through southwest to west in the Northern Hemisphere) with the arrival of a warm front.

The warm sector will pass before the arrival of the cold front. The warm sector is the mass of warmer, tropical air caught within the cooler, arctic air. Conditions are likely to be windy and typically cloudy, often with rain.

When a cold front arrives, there is usually a rapid shift in wind direction from west to northwest or even to north, an increase in wind strength for a short time, and deep cloud where condensation has occurred along a steep gradient. The cold front often takes the form of a line of towering thunderclouds with heavy rain or hail. As the wind shifts the temperature quickly drops.

A cold front generally passes much more rapidly than a warm front, giving way to colder, calmer conditions, often with clear skies or broken clouds and sun. At this point you are once more in the cold arctic air mass.

A cold front often takes the form of a line of towering thunderclouds.

In the Northern Hemisphere, the farther north the center of a low pressure system, the broader the warm sector will be, and the longer it will take to pass you.

When the center of a system passes close to the north of you, the cold front will follow right on the heels of the warm front with rapidly changing wind direction and no break in the rain. In fact, sometimes the cold front catches up with the warm front, pushing the warm sector up, so at ground level there is little or no temperature change, just the precipitation associated with both fronts and the shift in wind direction. This is called an occluded front.

When the center of the system passes south of you, the wind will "back" in direction, from south to southeast to east to northeast. When this happens you will experience no warm sector, and so no associated rise in temperature, frontal cloud formation, or rain. Any rain you get is not associated with the fronts. Effectively you remain in cold air, but experience the winds associated with the pressure gradient.

Wind

Wind is one of the most important aspects of weather for the sea kayaker. Wind is referred to by its direction of origin, so a south wind blows from the south. If you face south, the wind will blow in your face.

The wind speed is expressed as a number on the Beaufort scale, or as a speed most commonly measured in knots, miles per hour, kilometers per hour, or meters per second, depending on your location. This inconsistency can make interpreting a weather forecast challenging, so when you travel, carry some means to make an easy conversion to what you are most familiar with.

Wind speed is determined by the pressure gradient in the atmosphere. The greater the pressure gradient, the stronger the wind will be. Pressure gradient is the difference in air pressure over a given distance. If there is a difference of, say, 12 millibars over 50 miles, the wind will be stronger than if the difference were 8 millibars.

If the wind direction changes clockwise—for example, from south to southwest—then it is said to be veering. If the wind changes in a counterclockwise direction—say from northwest to west—it is said to be backing.

Wind blowing across the sea takes time to build up to a maximum sea state for the wind speed, although it will only reach this maximum if it blows at that strength over a sufficient downwind stretch of open water. That down-wind distance over water is called the fetch. An offshore wind may whip up a bit of spray close to shore, but you may see only small, windblown waves until you paddle farther from shore, where the fetch is greater and the waves are bigger. The apparent calm close to shore is deceptive. A capsized kayak will be blown into progressively rougher

This offshore wind offers a deceptive view of what it is like on open water.

conditions, and any distance you drift from shore will mean hard work paddling back against the wind. You will be paddling back toward a weather shore.

With an onshore wind, the prevailing sea state is more apparent when viewed from land. When you launch into the waves and wind, you know better what to expect. If you capsize you are likely be washed back toward this lee shore.

The weather side of the same island, with the same wind onshore, offers a better indication of likely conditions.

Mountains on the coast can greatly affect local winds. Onshore winds are deflected along the shore, and when they approach from within 22.5 degrees of even a low-lying coastline, they can speed up by as much as 5 to 10 knots. Offshore winds detour around mountain blocks. They funnel powerfully through gaps, and often sweep around either side of a peak and arrive on the coast from opposite directions. Wind speeds under these circumstances can increase from a force 3 to 4 on the Beaufort scale to perhaps force 9 to 10, if the mountains are steep. Downdrafts can be violent and sudden, lifting clouds of spray—and yet the general weather forecast may give little indication of such conditions. Expect tricky winds near steep, high coasts.

Admiralty Pilots (Sailing Directions) frequently note areas prone to violent squalls and places where katabatic winds are common. Katabatic winds are caused by cold air streaming down from the mountains, joining forces in the valleys to produce fierce offshore winds where the valleys meet the sea. They are well known in Greenland, Norway, and Antarctica.

The Beaufort Scale

Force 4 is a reasonable limit for proficient and self-sufficient paddlers to paddle as members of a group under competent leadership.

In the United States, a small craft advisory may be issued for expected winds of force 6 to 7 (23 to 33 knots).

In Canada, a strong wind warning may be issued for similar conditions.

Sea Breezes and Land Breezes

Sea breezes and land breezes are caused by convection. Sea temperatures remain fairly steady from day to night, but the land heats up during the day and cools at night, and is often warmer than the sea in the day and cooler than the sea at night. The warming air during the day becomes less dense, causing low pressure, so air flows in from the sea as a sea breeze. During the night the air over land cools and becomes denser, creating higher pressure, and air flows from the land as a land breeze.

Wind and Islands

Wind experiences more friction against land than against water, so it slows down and backs in direction by about 15 degrees when it hits an island. This causes the wind to be stronger past the side of the island where it converges with the wind blowing past the island, and weaker along the side where it diverges. That same demarcation between weaker and stronger streams of air will still be evident miles downwind of the island. Try to locate and make use of the weaker wind zone when paddling against the wind toward an island, and utilize the stronger wind zone when paddling downwind past an island. In the Northern Hemisphere, paddling straight into the wind, approach an island to the left to find the least wind. Paddling downwind past an island, the stronger wind will again be on the left side. In the Southern Hemisphere the opposite applies.

Backing and veering

In the Northern Hemisphere, a wind backs when it changes direction like a clock going back, such as from west to southwest to south. It veers when it changes clockwise, as from south to southwest to west.

In the Southern Hemisphere it is the opposite: A wind that changes direction from west to northwest to north, or from south to southwest to west, is backing. One that changes from north to northwest to west is veering.

Force	Speed in Knots	Description	Sea Conditions	Sea State
0	1 or less	Calm	Like a mirror	Smooth
1	1-3	Light air	Ripples like scales	Calm
2	4-6	Light breeze	Small wavelets, glassy crests, not breaking	Calm
3	7-10	Gentle breeze	Large wavelets, crests begin to break, glass foam	Calm
4	11-16	Moderate breeze	Small waves becoming longer, fairly frequent white horses	Slight

Force 4 is a reasonable limit for proficient and self-sufficient paddlers to paddle as members of a group under competent leadership.

In USA a small craft advisory may be issued for expected winds of force 6-7. (23-33 knots) In Canada a strong wind warning may be issued for similar conditions.

Force	Speed in Knots	Description	Sea Conditions	Sea State
5	17-21	Fresh breeze	Moderate waves, more pronounced long form, many white horses, possibly some spray	Moderate
6	22-27	Strong breeze	Large waves begin to form, white crests more extensive everywhere. Probably some spray.	Rather rough
7	28-33	Near gale	Sea heaps up with white foam from breaking waves	Rather rough
8	34-40	Gale	Moderately high waves of greater length, much foam	Rough

Force 8 is a reasonable limit for most paddlers on open water. Remember that it may take 2 days and sufficient fetch for the sea state to reach its maximum, so conditions in a force 8 can vary a lot.

Force	Speed in Knots	Description	Sea Conditions	Sea State
9	41-47	Strong gale	High waves, dense streaks of foam along the direction of wind. Crests begin to topple, tumble, roll. Spray may affect visibility.	Very rough
10	48-55	Storm	Large waves (up to 30 feet) overhanging crests, sea becomes white with dense foam, heavy rolling, reduced visibility.	
11	56-63	Violent storm	Large waves (up to 37 feet), white foam, visibility further reduced.	
12	64 +	Hurricane	Large waves (expect 45 feet), air filled with foam, sea white with foam and driving spray, little visibility.	

Hurricanes are classified in 5 categories. Category 1 has winds of 64 knots and above, while category 5 has winds of more than 135 knots (more than 155 mph, 249 kph)

The Beaufort Scale colored to highlight increasing levels of difficulty to the kayaker.

Modification of Weather near the Coast

- If the coast is formed by steep cliffs, or if the land rises rapidly inland, onshore winds are usually deflected to blow nearly parallel to the coast and with increased force.
- Near headlands or islands with steep cliffs, there may be large and sudden changes in wind direction and speed.
- In a strait, especially if it is narrow and steep, the wind will tend to blow along the strait in the direction most nearly corresponding to the general wind direction in the area, even though these two directions may differ considerably. Where the strait narrows the wind speed will increase.
- Similarly, in a fjord or other narrow, steep-sided inlet, there is a tendency for the wind to blow along the inlet.
- When a strong wind blows directly toward a very steep coast, there is usually a narrow belt of contrary, gusty winds close to the coast.
- Where there is high ground near the coast, offshore winds are liable to be squally, especially when the wind over the open sea is force 5 or more on the Beaufort scale.

Land and sea breezes may occur. In daytime, warm air rising over land draws cooler air from the sea, setting up a sea breeze. At night the land cools down rapidly, but the sea retains its warmth, and the warmer, rising air above the sea is replaced by the colder denser air from land. This pattern is often responsible for periods of calm in the morning and evening, when everything equalizes. It also means the welcome breeze that keeps the biting bugs at bay is often absent when you are setting up and breaking down camp.

Onshore sea breezes create the afternoon sailing conditions so popular among kayakers in southeast Australia. With the significant heat of the summer sun warming the land, onshore breezes pick up almost daily. When wind hits land, it backs in direction. In Australia, being located in the Southern Hemisphere, a backing wind turns to the right. The afternoon sea breeze will always come from the same direction.

Because the breezes do not start until the day heats up, it is possible to explore the coast in one direction, then to make use of the afternoon breeze to sail back.

Downdrafts can occur near cliffs with offshore winds. If the winds are strong, these vertical wind eddies can blow very hard toward the cliff. Kayakers in this zone will be carried to the base of the cliff, onto whatever rocks or shallows are there. Farther offshore, the wind will gust straight down onto the water, spreading in all directions. This is also awkward for a kayaker, as there may be little or no warning of which direction the wind will blow next. The wind becomes more predictably offshore as you go farther out to sea. Try to avoid paddling under cliffs during strong offshore winds.

Thunderstorms

Thunderstorms present a special danger to kayakers. Always get a weather forecast. If you are paddling on a day when storms are forecast, or are in evidence, be prepared to get off the water quickly. Stay close to land and watch for the buildup of thunderheads. Look into the wind for approaching changes. Stormy days are not for open crossings. Always wear your PFD; carrying one is not sufficient. You may survive a lightning strike, but if your body sinks the chances of anyone retrieving and resuscitating you are slim.

Thunderstorms present a special danger to kayakers.

You will see light from a lightning strike almost instantly if you are looking in the right direction, but because sound travels at only about 1 mile every five seconds, there will be a delay before the sound reaches you. Count the seconds between the flash and the sound, and divide by five to discover how far away the strike was in miles. Less than 25 seconds, and you should be off the water. The next strike could be much closer.

As you paddle, constantly update your strategy for landing and finding shelter. Size up no-landing areas, and estimate how long it will take to pass them. At the earliest signs of an approaching storm, seek a good spot onshore to shelter. Some paddlers imagine they are more vulnerable with an aluminum or graphite paddle, but it makes no difference what your paddle is made of.

Lightning normally joins cloud at the closest point. You may be that most prominent point above the surface of the water for some distance. If you are close to taller objects, such as boats, you are still in danger from electrical currents spreading through the water after a strike. This current can be enough to disable or kill you. Get off the water as quickly as possible.

Once onshore hurry to the shelter of a building if possible. Otherwise, sit or crouch on the ground on an insulating pad—your PFD for example—with your knees close to your chest and your arms hugging your knees. The objective here is to keep your contact with the ground in as small an area as possible. This way you avoid the possibility of ground current from any nearby strike taking an easy route up your arms, through your body, and down your legs.

If possible, choose a position partway up a slope on dry or well-drained broken ground. Although sheltering in woodland is generally okay, keep away from the tallest trees, and sit between trees rather than up against a tree. Avoid ridges, peaks, and prominent rises. Electrical currents will follow gullies, cracks, and pools—paths similar to those taken by water.

Do not shelter in caves, bunkers, or under boulders or overhangs unless you have at least 15 feet of headroom and at least 3 feet of space on every side. A current will run the shortest distance from roof to floor, and you do not want to provide the spark gap.

If you are with others, spread out 20 or 30 feet apart. That way if someone is injured, there will likely be others who can offer first aid.

Storms can move quickly. If you feel a buzzing or tingling charged sensation before you have found a good place to crouch, drop into your huddle position immediately.

Thunderstorms not only bring electrical activity, but also wind, rain, and even hail, combinations of which can rapidly chill you. It is better to seek good shelter well before a storm arrives than to leave it till the last minute.

Finally, lightning strikes often stun rather than kill immediately. Keep up to date with your first aid, particularly your cardiopulmonary resuscitation (CPR) methods. Your quick action could save the life of a companion.

Mirage Effect

Mirages present the strange navigation challenge of shape-shifting landmarks. What appeared close, suddenly appears to recede into the distance. You may see tall cliffs and distant mountain peaks that are not marked on the map. When you attempt to match the surrounding landmarks to the chart, nothing seems to correspond. How does this happen?

Superior mirages appear when the air temperature close to the surface of the water is colder than the air higher up. Called a temperature inversion, this is common in polar regions, where the water is very cold, cooling the air immediately above it, and the temperature increases with height above the water. The result is the refraction, or bending of light. This can give you a view of landmarks that would otherwise be invisible beyond the horizon. This is called "looming." Objects may even appear upside down in the sky.

"Towering" is when the refraction effect varies so the top of an object experiences a different degree of refraction than the bottom. The effect is to stretch the object, making it appear taller than it really is. For example, a single-story building might appear as a tower block.

When the temperature gradient fluctuates, you will see objects grow in height and also sink down. In the time it takes to consult your chart, an object can sink and vanish, even though it is obvious from the chart there should be something visible

This is an example of a "Towering" mirage effect.

there. In time, the object may reappear and then stretch taller than it should be.

Another mirage effect can appear where you would expect the horizon to be. Sometimes there will be an indistinct layer that you cannot focus on, with objects below and above it appearing clear. This is sometimes called fairy fog.

Mirages can be quite unsettling when you are kayaking, especially if you are alone. Your best approach is to keep note of your position by the direction you travel and the time, rather than relying on transits of landmarks. Attempts to visually judge distance can be very misleading.

Showers

Shower clouds usually build up when warmed air rises and draws in a light breeze from all around.

However, the first falling rain warms and evaporates before hitting the water, cooling the air. This cooled air falls with the continuing rain. As soon as the air has cooled sufficiently there will be a rain shower at the surface, together with a rush of colder falling air, which spreads out on the surface in all directions as a sudden squall. If the shower is short-lived, it will rain and the wind will blow for a while before dying away.

Bigger, cumulonimbus clouds will pull air up into one part of the cloud while air and rain is falling from another part. With this cycle the rain and the wind can last much longer.

The first effect of a shower cloud on a kayaker is a blocking of the sun, which usually means it gets cooler. Next, expect a drop in temperature due to the cooled air falling from the cloud. With

A shower cloud approaches.

Showers can chill you.

the rain and colder wind, you will experience wind chill.

This combination is why hypothermia is commonplace in places like Florida, in otherwise warm weather. It is too easy to go out on a hot sunny day and not consider the possibility or consequences of rain showers. Always worth carrying extra layers of clothing, just in case.

Fog

Fog can abruptly change your world from one where everything is visible to one where all landmarks have vanished. Even sounds may become difficult to pinpoint by direction.

You should always carry a compass on open water, and know roughly in which direction to paddle to reach land. You do not need to be far from shore to be surprised and disoriented by fog. I remember floating just 100 yards from shore at Brighton, England, a popular holiday beach crowded that hot, sunny day with sunbathers. In moments, haziness out to sea rolled silently to shore, dropping visibility to about 20 feet. I found the beach, and with easily identified pier

and groins I found my launching place. Yet it was memorable because of the suddenness of arrival, the density, and the chill of the fog. I learned from many subsequent experiences that this is not unusual. I learned to take note of the slight afternoon chill and almost imperceptible mistiness that often precedes the arrival of fog on hot days.

There are other visual signs of approaching fog, if you are watchful. On a hot summer afternoon on the beach, for example, you might notice the approach of a film of high cloud, perhaps the earliest signs of a warm front approaching. When it partially screens the sun, the temperature will drop, and if it drops below the dew point then you will get fog. In the English Channel, where the water is cool in spring, a warm moist breeze from the Atlantic will also trigger fog, so watch for changes in wind direction.

People often question whether conditions are misty or foggy. Fog and mist are the same phenomenon. Water condenses into the air as cloud. When that cloud is at ground level, we call it mist or fog. We differentiate only by the distance we can see. If visibility drops below 2,000 meters (1.25

Sea fog is enveloping the beach.

Keep together in fog. There are nine paddlers ahead in this shot.

miles), then there is mist. If the visibility drops below 1,000 meters (1,094 yards), then there is fog. That is clearly an arbitrary definition. In the United Kingdom, for driving, the definition of fog has been defined as less than 100 meters visibility.

Visibility is obviously very important to a sea kayaker paddling the coast. Imagine approaching a surf beach with low visibility, when you might be within the break line but still unable to see the nature of the shore.

Seasickness is often brought about or accentuated by the inability to see a horizon, especially when there is a gentle swell. We can deal quite well with an undulating surface when we have land features or a horizon to align to, but when these disappear in fog and we lose that orientation, it may trigger seasickness. It's not easy to paddle well when you feel seasick. If you think you might experience fog, it's not a bad idea to carry candied ginger. Sucking ginger often helps as a quick and easy way to alleviate the symptoms of seasickness. You might not need it yourself, but it could offer an easier solution than towing a seasick companion.

Convection Clouds

During the day land masses warm up, warming the air above, which then rises. Rising currents of air are known as thermals. Air is drawn toward thermals as surface breeze. Warm air can hold more moisture than cool air, so at altitude, where the rising air cools, the extra moisture condenses as clouds. These are known as convection clouds. During the day water temperatures over the sea will change very little, so convection clouds are not seen over water. Thus, convection clouds offer an easy way to locate a land mass from sea in clear weather. Convection clouds will form over even quite small islands.

Convection clouds form above the Åland Islands.

Seiche

A seiche is a tsunami-like effect created on a lake by severe weather. It is typically caused by a storm—especially a line squall—accompanied by a rapid change in atmospheric pressure crossing the lake with strong winds. An oscillation is set up on the surface of the lake, like the slopping of water in a pan, rising up on one side, falling on the other, while the middle stays at the same level. With different frequency oscillations, the pattern may result in several level sections, and water rising and falling in wave action between.

A seiche can have dramatic effects. One reported on Lake Michigan reached a height of 10 feet. On a lake, where one expects the water level to remain fairly constant, a seiche can drain shallow harbors, ground boats, and flood lakeside picnic areas. When storms are forecast over large lakes, consider the wind, the lightning, and the possibility of a seiche. When one comes up, best carry your kayak from the beach, tether it, and take shelter!

Storm Surge

A storm surge is caused by a combination of water blown by a strong wind into an enclosed space and low atmospheric pressure at the center of a storm, which allows a dome of water to rise higher than normal. Windblown waves running ashore add to the effect.

When such conditions coincide with high water and a spring tide, the effect can be a rise of sea level sufficient to inundate low coastal areas. A storm surge of 20 feet is not uncommon. Hurricane Katrina in 2005 caused a storm surge in the Gulf of Mexico, near the mouth of the Mississippi River, that measured more than 25 feet.

While hurricanes are responsible for the most devastating storm surges, it is worth noting that a drop of 1 millibar in atmospheric pressure allows a rise of 10 millimeters in sea level.

In the North Sea, there are about fifteen recorded storm surges per year when the surge is at least 2 feet. These are mostly recorded between September and April. When a surge of 2 feet coincides with a high tide, this is sufficient to cause flooding.

You might choose to stay onshore when a storm with strong winds is approaching, but if you are on an extended trip and camping on low ground, you may be in danger from flooding.

Tsunami

These are waves caused by submarine earthquakes. On open water they are not very high—just a few feet—but they can travel at hundreds of miles per hour. When they reach shallow water the waves slow down, and can rise to disastrous heights.

The first sign may be the draining of water from the shore, so if you are paddling in an area prone to tsunami and you see the tide falling quickly, or falling when it shouldn't, be aware of the possible implication. The time between crests is usually between ten and forty minutes, so you may only have a few minutes in which to act. There is usually a sequence of waves, building up to the biggest and then gradually diminishing in size before disappearing. Your best option may be to paddle into deep water as quickly as possible. The first wave is rarely the biggest, so keep going!

Navigation

This section outlines and elaborates on the main elements you should consider when planning a trip, including the effects of wind, tide, and current, and how fast and far you can paddle.

For many basic trips you may not need to consider tide or current, or make any calculations. But let's say you paddle at 2 miles per hour (mph) and want to paddle a 3-mile trip. It should take you 1.5 hours, right?

But imagine there's a 1 mile-per-hour current and you paddle with it. Your trip will only take you one hour. If you paddle against it, your trip will take three hours.

Double the length of your trip to 6 miles with the same current, and it will take you two hours with the current, or six hours against. That is a significant difference: enough to make it worth planning to go with the current.

It is worth planning your trip to take advantage of any current, tide or wind.

Consider Wind, Current, and Tide

Kayak navigation requires common sense when using the elements to assist rather than hinder you. It requires a combination of preplanning and final adjustment on the water. For the most part a kayak is a coastal craft, operating within a few hours paddling distance from a landing, so you can do much of your planning onshore. You need to consider the three most important influences: wind, current, and tidal streams. You can predict all of these fairly well from forecasts. For longer, open passages, where a kayak is perhaps not ideal, you will need to do planning day-to-day from your kayak.

Wind

The maximum wind strength you can paddle against depends on your paddling ability, fitness, and the distance you need to paddle. Beginners often have difficulty making progress against winds of force 3 on the Beaufort scale (up to 10 knots), whereas fit, experienced sea kayakers have been known to make miles of progress against 70 knot winds when the fetch was short. Progress is slow and hard work, in both examples. Far better to travel downwind if you have the choice, so long as you have a safe landing place ahead.

Current

Ocean currents usually flow in one direction, and are independent of tides. For example, offshoots of the East Greenland current and the northern extremity of the Gulf Stream circle almost the whole of Iceland in a clockwise direction, at a general rate of between 0.5 and 2 knots depending on location. Where there is significant current, it makes sense to use it.

Tidal Streams

Tidal streams vary in speed, direction, and duration, and can set up eddy currents along indented coastlines. Most journeys can be timed to take advantage of the tide whichever direction you choose to travel, but along some coasts it is possible to use the eddies to make good progress when the main stream is adverse.

Paddling Speed

Consider your paddling speed first when planning a journey. Your speed will vary according to your fitness, ability, and confidence in the conditions. The type of kayak you paddle, its load, and the sort of trip you are making also affect your speed. You can calculate your average speed, yet it is sometimes a good idea to plan for something slower. If you can paddle 4 mph, you still might enjoy a trip more when you average 2.5 mph.

Next, outside influences such as wind speed and direction, sea state, current, and tidal streams will affect your traveling speed more than they affect your paddling speed. When paddling 3 knots forward, you still may find yourself traveling backward as a result of a strong tidal stream. When sea conditions make you uneasy, you may paddle less confidently and less strongly, reducing your paddling speed to below what you expected.

Here is a very rough guide to paddling speeds, averaged out to include brief stops during the day.

- General purpose/whitewater kayak paddled fast, or a sea kayak paddled leisurely: 2–2.5 knots
- Sea kayak paddled fast: 3–4 knots
- Sea kayak paddled fast, without stops: 4–5 knots
- Sea kayak lightly laden, sprinting over short distance: 5–6 knots

One way to discover your average speed is to time yourself over distance in your own kayak and record the results. Another is to track with a GPS. Use your results to help you set reasonable goals when you plan a trip.

Let's say your measured average is 2 knots, including breaks. When you have eight hours available to paddle, you should look at journeys of 16 miles or less in length. If your average with breaks is 3 knots, then you might consider anything up to 24 miles.

In each case, when you factor in the help of tide, wind, and current, you will more quickly reach your destination. With adverse tide, wind, and current you will need to paddle just as hard to complete a much shorter trip.

Planning a Coastal Trip

Choose a stretch of coast you would like to explore. I begin by looking at a large area, then focus in on sections that look interesting for one reason or another. I might choose one stretch because it has an indented cliff line or small islands to explore. I might pick somewhere remote from development or the busy waterfront of a city.

Taking the potential launching places, I factor in distances and check for places that might be challenging in a fun way, or potentially problematic. For example, if I would like to paddle about 12 miles on my day trip and have no shuttle, I will need to return to my launch spot at the end of the day. That means I initially look for interesting sections of coast about 6 miles long. If I am not very confident, I must avoid rough water if possible—places with fast tidal streams and headlands with overfalls. These should be evident from the chart. If I estimate my paddling speed on average at 2 knots, I should allow six hours for 12 miles, plus whatever time I would like for breaks. That lends itself to a day-long paddle, with a lunch break at the turnaround. If there is tide, I can plan a day around the change in tide direction around lunch time, and then paddle with the tidal stream in both directions. From that start, I can look at the tide tables and study the chart to find possibilities.

Let's look at a chart (page 152) and check out a few possibilities without the initial constraints of paddling speed, distance, or ability.

On the chart, there are three obvious access points to the water from the road, A, B, and C.

First, use the scale on the left side. The easiest way to measure distance is using dividers. At this scale, if you set the dividers to 1 mile you will find it difficult to measure accurately around the head-lands, so set them to 0.5 or 0.25 mile.

From A to B measures about 2 miles (round trip = 4 miles).

From B to C measures just over 3.5 miles (round trip = 7 miles).

From A to C measures just over 5 miles (round trip = a little more than 10 miles).

Now look at the green part of the chart, which represents the foreshore. At A and B the foreshore stretches for 0.5 mile or more at the lowest astronomical tide. Both of these landings will be easiest around high water (HW) and more tedious at low water (LW).

On a real chart you should next look at the information under the title to find the tide levels referred to the chart datum. There it should show the heights of mean HW and LW for springs and neaps. If, for example, this indicates that at mean LW neaps the tide will be 2 meters above chart datum, you can check for drying heights greater than 2 meters to find where the tide will fall to at LW on an average neap tide. Or you could estimate the water edge at around midtide. In this case, assume that launching or landing at either the A or B sites will be easiest around HW.

At C, the water reaches land with no visible foreshore. There are low cliffs marked on the south side, but not to the north. You would need to check whether it is possible to launch here or not. For this example, let's assume that launching and landing is possible at all water levels.

Also assuming it is possible to park a car at each place, the next question should be about the tide. What time is HW? You can find that on a tide table (page 153).

Once you know the tide times, refer to the chart to find any tidal stream information. The tidal diamond A refers to the table showing the direction and strength of tides through the tide cycle at

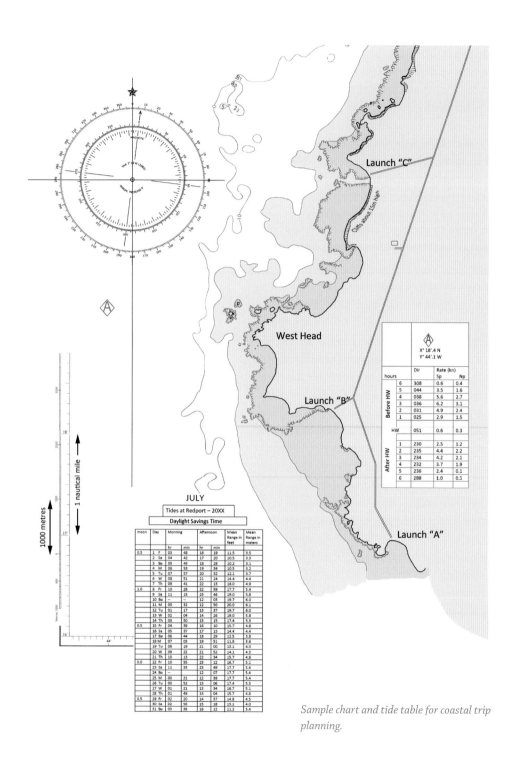

Launch "C"

Cliffs about 15m high

West Head

Launch "B"

Launch "A"

1 nautical mile

1000 metres

Tidal stream table

X" 18'.4 N
Y" 44'.1 W

hours		Dir	Rate (kn)	
			Sp	Np
Before HW	6	308	0.6	0.4
	5	044	3.5	1.6
	4	038	5.6	2.7
	3	036	6.2	3.1
	2	031	4.9	2.4
	1	025	2.9	1.5
HW		051	0.6	0.3
After HW	1	230	2.5	1.2
	2	235	4.4	2.2
	3	234	4.2	2.1
	4	232	3.7	1.9
	5	236	2.4	0.1
	6	288	1.0	0.5

JULY

Tides at Redport – 20XX

Daylight Savings Time

moon	Day	Morning hr	min	Afternoon hr	min	Mean Range in feet	Mean Range in meters
0.5	1 F	05	48	16	19	11.5	3.5
	2 Sa	04	42	17	20	10.5	3.3
	3 Su	05	46	18	28	10.2	3.1
	4 M	06	53	19	34	10.5	3.2
	5 Tu	07	57	20	32	12.1	3.7
	6 W	08	51	21	24	14.4	4.4
	7 Th	09	41	22	13	16.0	4.9
1.0	8 Fr	10	28	22	59	17.7	5.4
	9 Sa	11	15	23	46	19.0	5.8
	10 Su	--		12	03	19.7	6.0
	11 M	00	32	12	50	20.0	6.1
	12 Tu	01	17	13	37	19.7	6.0
	13 W	02	04	14	26	19.0	5.8
	14 Th	03	50	15	15	17.4	5.3
0.5	15 Fr	04	39	16	10	15.7	4.8
	16 Sa	05	37	17	13	14.4	4.4
	17 Su	06	44	18	29	12.5	3.8
	18 M	07	03	19	51	11.8	3.6
	19 Tu	08	19	21	00	13.1	4.0
	20 W	09	22	21	52	14.1	4.3
	21 Th	10	13	22	34	15.7	4.8
0.0	22 Fr	10	55	23	12	16.7	5.1
	23 Sa	11	33	23	49	17.7	5.4
	24 Su	--		12	07	17.7	5.4
	25 M	00	21	12	38	17.7	5.4
	26 Tu	00	52	13	06	17.4	5.3
	27 W	01	21	13	34	16.7	5.1
	28 Th	01	49	14	04	15.7	4.8
0.5	29 Fr	02	20	14	37	14.8	4.5
	30 Sa	02	56	15	18	13.1	4.0
	31 Su	03	39	16	12	11.2	3.4

Sample chart and tide table for coastal trip planning.

that location. From that, you can see the least tidal movement is around HW and LW, and that the rising tide floods generally north.

A trip launching 1.5 hours before HW at A on a neap tide would involve a short carry to the water. If you paddle at 3 miles per hour, you should reach C in 1 hour 40 minutes, not taking the tide into consideration. However, in the first hour you should get 1.5 miles of tidal assistance. That means you should travel 4.5 miles in the first hour. The final half mile should only take 10 more minutes, even without tidal assistance, so you can expect the outward trip to take about 1 hour 10 minutes.

If you leave one hour for a break, the return trip can be calculated in a similar way, bringing you back to A on the falling tide, and landing with a short carry up the beach.

Of course, the tidal streams along the shore are probably slower than those where the tidal diamond is located. But you can plan a suitable trip anyway.

Let's see when the best time to paddle this trip in July would be, bearing in mind you can only paddle at weekends. First, check the tide tables to find the neap tides. Look down the column marked *Mean Range* to find the smallest number, and see which date that occurs on. The smallest range occurs on Sunday, July 3. Since HW is in the evening on that day, (you would need to drive home afterward and work next day), you would prefer to paddle on Saturday. HW is at 1720 on Saturday (5:20 p.m.). If you launch 1.5 hours beforehand, at 3:40 p.m., it should take 1 hour 10 minutes to arrive at C, at about 4:50 p.m. After a break, you would launch again at about 5:50 p.m., to arrive back a little after 7 p.m. In July, this will still be daylight.

With the long beaches along this coast, the trip is more attractive around HW than LW. But the

JULY

| Tides at Redport -- 20XX |
| Daylight Savings Time |

moon	Day		Morning		Afternoon		Mean Range in feet	Mean Range in meters
			hr	min	hr	min		
0.5	1	F	03	48	16	19	11.5	3.5
	2	Sa	04	42	17	20	10.5	3.3
	3	Su	05	46	18	28	10.2	3.1
	4	M	06	53	19	34	10.5	3.2
	5	Tu	07	57	20	32	12.1	3.7
	6	W	08	51	21	24	14.4	4.4
	7	Th	09	41	22	13	16.0	4.9
1.0	8	Fri	10	28	22	59	17.7	5.4
	9	Sa	11	15	23	46	19.0	5.8
	10	Su	--	--	12	03	19.7	6.0
	11	M	00	32	12	50	20.0	6.1
	12	Tu	01	17	13	37	19.7	6.0
	13	W	02	04	14	26	19.0	5.8
	14	Th	03	50	15	15	17.4	5.3
0.5	15	Fr	04	39	16	10	15.7	4.8
	16	Sa	05	37	17	13	14.4	4.4
	17	Su	06	44	18	29	12.5	3.8
	18	M	07	03	19	51	11.8	3.6
	19	Tu	08	19	21	00	13.1	4.0
	20	W	09	22	21	52	14.1	4.3
	21	Th	10	13	22	34	15.7	4.8
0.0	22	Fr	10	55	23	12	16.7	5.1
	23	Sa	11	33	23	49	17.7	5.4
	24	Su	--	--	12	07	17.7	5.4
	25	M	00	21	12	38	17.7	5.4
	26	Tu	00	52	13	06	17.4	5.3
	27	W	01	21	13	34	16.7	5.1
	28	Th	01	49	14	04	15.7	4.8
0.5	29	Fr	02	20	14	37	14.8	4.5
	30	Sa	02	56	15	18	13.1	4.0
	31	Su	03	39	16	12	11.2	3.4

Tide table.

1.5-knot stream at the rocks offshore West Head will create a tide race. If you are not comfortable with this, you could plan the trip in reverse, starting at C, arriving at A around LW, taking lunch on the beach, and returning on the rising tide. Sunday would be slightly later, making for a better lunch time. With weaker tidal streams around LW than around HW, paddling conditions should be more straightforward. The LW carry to the launch is much shorter at C than at A, so this trip idea is certainly an option.

For the advanced kayaker: Paddling from A to C on a rising tide, take a look at what happens around midtide on a spring tide. At the tidal diamond the streams show as 5.6 and 6.2 knots during an average spring tide during the middle two hours. There would be a longer carry down the beach to launch, but with tide, plus say a 3-mph paddling pace, you would travel at more than 9 miles per hour.

The tide running around the rocks off the headland north of B will cause the tide to funnel into a tide race, or overfalls, even though you do not see the symbol marked on the chart. If there is any wave action, especially from the north, it will make conditions even more exciting here. You could time your arrival at the rocks to coincide with the fastest current, play until it calms down, and then take an extended break at C to wait for the southerly tide before returning.

The biggest weekend tide in the month, on Sunday, July 10, shows 19.7 feet HW occurring at 12:03 p.m. To launch at 8 a.m. would offer plenty of play time around the rocks, with the option to then drift on to C at any time. After lunch, the return journey would be more or less exciting depending on how soon after HW you leave. The tide gathers speed quickly, reaching 2.5 knots by one hour after HW (about 1 p.m.).

These are three options, and of course, there are more. There is the easier A to B and back, best at HW. You could choose the fastest part of the tide on a neap tide to find less extreme conditions at West Head. There is likely enough of an eddy to reach West Head from C during the flood tide, offering a way to reach the tide race with an easy return once you have had enough. Planning a day

trip is about exploring all the possibilities, and then choosing the one that suits you best.

Other Considerations for Planning a Trip

- Whenever there are potential areas of danger, such as those with tide races or overfalls, plan to pass while the tide is weak, unless you are looking for excitement.
- Consult a timetable of ferry departures and arrivals if you plan to cross the mouth of a ferry port.
- If there is more than one tidal diamond within the section of coast to be paddled, interpolate to decide how the tide is likely to behave in between.
- If wind is forecast, modify your plans to suit the conditions. This may mean paddling somewhere else.

Planning Open Crossings

There are several ways to plan an open crossing. Here are five examples, each taking the tidal stream into consideration, but excluding the effect of ocean current and wind for simplicity. The approaches should help you make sensible choices for different situations.

Example 1

Consider crossing to an island in an area where there is either no tide, or where there is a long enough period of slack water to complete a crossing on slack water.

Measure the distance: Draw a straight line from your starting point to your destination on the chart, A to B. Measure the distance from A to B. In this case, the distance is 4 miles.

Find the true bearing: Find a true bearing from A to B. You can do this by using parallel rules and transferring from your drawn line to a compass

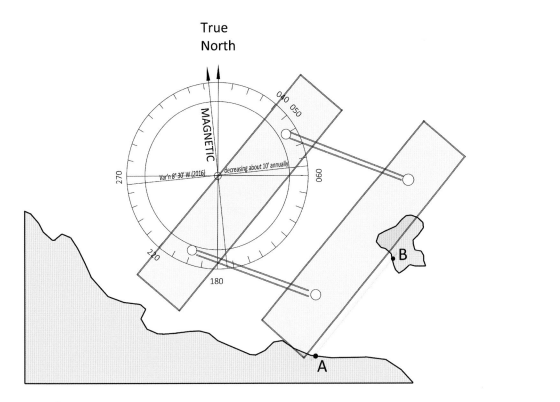

Example 1

rose on the chart, reading the true bearing from the compass rose. In this case, the reading is 40 degrees true (it will need to be corrected for magnetic variation).

Check your direction: Check your course by comparing your compass bearing with the approximate direction you will travel—north, south, east, or west—to make sure you have read the compass rose correctly. It is a common mistake to read the figures from the wrong side of the compass rose. In this example, the island is roughly northeast. In this case, the incorrect end of the parallel rule would indicate 220 degrees (roughly southwest), so the check will immediately reveal the mistake. At the other side of the compass rose, roughly

northeast, the bearing is 40 degrees. This is correct.

Correct for magnetic variation: In this example, the information in the center of the compass rose indicates the magnetic variation in 2016 was 8 degrees 30 minutes west, decreasing by about 10 minutes annually. So if you use this same chart in 2019, you will need to subtract 3 x 10, or 30 minutes, from 8 degrees and 30 minutes, for a variation of 8 degrees west. The variation in this case is west of true north, so add 8 degrees to the true bearing of 40 degrees, which gives a compass bearing of 48 degrees. From point A, you will paddle on the compass bearing of 48 degrees to reach point B.

Making the crossing: When you actually make your crossing, you may paddle using the compass reading at 48 degrees, or you may prefer to simply aim at the island, keeping your bearing as a safeguard in case of poor visibility. If you can see the island, point your bow to it at the start, and confirm the accuracy of your compass reading. It should show 48 degrees in this case. The straight line distance from A to B is 4 miles. If you paddle at 2 knots, you will reach the island in two hours.

Example 2

A well-used method of making a crossing when the tide runs across the path is to balance out the

effect of the tide in one direction against that of the tide in the opposite direction. Make the crossing over the period straddling slack water. In this example, the northerly tide in the hour of high water is compensated for by the southerly tide in the hour after high water.

The compass bearing you will need is from C to D. Your path will not follow the straight line C to D, as the tide will carry you to the north, then back to the south. You must follow the compass bearing rather than aim for the island. Your course will resemble that shown by the dotted line on the diagram. But although your traveled distance will be farther, the distance you actually

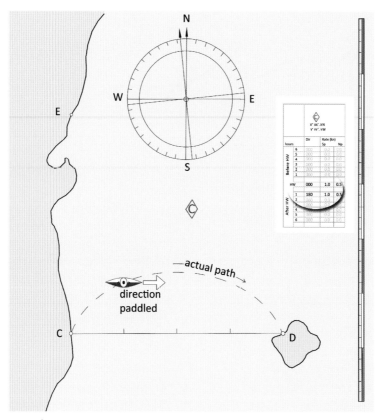

Example 2

paddle will be the straight line distance C to D (4 miles). Your paddling time at 2 knots should be two hours.

Example 3

A good way to make an open crossing when the tide is running in one direction only is to depart from a position uptide of your target.

Let's use the same island, D, as in the previous example. If the tide is running south at a rate of 2 knots for two consecutive hours, then by setting off from a point 4 miles north of C, at point E on

the diagram, and by paddling on the bearing C to D, you should reach target D in two hours.

Once again, you cannot point your kayak toward the island while you make the crossing, but must follow the compass bearing, allowing the tide to sweep you down onto your target.

This method of navigation keeps your paddling distance to the minimum, as before. It can be used to good effect on a crossing where the previous method would have you arrive at the destination when the tide is running fast. By this method you can calculate to arrive when the tide is approaching slack.

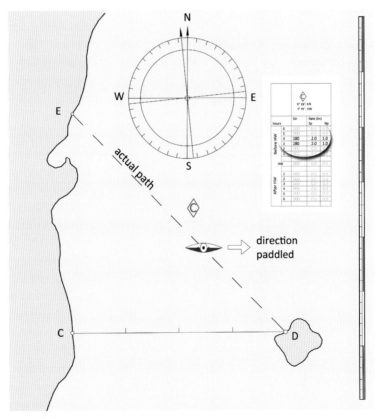

Example 3

Example 4

This method makes a straight-line crossing using the compass to point the kayak up into the tide to compensate for the stream. It is effectively a ferry glide.

Mark a line E to F to represent the crossing you will make. The measured distance is 4 miles.

From the tidal diamond information, the period used for the crossing will be five, four, and three hours before high water.

In the first hour of the crossing (five hours before HW), the 1-knot tide at 180 degrees will carry you 1 mile south. Start at point E on the chart, and measure one mile south to point G. This represents the total effect the tide should have in the first hour of paddling.

Now, measure your paddled distance for the first hour (at 2 knots, that will be 2 miles) from G to the line E–F. Use dividers to do this. I have marked that point on line H. This represents the point you will reach at the end of your first hour of paddling. The bearing you will need to keep to reach this point is "a" degrees marked on the chart. Use your parallel rules to transfer the line G–H to the compass rose to find your true bearing.

Repeat the process for the second hour, starting from H. The tide now carries you 1.5 miles south, so your 2 miles of paddling does not carry you as far along the line E–F as the first hour's paddling did. The compass bearing you need to keep is different, marked on the chart as "b" degrees.

In the third hour the tide is stronger at 1.9 knots, but still south. Your compass bearing "c" degrees will point you more steeply into the tide, so you will travel an even shorter distance along the line E–F.

When you make your crossing you will use three separate compass bearings, each corrected for magnetic variation, and you must change bearings each hour. The actual path your kayak follows will approximate the straight line E–F, so you could use transit marks to confirm your course.

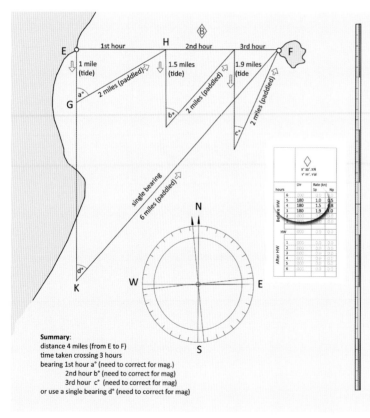

Summary:
distance 4 miles (from E to F)
time taken crossing 3 hours
bearing 1st hour a° (need to correct for mag.)
        2nd hour b° (need to correct for mag)
        3rd hour c° (need to correct for mag)
or use a single bearing d° (need to correct for mag)

Example 4

Changing your bearing every hour is something you can avoid by first measuring the distance and direction the tide would carry you during the whole crossing. That is 1 + 1.5 + 1.9 = 4.4 miles south from your starting point. I have marked that as point K on the chart. Take the single bearing from K to F, marked here as "d" degrees. You can measure the distance you must paddle as the line K–F, (6 miles).

Paddling on the single bearing across a tide that increases from 1 to 1.9 knots, you can expect to make progress to the north of the line E–F to begin with, before being swept back by the stronger tide to end up at F. In this case, you cannot use a single transit line to help you navigate visually, but must follow the compass.

Note that in Example 4, it takes three hours to make a 4-mile crossing, paddling constantly at 2 knots. Your paddled distance is 6 miles. This is not as efficient as the previous examples because you are paddling against the tide.

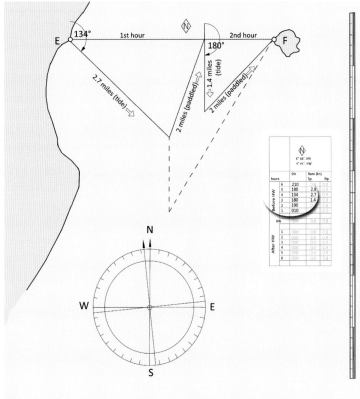

Example 5

Example 5

It is quite usual for the tide to vary in direction from hour to hour, so you need to consider both the direction and the speed of the tide.

The procedure in this example is the same as in Example 4, but you will need to scan the tabulated stream directions to find the period when the tide will help rather than hinder you. You can still work from several compass bearings, changing each hour, or adjust to a single bearing for the whole crossing.

Note: In the example, you can cross 4 miles in two hours because, despite the streams being faster than in Example 4, their direction is more favorable.

Other Navigation Techniques

Here are some strategies for crossing current, gauging progress and how to make chart and tidal information accessible on your deck.

Aiming Off

On long, open crossings it is often best to aim toward a target that will be uptide of your final destination. Then, at the end of the crossing, if you have made a slight error you will have a downtide run to your final destination. You may have to paddle a little farther, but in poor visibility you will know which way to turn, even if you are no longer certain about how far you need to go. If you are late, you are still likely to reach your destination. If you are making a long crossing with a strong tidal stream running across that you cannot use to your benefit, it is better to cross during neap tides, when any small errors will be minimized.

Using Transits

Transits (ranges) are the sea kayaker's most useful navigation aid. When making short crossings, keep two objects in line, one behind the other, to maintain a straight course. Adjust the angle of your kayak against the tide or wind to prevent yourself going off the line.

When you are paddling along a coastline, refer to points in transit alongside your path to tell whether you are moving forward slowly or quickly, or whether the wind or tide has effectively stopped you or started to push you backward. If the closer transit is falling behind the farther, you are moving forward. If the more distant transit is falling behind the nearer, then you are moving backward. If there are good transit points behind you that you can line up with your stern, then you can also use these.

Your constant reference to transits will keep you in tune with any change in conditions affecting your speed, position, or drift. This sensitivity and awareness is the mark of a good sea kayaker.

current:

angle into current
to keep the two objects
in line as you approach

If the near object (green buoy) appears to the right of the far one (red buoy) move right until they line up again

If the near (green buoy) appears to the left of the far (red) move left until they line up again

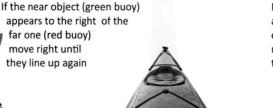

Use a transit (range) to keep a straight course in current, in this case using two objects ahead.

Crossing Fast Tidal Streams

When you want to cross a tidal gap where the water is flowing faster than you can paddle, you can either be carried downstream or you can ferry glide.

If you start with a ferry glide, but maintain a steady angle, you will finish up at the far side of the gap lined up parallel to the eddy line, and paddling directly against the stream. To avoid this, change your angle before you reach the eddy line,

To start a ferry glide, angle steeply into the current as you cross the eddy line at speed.

When crossing current in a ferry glide, change direction to cross the final eddy line at right angles.

eddy

turn at eddline
until broadside
to current

current

Cross the current broadside for the shortest crossing. Make up lost ground using the eddy on the far side.

and cross the eddy line at right angles. You can start to change the angle midstream.

Alternatively, you can cross the gap keeping broadside to the stream the whole way across. Your kayak will be carried downstream, but you will paddle the shortest possible distance to reach the far eddy.

Either way, once you reach the eddy, you can use it to make up lost ground.

Using Charts and Maps Afloat

Maps and charts are awkward to use on the narrow deck of a kayak. When using a clear waterproof chart case, fold your chart so the part you need is visible, and then check for details like the scale and compass rose. If they are no longer visible, copy what you will need onto the visible part of the chart, which should include a scale and a north-south line for measuring bearings. If you need to refold your chart partway through a trip, copy needed information onto each section you will use.

Seal the map case, carefully flattening out as much air as possible. If possible do this in a warm place. Otherwise, if your map case heats up during the day, the air inside will expand, making the case bulge and making it more difficult to read the chart inside.

Flatten out as much air as possible from your chart case before sealing.

You can cut, notate, and laminate sections of charts for areas you visit often, or for a longer trip where it may be convenient to simply switch sections rather than refolding and packing a larger chart. It is convenient to be able to see adjacent sections of chart edge-to-edge, so avoid sealing adjacent sections back-to-back when laminating.

I like to mark measured distances between prominent points and across bays, together with bearings, on charts. That way I can see at a glance how much farther it will be to follow the shore or cross a bay, or how far it will be to detour around an island. I also have an accurate bearing to quickly and definitively identify landmarks. This preparation helps me learn more about the area I will paddle before I set out. I also add points of interest from other sources.

You can also note the relevant tide times for slack, high, and low water, and perhaps the time of sunset, on a separate sheet and laminate that for reference. You can also use a waterproof notebook or a board, or mark such details directly on your fiberglass deck with pencil, waterproof felt-tip pen, or grease pencil (chinagraph).

A laminated section of chart is usually easier to read than a chart in map case.

A laminated chart can get washed from under your deck elastics, so leave a generous margin around the edge, and punch a hole for a tether.

Some kayakers have better sight than others. You can photocopy a section of chart, blowing it up in size to make it more easily readable. Another trick I learned from a Swedish man was to carry a magnifying glass on a retractable tether, the type you might find in use for a ski pass. It may be easier for quick and frequent use than a pair of reading glasses, deploying and packing away almost instantly.

Tide Tables

Tide tables show the time of high water at a particular location on a particular date. It is essential to have the correct date. Depending on the tide table, it may also show the time of low water, the range for that tide or the mean for that day, or the height of the tide at low water and at high water as measured from a given datum (typically chart datum). Because tides are associated with the moon, the moon cycles are often shown.

Be sure to check what the times represent. They may be shown in standard time for a particular time zone, such as Greenwich Mean Time, even in summer, when daylight saving time applies. In that case, you need to add one hour to get summer time.

Tide tables are produced for standard ports, which are the major harbors. You may not be able to find the tide table for the place you want to paddle, but you should be able to find a tidal constant (available for "secondary ports"). This is the time you need to add or subtract from the standard port tables to get the correct tide time for your location.

Imagine a tidal estuary with a standard port at its mouth. The rising tide moves progressively up the estuary from the mouth. If it takes two hours for high water to reach a location farther inland, the tidal constant will be +2 hours in relation to the standard port. Add two hours to the time of high water at the standard port to find high water at the upstream location.

If the major port is farther inland, the tidal constant for a location at the mouth might be -2

hours, as high water will occur earlier at the mouth than at the standard port.

The same principle applies when the tide rises along a coast—for example, rising in a generally northerly direction and falling in a generally southerly direction. The expectation might be that a port farther north would experience high water later than a port farther south, and that a location between the two would experience high water at some time between the two. If this were the case, and you had the tide tables for the middle port, then a tidal constant (sometimes called a tidal difference) for the southernmost port might be -39 minutes, indicating that high water occurs there before high water at the standard port. The northernmost port might show a tidal difference of +51 minutes, indicating that high water occurs there later than at the standard port.

Although the concept serves well for explanation, a linear advance of tide seldom seems to work as expected, especially given that ports are often located within estuaries. You need to find the correct constant to apply to the appropriate tide tables. Local tide times are often available online, and at kayak, fishing, and marine stores.

This table shows July tides for Redport at Greenwich Mean Time (GMT). But it is British Summer Time (BST) in July, so you need to add one hour. Typically, you will find a note in small print to remind you of the dates when BST applies, but many tide tables will be corrected for daylight savings before printing. Why not this one? GMT is a standard time used in navigation, and ships travel the world using only GMT as shipboard time. It is more appropriate for ships to carry tables referring only to GMT. Always check, to see which time is applied.

Glance down the columns on the right and you will see the numbers reach a low of 10.2 feet/3.1

moon	Day		Morning		Afternoon		Mean Range in feet	Mean Range in meters
			hr	min	hr	min		
0.5	1	F	03	48	16	19	11.5	3.5
	2	Sa	04	42	17	20	10.5	3.3
	3	Su	05	46	18	28	10.2	3.1
	4	M	06	53	19	34	10.5	3.2
	5	Tu	07	57	20	32	12.1	3.7
	6	W	08	51	21	24	14.4	4.4
	7	Th	09	41	22	13	16.0	4.9
1.0	8	Fri	10	28	22	59	17.7	5.4
	9	Sa	11	15	23	46	19.0	5.8
	10	Su	--	--	12	03	19.7	6.0
	11	M	00	32	12	50	20.0	6.1
	12	Tu	01	17	13	37	19.7	6.0
	13	W	02	04	14	26	19.0	5.8
	14	Th	03	50	15	15	17.4	5.3
0.5	15	Fr	04	39	16	10	15.7	4.8
	16	Sa	05	37	17	13	14.4	4.4
	17	Su	06	44	18	29	12.5	3.8
	18	M	07	03	19	51	11.8	3.6
	19	Tu	08	19	21	00	13.1	4.0
	20	W	09	22	21	52	14.1	4.3
	21	Th	10	13	22	34	15.7	4.8
0.0	22	Fr	10	55	23	12	16.7	5.1
	23	Sa	11	33	23	49	17.7	5.4
	24	Su	--	--	12	07	17.7	5.4
	25	M	00	21	12	38	17.7	5.4
	26	Tu	00	52	13	06	17.4	5.3
	27	W	01	21	13	34	16.7	5.1
	28	Th	01	49	14	04	15.7	4.8
0.5	29	Fr	02	20	14	37	14.8	4.5
	30	Sa	02	56	15	18	13.1	4.0
	31	Su	03	39	16	12	11.2	3.4

Table title: **Tides at Redport -- 20XX** / **Greenwich Mean Time**

Tide Table relating to Greenwich Mean Time. From the columns on the right see when the maximum (spring) and minimum (neap) occur relative to the moon cycle in the left side column.

meters, on July 3. From the left-hand column, you can see this is three days after the half-moon. This

represents neap tide. Farther down, the right-hand column the numbers reach the maximum of 20 feet/6.1 meters on July 11. This represents spring tide. The left column reveals that occurs three days after the full moon.

Continue down the table and you will find the next neap tide on the 18th, and spring tide on the 24th. Check the times of HW for springs, and you'll see they occur around 1 p.m. GMT (2 p.m. BST). Neaps occur roughly between 6:30 and 8:00 p.m. GMT (7:30 to 9:00 p.m. BST).

That distilled information is needed for general trip planning. The best potential for currents around headlands, and the easiest long-distance travel, would be at the first spring tide in July. For weekend paddling, that would mean from July 9–10. Second best would be July 23–24. For gentler tidal conditions choose the other weekends.

This is based on the range of the tides as an indicator of the strength of the stream. You also need to find the direction of the stream and its speed. For that, refer to the chart, and perhaps also to a stream chart.

Moon Cycles

Tides follow the monthly moon cycle, with a lag of about two days. When the moon shows full or new, tides are approaching the maximum range. Expect a neap tide with the least range about a week after a spring tide.

Florida's spring-fed rivers offer crystal clear warm water. Weeki Wachee River.

Wave and Sea Theory

Dumping waves pound the flint cobbles of England's Brighton beach.

Although we can choose where we paddle, occasionally conditions are beyond our experience. Kayak handling skills are only part of what we need. We must also understand the environment we explore. This includes elements such as wind, waves, and current. When these elements encounter obstacles or tides, the effects are modified in some way. This chapter explores some of the fascinating aspects of the environment we paddle in.

Waves

I'll describe three categories of waves: waves that are produced by the wind, swell that has been produced by wind elsewhere, and waves modified by ocean current or tide.

Let's look at the formation of waves in deep water first. The types of waves kayakers normally encounter are gravitational waves and capillary waves. Capillary waves are the streaming wavelets that tear across the water surface heralding gusts of wind. These travel at the same speed as the gust, and die away immediately as the wind dies. We use capillary waves as early warning indicators that we are about to be hit by a gust.

When the wind blows steadily across the water over time, bigger waves called gravitational waves are formed. These travel more slowly than the wind that creates them, but they frequently outstrip the weather systems around which these winds blow, and can arrive at a beach long before the weather system arrives, warning of its approach.

Windblown waves tend to be irregular, sharp-crested, and chaotic, particularly when the wind direction changes as the weather system advances. With winds circulating around a weather system, waves will radiate out in all directions, sometimes combining and sometimes flattening each other. Seafarers call this chaotic spawning ground a "sea." However, at a distance from this wave generator,

the waves begin to sort themselves out into more even wavelengths. The wave form becomes more rounded at the crest. This type of wave is called a swell. Swells can travel thousands of miles. As they travel their wavelengths—the distance from crest to crest—and their speed increases. Young swells are steeper, slower, and closer together than mature swells.

Old swells attain speeds greater than 50 knots and have been observed with a period (the time taken for successive crests to pass a given point) of as much as 30 seconds.

Gravitational waves gain size according to several parameters. The stronger the wind, the more energy is available to build up waves. The greater the expanse of uninterrupted water over which the wind can blow, called the fetch, the bigger the waves can get. The longer duration the wind blows in the same direction, the bigger the waves can get. In the Southern Ocean storms create strong winds that can blow uninterrupted, creating waves that circle the globe without hitting land. These are perfect conditions for producing huge swells: strong winds blowing for long periods of time with infinite fetch. On the other hand, gale force winds blowing without end will not produce large waves on a small pond. There is insufficient fetch. Neither is there the possibility of huge waves being formed by a gale blowing on open water for just a few hours. There is insufficient duration for them to become very big.

Because waves travel at different speeds, those traveling faster will catch up with and pass slower ones. When one catches up with another, the combined wave will be larger than either of the component waves. But when the waves are out of phase and one crest coincides with the trough of another, the two cancel each other out to flatten the water. In this way we experience a series of larger waves, called a set (or a wave packet on open water), followed by a lull, when we see much smaller waves or no waves at all. We can make use of these natural patterns to choose a lull for launching or landing through a surf zone, or to pick a bigger wave during a set for surf-riding.

Weather systems move, and as they intensify, the wind increases. When they dissipate the winds diminish. From any one weather system far out in the ocean, you may see waves at the shore from a variety of directions and of a variety of sizes, and the variety may arrive simultaneously because different-size waves travel at different speeds. When waves cross each other at an angle you will see peaks and shoulders form along the length of a wave. On open water this creates a crisscrossing effect of mounds rather than simple walls of water. The visual effect and the paddling experience become quite different.

Tide Races and Overfalls

Tidal races and overfalls can be described as **tidal rapids.** They are caused by constrictions in a tidal stream, so unlike river rapids they will change considerably with the state of the tide, the size of the tide, and also with general sea conditions. The rate of flow at any water level depends on the range of the tide, whereas river rapids have a constant rate of flow for any given water level.

Overfalls are caused by constriction in the depth of a tidal stream, while tide races are caused by constriction in the width.

In both races and overfalls, water accelerates past the constriction, which is followed by an area of rough water with waves steepening and often breaking against the direction of the stream. The rough water typically calms farther downstream as the current slackens.

Tide races and overfalls are potentially hazardous, and require care and planning, especially in swell or wind. Waves break more powerfully when they oppose the tide, so even a light breeze will produce waves sufficient to generate a rough sea. When you travel with the tide you meet the breaking waves. If you find yourself surfing the waves, you are traveling against the tide.

Tide Race

A tide race is caused by constriction in the width of the tidal stream—perhaps a gap between islands, between an island and a headland, or simply at a prominent headland.

This is an overview of the tide funneled between islands into tide races. The position of the eddy lines are highlighted in blue.

From slack water, when there may be little surface indication that a race will form, the first indication of movement will be the water streaming in one direction. As the flow increases, the lead-in above the rapid becomes smoother, accelerating into a tongue or chute of water starting at the narrowest part of the channel, the most salient point if the race is caused by a single headland.

The tongue of water narrows as it runs into slacker water beyond the constriction, and waves appear, running against the current.

As the current picks up speed through the tide cycle, the waves steepen against the current and creep closer together. They also curve, because they travel faster in the slower water at the edges, and travel slower in the middle, where they move against the fastest current. This refraction sends waves toward the middle of the stream from both sides, and the waves crisscross as steep peaks that begin to break randomly when the tide gathers speed. Each wave works slowly upstream until it flattens and disappears into the smooth tongue, to be followed by the next.

As with other sequences of waves, you will see sets of larger waves as the wave groups travel in packets, each packet separated by a lull.

Eddies form behind the obstacles that cause a tide race. Immediately behind the obstacle, the eddy direction is usually opposite the main flow, separated by a shear line or eddy line. This line spreads downstream into a wedge between the current and the eddy, with the edges marked by vortices or whirlpools that move slowly downstream, intensifying and deepening as they go and then gradually filling and dissipating.

The main stream, although fixed in position at the top by the obstacles that cause the rapid, does not run in a straight line from there on down, but snakes from side to side, squeezing the eddy to

one side while allowing the eddy on the opposite side to spread, and then squeezing the eddy on the other side. But the waves always break into the current, so it is possible to tell the actual water direction at any point by the direction of the waves. It is also possible to keep to the main stream by threading the line between the whirlpools rotating clockwise on the right side, and those rotating counterclockwise on the left side, although the rougher the conditions, the more difficult it is to see these.

Overfall

An overfall is caused by a constriction in the depth of the stream. Patterns of coastal erosion often leave wave-cut platforms at headlands, creating the shallow water over which the tide accelerates as an overfall. Overfalls can also occur farther from shore, over rocks or shoals in areas of strong tide.

Overfalls exhibit most of the features of a tide race, but can also cause standing waves, which remain in the same place immediately downstream of a ledge, and stoppers, which break constantly in one place. Interference from swell will cause a stopper to fluctuate in strength.

Water deflected by submerged rock features will surface downstream as eddies, making the surface currents more complex than in a straightforward tide race.

Wave Reflection

Waves can reflect off steep cliffs and walls, running out to sea almost unchanged except for direction. However, most obstacles that waves hit are less than perfectly vertical walls, so waves tend to reflect in a variety of directions. Think of the difference between light reflecting straight back from a flat mirror, or from a mirrored disco ball, bouncing light in all directions.

When a wave reflects off a flat wall, the reflected wave will pass through the next wave, combining for a moment to produce a much bigger wave. If the water depth is insufficient to support the combined height the wave will break, exploding in all directions. This is called *clapotis*.

Clapotis, a reflected wave meeting an oncoming wave, rears up and explodes.

What remains of the reflected wave will continue on its track out to sea to meet the next incoming wave, causing that to rear up for a moment, and onward, making each wave in turn jump up as the reflected wave heads offshore.

The breaking water seen here, called clapotis, is caused by waves meeting rebounds from a distant cliff.

Perfect reflecting walls are rare. Natural cliffs tend to be more like the disco ball, with facets facing in all directions. The resulting reflected wave is broken into parts traveling in different directions. These waves may still cause clapotis, and will make the incoming waves jump and peak, but the overall effect of the sea is one of considerable confusion, with waves crisscrossing in all directions and combining to break chaotically.

The unsettled effect of rebounding waves can be felt more than a mile offshore of cliffs, and becomes more intense closer to shore.

Combine the effect of refraction (see below), which focuses wave power onto headlands, with reflection and clapotis from headland cliffs, and the acceleration of tidal streams around headlands as tide races or overfalls, and you can see why headlands can be potentially hazardous places, with much rougher conditions than those found inside a bay.

Clapotis around a harbor wall in windy conditions: Each wave is reflected in many directions by the irregular harbor wall, creating random breaking peaks instead of a solid wall.

Wave Refraction

Waves change direction by refraction. In simple terms, if something causes one part of a wave to travel more slowly while another part of the wave continues at full speed, the wave will bend so different parts travel in different directions.

Waves approaching a bay, for example, will slow down in the shallower water approaching the headlands to either side before they slow in the middle of the bay. The wave stretches to a longer curve as it progresses deeper into the bay. When it finally reaches shore it will have spread to contact the whole coastline, from one headland around the bay to the other headland. In spreading it becomes less powerful, so when it breaks on the shore it will be smaller than when it was on the open ocean. This stretching is called *divergence*.

The opposite effect occurs at a headland, where the wave slows down on either side and wraps toward the headland with gathering power and increasing wave size. This is called *convergence*. Assess the waves when you launch from a bay and expect more powerful ones when you reach a headland.

Wave Diffraction

This occurs when a wave spreads after it has passed through a gap. Waves at the entrance to a harbor can be big, but as soon as they pass through the entrance they fan out to reach most of the inside of the harbor, shrinking in height as they spread. The total energy spread around the shore of the

A diverging wave wraps around the shore of a bay.

Waves diffract or spread after passing between rocks.

A swell converges on a shoal.

harbor is limited to the energy of the part of the wave that passed through the narrow gap of the entrance. Bottle-shaped bays tend to offer sheltered landing places because of diffraction.

Breaking Waves

Swells begin to change shape when the depth of the water becomes less than half the wavelength. A swell with a wavelength of 300 feet (90 meters) will "feel bottom" when the depth is less than 150 feet (45 meters).

Offshore winds can hold up a wave until the depth is less than three-quarters the height of the wave.

Once waves feel bottom they begin to slow down, become closer together, and steepen. If the wavelength is fifty times greater in length (or more) than the wave height in deep water, the wave will also increase in height when it reaches shallow water. This applies to old swells that have traveled from distant storms. In the Pacific, for example, wavelengths from distant storms are often more than 3,200 feet long, but the wave height becomes less with distance. When such a swell reaches shallow water it will increase in height.

When a wave encounters water that is about 1.3 times the height of the wave, the wave will break. Onshore winds will cause waves to break in deeper water, maybe even at a point where the water depth is twice the wave height. With an offshore breeze, old swells with a long wavelength may be held up until the depth of water is less than three-quarters of the height of the wave.

If you are technically minded I recommend the book *Waves,* by Fredric Raichlen, published by the MIT Press.

How Waves Break Depends on What Is Underneath

The way waves break depends on the shape of the seabed, not only at the beach but also farther offshore. Shoals can cause diffraction, distorting the path of waves toward shore and causing them to vary in height and direction as they approach.

Spilling Waves

Assuming a shallow and regular seabed incline, waves will gradually steepen and then break at some distance from the shore, reforming to break again with diminishing power the shallower the water becomes. Waves that break in this way are spilling waves; the crest tumbles forward and spills down the wave face. This is the gentlest form of breaking wave.

Pitching or Dumping Waves

When a shore shelves steeply, then waves will approach close to shore before they steepen abruptly, then pitch forward to break violently. Such waves can break or dump onto a beach with explosive force, hence the name "dumpers." Dumpers can be very dangerous, not only because the full power of the break crashes directly onto the shore, but also because they can produce strong undertows, which are currents that run out to sea along the seabed.

Surging Waves

Waves that run onto a ledge-shaped shore can run ashore without breaking. These are called surging waves. The power is dissipated as the wave rushes uphill.

Spilling waves are great for surfing.

Pitching and dumping waves break with explosive power.

Rocks, Shoals, and Boomers

Isolated rocks and shoals are marked on the chart. In swell conditions, it is important to note where they are because small swells may pass across them without any noticeable effect, but larger ones may converge and break. Such intermittent breakers are called boomers.

Swash and Backwash

When a broken wave pushes water up the shore, that surge of water is called the *swash*. When the water sucks back toward the next oncoming wave, it is called the *backwash*.

Swash surges onshore.

Backwash sucking back out to sea: The scalloped effect suggests there will be strong undertow.

Judging Wind and Waves: Reading the Water

An experienced sea kayaker can tell you a lot about the water just by looking at it: whether the tide is running; if so, in which direction; whether the sea conditions are likely to get worse or better.

Let's consider a simple scenario. Imagine the tide runs first in one direction, and then the other, along a strait, to a maximum of a knot or two. Let's also imagine windblown waves from a steady 15-knot wind along that channel, and that the wind has been blowing long enough to build the average wave height at least 1 foot. When the tide is slack, you see waves breaking as white horses. At slack water, the sea conditions should indicate a Beaufort force 4 wind.

When the tide begins to run in the same direction as the waves, the waves settle down and stop breaking, until at midtide, when the current is at its fastest, the sea appears fairly calm. You might imagine the wind has dropped.

As the current slows down again toward slack, the sea gets steadily rougher, until the white horses reappear.

When the tide turns against the wave direction, the wave height will increase until breakers appear everywhere. The wave height will likely double and the wave length will shorten, making the waves steepen and repeatedly break. The wind may still be blowing a constant 15 knots, but the wave action now suggests a much stronger wind.

With a stronger current, the effect is magnified. A small amount of swell against the current can create big seas. Wind accentuates the effect.

But the wind is primarily a wave generator in this example. If the wind stopped but the swell continued, you would observe the same effect of calming when the swell and current moved in the same direction, with considerable roughening when the current ran against the swell. Likewise, a wind suddenly springing up will show little effect until it begins to build waves. It is the waves against the current that produce the rough seas. The wind merely accentuates the effect, causing the waves to break earlier.

When you know there is a tidal stream, it is good to check the stream charts to find out in which direction it flows, and when, and to plan your trip to take advantage of the tide. But you also should check on swell size and direction: Swell against current will cause rough seas. You should also check the weather forecast for wind direction and strength. The stronger the wind, the bigger the wind waves; the bigger the wind waves, the rougher the seas when waves run against current.

Paddling areas of strong tidal streams and indented coast, the main currents will create

strongly running eddies. Sometimes the main currents will be fairly calm but the eddies will appear rough, or vice versa, depending on the swell direction. When these patterns emerge, it is easy to see where the currents run, and to use them to advantage. From the waves breaking against the current, you should be able to spot when a stream has changed direction, perhaps earlier than expected from your original on-land data.

Long-Shore Drift

Prevailing weather conditions cause waves to push beach material gradually along coastlines, piling it up at the downwind ends of beaches. This is known as long-shore drift. Groins are often built to slow this action and keep beaches from eroding, especially upwind of building projects such as marinas and harbor entrances, where efforts have been made to stop migrating material from silting

Accumulation of material on one side of each groin and erosion on the other shows the direction of onshore drift.

up boat passages. These groins are often built quite close together, making each beach section narrow.

For kayakers, groins can offer challenges. The conditions that cause long-shore drift tend to push a kayaker, waiting to land, sideways toward the next groin. Material carried by long-shore drift piles steeply against the groins, so there is frequently a violent shore break at the downwind end of each beach section, and a more gradually shelving profile at the other end. It is important to aim for a landing at the easier end of the beach, and to avoid being carried by the waves onto the steep, dumping shore against the next groin.

In event of a bad landing, a kayak or a swimmer will likely be carried up against the exposed side of the next groin, downwind into the dumpers where the beach is steepest, or from there carried out to sea by the undertow and rip along the exposed side of the groin. Neither option is much fun.

Sandbanks

Sand coastlines can develop features that present special challenges to kayakers. Much of the East Coast of United States, the Netherlands, and the south coast of Iceland are sand.

Sand coasts are shaped by tidal streams, currents, the prevailing wind and wave direction, and storms. They are dynamic coasts, constantly building in one area while eroding in another, so although beachfront properties are attractive, in the natural scheme of things the shoreline will always be moving.

When barrier islands form offshore, connecting and extending sandbanks, tidal streams are channeled and maintain deeper passages with faster currents. Surf rolling across barely covered sand banks fuels the flow at exit channels, often called passes, working in the same ways as rips on a surf beach, but on a much larger scale.

When the tide rises against a large sandbank, the current will flow around it. When the wind is blowing opposite the main direction of tide, there will be a sheltered area of water behind the sandbank experiencing an offshore wind, while the other side of the sandbank may be quite rough, with the wind blowing onshore.

Be alert. As the rising tide covers the bank, the current will run swiftly over the sand with insufficient depth for a kayaker to paddle strongly. When that current meets the oncoming waves, it will steepen them. Conditions will quickly get rougher. It is really easy to be carried by the fast, shallow water across a sandbank into deeper, rough water with no easy way back.

Deep channels may be cut into the sand by water draining when the tide falls. When the tide rises into these channels, waves can run as far as bends in the channels, dumping abruptly over the steep shore. Once these channels are covered by sufficient water, the underwater topography may not be obvious, but there will still be a violent dumping break at the spot where the depth changes abruptly.

Sandbanks at the mouths of estuaries can remain more or less in position but change in form with storms. As waves or swells approach a submerged sandbank, they are refracted inward, creating horseshoe breaks at the seaward end. Farther down the sandbank, the refracted waves continue to focus inward, creating a crisscrossing sea with peaks occurring wherever waves cross one another. In the shallow water the peaks may break and roll, moving position as the waves move across one another like the blades of scissors closing. Sometimes a wave will approach from one side, sometimes from the other.

Sandbanks are rarely regular in shape, wave patterns are rarely regular, and so the result is an area of chaos. With a rising tide, waves tend to gradually increase in size, but the likely outcome of a swim would be that waves and current would sweep you into the more sheltered estuary where a rescue may be controlled. On an outgoing tide the reverse is more likely. You are likely to be swept out into bigger waves, and rescues will be more demanding.

Spilling waves peaking over a sandbar, La Push, Washington

Applying
Skills

Letting a wave do the work, Cape Flattery, Washington, USA

The paddling techniques you learn and practice in a calm setting can be applied to a wide variety of different conditions. In a calm setting, any one of a number of turning techniques may seem to work equally well for a situation, but when you are in wind, on a wave, or in current you will need to be more selective. Particular techniques work well for certain situations, and not so well for others. You will get better results when you modify your forward stroke, your maneuvers, and even rolling according to the situation.

This section on applying skills offers some guidance and solutions for operating accurately and efficiently in harmony with wind, waves, surf, current, and around the rocks, building on what was learned in the previous sections on wave and sea theory, as well as wind and weather.

Open Water Wave Zone

Waves on open water are often a combination of windblown waves and swell from a more distant source. As a result, waves travel at different speeds and in different directions. If you paddle into the waves for any distance you'll see the wave size vary, and a pattern of sorts will emerge. You will encounter a series of fairly small waves, then the size increases to a maximum, then diminishes again. If you turn around, pick one of the biggest waves, and start to surf it, you will find the wave will soon diminish in size, leaving you surrounded by smaller waves. This is because waves of different wavelengths interfere with one another, combining to increase in size, or when out of phase, flattening the water.

This effect causes sets and lulls on a surf beach, but on open water the effect is to produce wave packets, or groups of waves. A wave packet is a group of waves that are in sync. This is *constructive interference.* Ahead and behind the wave packet are calmer areas of water, where the waves are out

of sync. This is known as *destructive interference,* where waves cancel each other out.

An interesting feature of a wave packet is that waves from bigger wave patterns pass through the wave packet from behind, building in size to the middle, then fade out when they reach the front, traveling at roughly twice the speed of the packet itself. Waves from smaller wave patterns pass through the wave packet from the front, building in size to the middle and fading when they reach the back.

A wave packet is a traveling group of larger waves caused by wave interference.

When surfing on a following sea, it is often easiest to catch one of the bigger waves close to the back end of a wave packet, one that is still steepening and building. Once on the wave, you will accelerate toward the front of the wave packet, where the wave will begin to diminish in size, and you'll most likely lose it.

Depending on the size of the wave packets and the distance between them, you may keep enough speed to sprint forward and catch the tail end of the wave packet ahead of you, in which case you can try to work your way forward through this packet too.

Otherwise when you reach the front of a wave packet, you will find it more difficult to catch a wave for a time. Continue to paddle forward, and eventually you will either catch up with the packet ahead, or the one behind you will catch up with you, and you will experience bigger waves again.

With larger wave patterns, you may find the bigger waves impossible to catch, in which case you should go for the smaller, slower ones.

Catch a wave near the back of a wave packet to ride it until it reaches the front. Each kayak here is in a good starting position, but on a different packet. Notice the smaller waves between the packets.

Try to get used to the rhythm of the wave patterns so you can best use the wave energy. Sometimes it pays to paddle along gently, accelerating to catch waves only when you are in the ideal position in a wave packet. It is usually more productive to relax while you surf a wave, letting the wave go when it diminishes in size rather than working hard to keep with it. Use your energy to catch the next steepening wave that approaches from behind. This way you have a short sprint of three or four paddle strokes, followed by a break while you ride the wave and steer. Then, when that wave drops you, pick the next suitable wave to repeat the process.

You can see wave packets in action if you watch a boat wake as it spreads outward. Individual waves progress through the packet until they reach

Look ahead. Accelerate to catch a wave when it lifts your stern. Steer for the deepest part of the trough ahead.

Relax and use a stern rudder to steer when pushed by a wave. When you stall, wait for the next suitable wave to lift your stern before accelerating.

Traveling downwind with the help of waves is rapid. The distant kayak is surfing on one wave packet, with a calmer zone separating the kayaks.

The paddler on the left might catch this following swell. The others are too late.

the front, where they disappear, to be replaced by the next in line. The packet travels more slowly than the waves. You see the same effect in a tide race, where steepening waves creep forward against the current, only to disappear when they reach the top end.

Longer wavelengths travel faster, so it is difficult to catch open water swell unless it has been steepened by shallows, current, or by interference with another wave pattern. You can usually get better wave-riding results on windblown waves.

The Wind Zone

One of the big factors to affect sea kayakers is wind. Knowing a few relevant points about wind, will help you use it to your advantage when controlling your kayak.

Offshore and Onshore Winds

Wind blowing across water produces waves. On a small lake, no matter how strong the wind, waves will never get as big as on a larger lake. The wind must blow over a long distance of open water to produce big waves. That uninterrupted open-water distance is called the "fetch." A gentle breeze needs only a short fetch and a short time to build its biggest possible waves. Stronger winds need a longer fetch and more time to produce maximum wave heights.

An onshore wind creates waves you can see from the beach. This is the downwind end of the fetch, so the waves are biggest. You can see from shore what to expect farther out. Onshore winds are generally safer because if you can't cope with the strength of the wind and waves, you will be pushed back to shore.

With an offshore wind, the fetch increases the farther from land you go. Seen from the beach the sea looks calm. Paddling out is easy with the wind pushing you along. The danger is you don't know if you are capable of paddling back to shore against the wind until you turn around. The farther from shore you are blown, the longer the fetch, so the bigger the waves will be. You can easily get uncomfortable with the increasing wave size, and find it difficult to make it back to shore against the wind and waves. Always be wary of offshore winds.

Judging Wind Strength by Wave State

The Beaufort scale (page 141) judges wind strength on open water according to the sea state, using signs like breaking crests, spray, or streaks of foam. You match what you see against the descriptions to figure out where on the scale the wind falls. Each section on the scale encompasses a range of wind speeds. Work with the Beaufort scale until you

Kayakers visually assess the wind from shore by wave appearance.

can judge from a distance whether you would be comfortable and competent out on the water. Aim to be able to visualize the effect at sea of any wind speed, given in a weather forecast, since the wind blowing now is not necessarily the strength that was forecast.

A handheld anemometer/wind gauge can be useful for checking the actual wind speed against the conditions you see.

A handheld anemometer (right) can accurately measure wind speed.

Wind in Relation to Direction of Current/Tide

When the wind blows in the same direction as a current, the sea becomes calmer. When the wind blows against the current the sea becomes rougher.

A tidal flow can be strong enough to change sea conditions radically, even in quite light winds. The sea will be calmer than expected for the wind speed when the tide flows with the wind, but much rougher than expected when the tide changes direction. The appearance of a steadily increasing wind may actually be a tidal stream that was flowing in the same direction as the wind slowing to standstill, or reversing direction and speeding up against the wind.

Paddling Across the Wind

Sea kayaks at rest typically turn side-on to the wind. When you start to move forward, the kayak turns toward the wind. The kayak turns from the wind when you reverse.

When you paddle forward there is more water pressure against the bow than the stern, so the wind blows the stern sideways more quickly than the bow. The stern being blown downwind makes your kayak turn. To track straight across the wind you have to correct the position of the stern, not the bow.

Imagine the stern of the hull of a sea kayak as a "V." When the kayak moves forward across the wind and the stern is pushed sideways, water flows under the stern down one side of the V and up the other. If you edge the kayak into the wind (low side to the wind), the V tilts to an L-shape. The more vertical face on the downwind side resists the sideways push better than the slope of the V, so your kayak tracks straighter.

The effectiveness of edging to aid tracking depends on the design of your kayak. The more

Most kayaks tend to weathercock (turn into the wind) when paddled across the wind. To prevent this, edge into the wind, make corrections at the stern, or drop your skeg. To turn toward the wind, lift your skeg, edge from the wind, and maintain forward speed.

pronounced the rocker (or banana shape) of your kayak, the less your stern will grip the water. The wider your kayak is amidships, the more your stern will lift when you edge, and the sooner the stern will lose grip. Convex or bulging sides at the stern also grip the water less. Narrow kayaks with a straight horizontal keel and sterns with steep or concave sides underwater will make the best use of edging to aid tracking.

Even with edging you will likely not prevent all the turn into the wind. Make corrections with your paddle at the stern. To slow you as little as possible, a stern draw at the end of your forward stroke on the upwind side is probably the most efficient correction. It drives your kayak forward a little, in contrast to a push with the back of the blade on the downwind side, which slows you down. Also, it need scarcely interrupt your paddling rhythm.

Add the steering component to the end of your forward stroke. When your blade is ready to leave the water at the end of the stroke, slice it diagonally back and away from the hull, continuing your torso rotation. Bring your onside elbow to your hip until your blade is in neutral and behind you, about 8 inches from your hull. Now push across your kayak with your offside hand at shoulder height. As you push across your blade will open, with the leading edge angled slightly out. Check that your kayak is edged toward the blade and the blade face is engaged. Your kayak should begin turning from the wind. Hold your edge as you slip the blade from the water and continue with your next forward stroke on the downwind side.

Repeat this correction as necessary. You probably won't need it after every stroke on the upwind side, but try to use it before the kayak goes far off course. Small corrections more often are better than a big one. Hold the blade in the "steering" mode longer if you need more effect.

You can use a rudder, a retractable skeg, or both to aid tracking across the wind. Using the skeg, drop it only halfway down to begin. You need to reach cruising speed before you can tell how well this setting will work. Then, if the kayak is heading into or off the wind, you can fine-tune by lowering or raising the skeg a small amount, respectively.

Note: In very strong winds you may find it easiest to paddle across the wind, because your kayak will be blown sideways hard enough to create pressure along the whole length of the kayak. In lighter winds the pressure builds against both sides of the bow, with turbulence forming on both sides of the stern. As the wind increases, the kayak is pushed sideways more strongly. Water flows from the downwind side past both bow and the stern, making the side of the kayak act as a bow. The effect of the pressure you create at the bow through forward speed diminishes as the effect of the kayak moving sideways increases. It becomes easier to track across the wind, and more difficult to turn to or from the wind, as the wind speed increases.

Paddling into Wind

Often the easiest course for tracking: Lift your rudder and raise your skeg.

It is relatively easy to keep straight when paddling into the wind in gentle conditions, if you keep your speed up. The pressure you build against the bow will anchor it, letting the wind blow your stern like a wind vane.

Keep your paddle strokes short, with the blade catch as far forward as possible, lifting the blade from the water sooner rather than later. The wind kills the glide between strokes, so make the switch over from a blade engaged on one side to a blade engaged on the other as rapid as possible. Move your hands slightly farther apart on the paddle shaft for a lower gearing.

Keep your speed up. At slow speeds there is less pressure difference between bow and stern, so your kayak will turn side-on to the wind. If that happens, focus your energy in short sweep strokes at the bow on the downwind side to turn your bow to the wind, and increase your forward speed.

In stronger winds you get a strong turning effect when the bow leaves the water at the crest of a wave and catches the wind. For a moment there is no resistance or pressure from the water at the bow, so the wind can carry the bow faster than the stern, turning you sharply off the wind. To minimize this effect, use a bow rudder to hold the bow on track as you burst over a crest, or use a forward sweep stroke at the bow on the other side.

In very strong winds you will make slow progress across the water. With less pressure difference between bow and stern, the kayak will have a strong tendency to sit side-on to the wind. Remember, the faster you paddle forward, the greater the pressure difference between bow and stern, and the easier it will be to keep on course or turn any degree upwind. Focus on correcting the slightest turn from the wind immediately to prevent the wind from turning you sideways. Reverse to turn downwind.

Break Your Journey into Sections

Paddling against wind can be demoralizing, especially on open water where you see little gain for all your effort. Whenever possible break your journey into short bursts from one sheltered place to the next. Under cliffs, you can often find shelter enough behind little headlands to take breaks from the wind. You may find shelter behind a stone breakwater or pier, or even behind a large channel marker. The energy you apply countering the force of the wind depends on the length of time you are in it. To minimize that time and reduce the overall amount of energy you use, make quick sprints from one shelter to the next.

Watch for Gusts

Watch for signs of gusts and lulls before they reach you. These are easiest to see when there is less fetch: for example, when you approach shore against an offshore wind. The racing edge of a rougher patch of water heralds a gust of wind, and a slightly calmer surface indicates a lull. In heavy winds it may be all you can do to hold the bow to the wind against gusts, so it's really important to sprint for shore during lulls to make progress.

In stronger winds, gusts approach as walls of spray ripped from the surface. Keep a firm grip on your paddle, aim directly at the gust, lean your weight forward, and paddle hard.

If you want to become familiar with strong, gusty offshore winds, choose a lake or enclosed bay with a short fetch and practice near a downwind beach. If the wind gets too strong for you to paddle against, you'll be blown to a safe landing.

Gauging Progress

Watch the shore to gauge your progress. When you move forward, distant objects should appear to move forward in relation to closer ones. If you see no movement between them, you are not moving forward. When you have nothing visible to the side to gauge progress, use landmarks that line up ahead of you, one more distant than another. Move off course to one side, and come back to see the objects open or close from one another. The closer you get, the bigger the effect, until simply moving your head from one shoulder to the other will be enough to see the effect.

Group Behavior

Paddling against the wind as a member of a group requires self-control. It's easy to put your head down and paddle fast, knowing it's the most efficient way to deal with wind, but you could leave weaker paddlers far behind. Sounds are carried away by wind. If slower paddlers are unable to attract your attention, your group safety will be compromised. Instead of paddling faster than your companions, put yourself in a supportive position alongside and just a little behind the slowest paddler. This gives the impression that the person is paddling faster. The slower paddler will feel more positive and perform better.

Turning in Wind

The easiest ways to start a turn in wind are to paddle forward to turn into the wind, and to reverse to turn from the wind.

Turning into the Wind

Fully raise your skeg/rudder.

When you edge from the wind and paddle forward, your kayak should start to turn. If this is not enough, then add a bow rudder as far forward as you can easily reach. If you run out of speed and need more turn, use the front third to half of a sweep stroke on the downwind side, from the bow to the midpoint, which turns you while adding

A kayak at rest usually sits side-on to the wind.

forward speed. Then apply another bow rudder. Hold your edge throughout.

In stronger winds, repeat only the first short section of a sweep at the bow. Push the blade sideways from the hull, not back toward the stern. Mimic the effect of a bow thruster on a ship, which pushes the bow sideways.

Turning from the Wind

Drop your skeg/rudder fully.

Reverse across the wind to start turning downwind. Add to this, if necessary, by edging from the wind and applying a stern rudder on the inside of the turn, grabbing the water near the stern and pivoting around the paddle blade. You can also use the stern half of a reverse sweep on the downwind side.

To turn downwind without reversing, use the last half of a forward sweep stroke, starting level with the cockpit and moving to the stern, then repeat. This anchors the stern and pulls it to the wind. This is effective at slow speeds, but decreases in effectiveness through the last 20 to 30 degrees of turn downwind, when the wind at your back starts to push you faster. When that happens, make use of that forward speed by steering with a stern draw on the upwind side, or by steering with the back of the blade on the downwind side. Any reverse sweep from the stern to midsection will do much the same as a stern draw, but you will lose a little more speed. However, it is effective and the wind adds to your speed anyway.

Sit your kayak upright as soon as the wind is directly at your back.

Paddling Downwind

This is the most difficult direction to hold straight, because the bow creates high pressure and the wind pushes the stern. It is like trying to balance a wind vane tail to wind. As soon as the vane swings slightly, the wind catches the tail and forces it around.

To help, drop your skeg or rudder for extra grab at the stern. You can also lean back a little to weigh down the stern. Control your direction using a stern draw at the end of your forward stroke whenever needed, or a stern rudder, trailing the blade with the back of the blade engaged rather than the face.

The farther downwind you paddle from land, the greater the fetch. You will be affected by waves from behind, as well as the wind. To learn more about catching waves when paddling downwind, see page 181 on the open water wave zone.

Rock Gardens

To paddle in rock gardens, you first need the kayaking skills to negotiate gaps without touching the rock either side. Challenge your skills by negotiating passages on a calm day to find out how accurate you can be.

The level of difficulty increases with sea conditions. You also need to understand how the water moves, and be able to read and interpret it. Try a day with gentle regular wave action to add the up-and-down motion, which requires timing. Work on your timing to pass through gaps at the optimum moment for water level, and to work with a surge rather than against it.

Once waves start breaking through gaps timing is more critical, and the consequences of bad timing become greater. Pay attention to the pattern of sets and lulls and, when you feel ready, try some straightforward moves into safe areas.

With more swell action you will find turbulent water everywhere, causing strong, changing currents and a bigger rise and fall. Your kayak control must be automatic, and you must be quick to

A kayaker enjoys easy conditions.

Progress from calm conditions to find a little wave action.

recognize and react to currents, and to anticipate the effects of approaching waves.

An Overview

Rocky coastlines with cliffs, stacks, offshore rocks, and other features consistent with erosion are referred to, in general terms, as "rock gardens." Rock gardens are typically formed where a coastline is battered by waves, although you will also find them in places like Sweden and Finland, where new islands and rocks are gradually appearing as land levels rebound (the land was weighted down under ice during the last ice age).

When checking out a rock garden to decide whether it is a good place to explore by kayak, I find it useful to categorize the rock I see as:

- always above water;
- alternately covered and exposed by waves;
- always covered by water, but close enough to the surface to affect the way waves will behave

Rock such as sandstone and chalk erodes fast. Waves cut a platform or ledge, beyond which stands a steep or vertical wall or cliff. Waves erode the base of the cliff until the soft rock above

Rock gardens come alive with wind and waves.

collapses. The waves then wear away the fallen rock, eventually reaching the base of the cliff again.

This type of cliff is not ideal for rock play. At low tide, the sea breaks as surf across the wave-cut platform, and at high tide the waves hit the cliff and rebound, creating a confused sea with clapotis. Fallen piles of rock at the base of the cliff do not create a good rock garden.

Rock that is more resistant to erosion, especially when it has natural fault lines with bands of weakness, is more interesting. Waves beat into cracks to create caves, which join to form tunnels, which collapse into archways, which collapse again

to leave stacks. Remnants of worn stacks stand as low, exposed rocks, often offshore, creating pour-overs. Such coastline is wonderful to explore in calm weather, when all the narrow channels, caves, and tunnels are accessible to a sea kayak. Cruising between rock features on a calm day is like studying a whitewater river at low water flow, with deep clear water between obstacles revealing all manner of life.

But with a little swell the area springs into action, with surging water, crosscurrents, breaks, and rebounds. Suddenly, everything requires not only more skill to negotiate, but also some understanding of what is going on.

In rougher conditions, expect strong currents and broken water, as well as a rise and fall between the rocks.

As the wave action increases, you will experience the rise and fall of water, with isolated pour-overs and surges to run, and you will get turbulence everywhere, with powerful crosscurrents that change direction. Amid rocks that will reveal themselves as the water drains, you will have to deal with the power of waves breaking violently enough to push you against your will. You will require technical skill in negotiating currents and waves, and a sound awareness of how the lulls and sets will affect your situation. You also need to realize the potential for disaster, and have a rescue strategy. This is where the risk increases, not only through a mistake or misjudgment on your part,

but because a slightly bigger wave could cause disaster.

I recommend plenty of exploration in gentle conditions to become familiar with what you might find in a rock garden. Here are some features you might enjoy.

Flat Ledges

Flat ledges often occur at about water level, especially in areas of relatively soft sedimentary rock. They are known by geographers as wave-cut platforms, which perfectly describes how they are formed. They can offer an interesting place to play.

This wave breaking across a flat ledge will dissipate when it reaches deeper water.

Look for platforms surrounded by deeper water. To visualize paddling on a flat ledge, imagine an isolated platform of rock surrounded by deeper water. With ledges extending from shore, you run the likelihood of being grounded when the water shallows. I make the distinction between flat ledges and reef breaks by the water depth, and by the way waves break as a consequence.

Depending on the water depth, you may see the rock exposed between waves, or covered in shallow water. Either way, when a wave approaches, the preceding trough will drain water from the rock before the wave washes across. Because of the shallowness, a wave typically breaks at the first edge it reaches and rushes across the entire ledge as broken water (soup).

Friction will cause the wave to refract, so it will peel diagonally onto the rock from each side, combining to peak with greater power toward the midline. This is the same convergence you see on reef breaks, but you tend not to get the unbroken wave, only the soup. Beyond the rock, the refracted wave will continue to intersect, peaking along a line toward shore. When refraction is great enough, the wave will wrap around to approach from almost opposite directions, intersecting along the midline like the cutting point between the blades of closing scissors. The resulting "zipper" is a plume of clapotis that races toward shore.

Beyond the rock the refracted waves will continue on their modified paths, interacting with subsequent waves as they spread outward.

To cross a ledge of this kind, it is essential to keep your kayak just behind the wave front as it crosses the rock. If you surf onto the front of the wave, your kayak will plow into the exposed rock ahead. Too far behind, and you will run aground.

Waves cross sandbanks in a similarly way, so sandbanks make a good place to practice your timing without such harsh consequences should you make a mistake.

Pour-overs

Pour-overs frequently occur when a wall of rock runs parallel to a cliff. Waves may repeatedly, or occasionally, lift high enough to wash right over the top of the wall. To negotiate a pour-over, check your landing area first, watching it through at least one full cycle of set and lull to see what happens. Perhaps a pour-over will have insufficient depth to paddle over during a lull, but may offer too shallow a landing or too wild a landing pool during a set.

Pour-overs often have a low spot or slot in the parapet. The pour-over will be deeper here, so it is usually the best place to aim for. But check the shape of the slot when the water drains away. A slot that narrows down to a kayak-width or less may trap you if you make a mistake. Look to see how sharp the edges of rock are, and how large the barnacles or other hazards. A clean gap with smooth bare rock promises a safer passage than a narrow, sharp-edged slot with shellfish.

Look to see how open your landing will be once through the slot, especially when a large wave has passed and the water level has fallen. You may have enough water to land in during a lull, but a rock landing during a set.

A funnel-shaped approach toward a gap between two rocks will cause the wave to squeeze narrower and build in height. This accentuates the difference in levels between the water in the gap and the water ahead, and may also make the wave break in the gap. Beyond the gap, the wave will diminish in height and stop breaking if the water is deep.

Watch to see what happens, and rehearse in your mind to get a sense of the correct timing. Approach this kind of feature with the same

As a trough approaches from the ocean, water pours out to sea over this pour-over.

The approaching swell has now leveled the pour-over.

The swell has arrived; water pours from the ocean side.

timing as with a flat ledge: chase immediately behind rather than going ahead of the wave peak. The wave will rise, maybe break, and then explode from the gap, perhaps with a pronounced drop and a waterfall effect. Even if the water is deep and the wave spreads and diminishes in height, a kayak barreling through the gap and "over the falls" will exit at speed, so make sure you have sufficient room to maneuver.

Stoppers in Pour-Overs

A steep fall will cause a vertically recirculating eddy of water: a stopper. This can pull the surface water back toward the falling water, slowing or stalling a kayak, which may then be in danger of being pulled back over the fall in the other direction when the fall reverses. You should be able to spot this when you check out the landing area, and be able to decide whether to give it a miss. When encountering a stopper, push through at speed

As water pours down through this gap (A), surface water is drawn toward the gap from the other side (B). With this gap, a stopper did not form with every wave.

immediately behind the peak of the wave and continue to paddle until you are clear.

A rock barrier with a slot might not produce a reversing fall. Some only work in one direction.

Reversing falls are at their most powerful when the wave causing the pour-over in a barrier wraps around the ends of that barrier to make the cliffward water level peak in height as the next trough approaches from seaward. Water naturally pours back over the ledge. Reversing falls involve more risk than one-way falls. If you pass through a gap too soon, too slowly, too late, or capsize on your way through, you run the risk of being taken back through, upright or not. You may find yourself carried to and fro several times before you can break free.

Assess the dangers, and choose places with potential excitement but low risk rather than low excitement with high risk.

Timing for a Pour-Over

Time your approach to reach the slot immediately following a peak, so you ride high on the back of the wave up and over the rock. Too soon, and

Be ready to brace to prevent loss of balance, or to roll to regain it.

you'll surf, typically broaching and hitting rock: you'll almost always lose control. Too late, and you risk landing on the rock, which seldom has a happy ending. You can practice timing on shore breaks, riding the back of each wave onto a beach. The required timing is similar. With a pour-over, you typically need some speed to clear the drop beyond. Be ready to use a low brace to keep balance when you land.

Passages Between Cliff and Rock

Running perpendicular to approaching waves, passages are either safe or not. If waves break as they run through a passage, then you probably want to find somewhere else to go, or should wait for a calm period. In passages running parallel to approaching waves, the effect is different. The wave will build up and fill the passage often from both ends simultaneously, peaking to a high point in the middle then draining back out in both directions.

A passage like this can be fun to paddle, entering with the swash with enough speed to reach the midpoint where it peaks, and accelerating out the other end with the escaping water. You really get a sense that you're climbing in and running downhill on your way out. You will rise much higher than you would expect given the swell size, but remember the opposite effect also occurs. The trough may expose rock in the middle when the wave drains, or the slot may be narrower than a kayak. Watch

This wave has peaked and will drain (see arrows), offering a downhill opportunity between the rock and the wall.

The wave and water is pushing from behind the paddlers, downhill toward the far end, while a pour-over through a gap into the channel causes a current to push toward the left wall, as indicated by the arrow.

to see what happens, and rehearse the run in your mind to gauge your timing before you go. You do not want to mistime it and get stuck in the middle waiting for walls of water to pile in from both ends.

Rockhopping

Rock gardening and rockhopping are terms commonly used for playing in a rock garden, but rockhopping can more accurately describe taking a wave over a rock while it is submerged by a wave. Timing is crucial, as you must approach the rock at speed to arrive at the same time as the upsurge of water from the wave enveloping the rock. Judgment

is also crucial. Too small a wave and you will simply collide with the rock, or lodge on top of it. Watch to see what happens with the biggest waves and the smallest wave in the cycle. Visualize how you might fare with each wave.

In the sequence shown on the next page, the paddler is approaching while the rock is clearly completely uncovered and is lifted over the top. The wave was just sufficient for success. Notice how the bow launches into air beyond the rock before the kayak pivots nose-down. Be ready to brace when you land, or perform a recovery stroke as needed. The second sequence shows the same rock with a larger wave. Notice the more turbulent landing zone.

Visualization will help your timing and choice of wave when rockhopping.

Rockhopping requires good wave selection and precise timing. These sequences compare the effect of two waves of different size on the same rock.

Caves and Tunnels

Underground features are best explored in calm conditions. Caves can be very dangerous. There are few scarier experiences than watching a big swell funnel into a cave until it reaches the roof and blocks out the light, or to see a rogue swell funnel in, steepen, and break toward you when you are in a cave. Always be watchful for rogue waves, and prepare an escape strategy. In some places, passing ships or ferries can cause breaking waves in caves on flat calm days. Consider reversing in so you can escape more easily. A narrowing, funnel-shaped entrance will squeeze a wave progressively taller. A cave that opens wider beyond the entrance is safer

Waves are squeezed narrow but taller in caves, and also create strong currents. Notice the wave behind the paddler.

if the water is deep enough. Favor caves that are protected from waves.

Blowholes

Blowholes occur when a wave completely covers the mouth of a cave, pressurizing the air inside. The air then escapes under pressure, spraying water and foam out through the entrance or through cracks in the rock elsewhere. Where a second exit occurs, then water and spray may be

On calm days caves offer an underground wonderland.

A swell seals the entrance to a cave, compressing air that blasts back out as blowhole.

sent upward as a geyserlike jet. If water is funneled into a narrowing channel before it reaches and seals the cave entrance, the height of the wave will increase, adding to the pressure exerted on the air in the cave and creating a more impressive blast.

It is not a good idea to get too close to blowholes, although it can be fun to receive a sudden dousing from nearby. Normally, blowholes work when the top of the cave entrance is low to the water, so an oncoming wave can completely seal the entrance. If the entrance is incompletely sealed, you may get only a little spray, or none at all.

Currents

Sometimes waves breaking into the entrance of a passageway will force water toward a different exit. There, you would experience pulses of current. Less frequently you will find a current running steadily rather than pulsing, indicating tide running through the headland.

The current, in both instances, indicates a through passage that may or may not be suitable for a kayak. If you cannot see the far end and wish to explore, allow plenty of time to get out before the tide is next due to change direction, and explore from the exit end, rather than letting current carry you in.

Waiting Places

To wait for optimal conditions out of reach of bigger waves, you can often find a place behind a rock, so long as the waves are not big enough to break over the top. But you can also safely wait out waves in a deep pool full of turbulent water, so long as you have good control and balance. In a deep pool the water may surge with crosscurrents and fill

with foam, but mostly the water goes up and down without actually breaking.

Rescue

Moving through a rock garden, you will find gaps you can dodge through with good timing, and others where you could sit all day in peace. You'll find places you can pass only during a lull, or only during a set. Sometimes the consequences of a mistake, such as mistiming your entry, will be benign. Perhaps you'll be stuck in a passage waiting for the next wave, perhaps capsized but washed by the next wave into a pool where you can sort yourself out with or without help. But other places are less forgiving. Watch for strong reversing current in channels between the rocks that might make escape difficult in either direction.

Always consider "what if?" Recognize the dangers and weigh up the potential consequences. Avoid places with high risk for little thrill, and also places where you cannot reason a clear and easy strategy to deal with possible consequences. There is plenty of fun to be had without damaging yourself or your gear.

Given someone else's disaster, watch and wait your moment. There is little to be gained by getting two people stuck in the same place. Figure out your best option, which may involve paddling a different route to get to the other end of a gap. Perhaps your best rescue would require climbing onto a rock and throwing in a line to tow out.

For the paddler in trouble, the challenge is fending off contact with rock or sharp shellfish while attempting to escape by the safest-looking route. This might not be easy, and you may need to wait out a complete set of waves before escape is possible. You'll realize the importance of a helmet, sturdy clothing, and good footwear.

A slight mistiming has resulted in stranding on a rock.

What will happen when the approaching wave hits?

Technique

Here are several techniques that can enhance your control and safety when kayaking in rock gardens.

A Sharp Turn on a High Brace

When you ride a wave or surge along a passage only to reach a dead end or a sharp turn, you will likely have too much momentum to stop by reversing. The quickest way to halt is to make a sharp turn onto either a low brace or a high brace. Which you choose depends on your kayak, and how quickly it will turn when edged. Either edge as far as possible on a low brace, or drop your shoulder into the water onto a high brace. Start with your brace angled about 45 degrees behind you. Raise the leading edge of your blade to about 45 degrees to the water to gain both support and resistance, and drag the blade forward to power your turn. Use the last part of the arc, from mid-kayak forward, as support to right yourself. You should be able to kill your forward speed and turn 90 degrees in one swift move.

Hovering Using Vertical Strokes Alongside

Vertical paddle strokes are often considered flatwater skills, but they are essential for fine control when holding your position in surging water. Make positional adjustments by drawing or prying sideways at the bow, stern, or mid-kayak. Keep your blade engaged throughout as you maneuver. Use while you wait out sets behind a rock or in an eddy. The spin stroke, described in the section on turning (page 57), is a useful exercise.

Work the Surges and Currents

Timing is crucial. Watch how swells force water along passages or over ledges, and watch how the water drains afterward. Negotiating routes between rocks is all about using the water. Time your entry so a surge will carry you to a safe spot before it changes direction. With perfect timing, you may only need a few strokes to start before relaxing to enjoy the ride. At other times you will need to paddle hard all the way through.

Take time to watch and imagine paddling through. By visualizing beforehand what would happen if you started late or early, it's easier to get your timing right. Watch for currents as well as the wave peak. Judge how far they will carry you and how hard you'll need to paddle.

SUMMARY

Rock gardens can be a joy to explore, but they are impact zones where waves expend all their energy. Carry emergency gear, practice rescue skills, and work together as a group. Watch and spot each other to minimize danger. Use your own best judgment rather than bowing to pressure from your peers.

The Surf Zone

The surf zone is an exciting place to ride waves for sheer exhilaration. It is also an excellent place to hone skills. Surf features, technique, and some safety guidelines to avoid common injuries are covered in this chapter.

Choose a Beach

Find a gently shelving sand beach causing waves to spill. Refer to a sea chart to see the nature of the seabed farther from shore. This will show whether the waves approach cleanly in deep water, or whether there are banks and shoals that may modify their progress. Offshore shoals may help diminish the force of waves, while clear, deep water will allow bigger waves to reach the surf zone. Surf may be bigger toward high tide, once the water is too deep for waves to be influenced by shoals and banks farther out.

Learn as much as you can by walking the beach at low tide. Check the profile of the beach from the low-tide level to where it will reach at high tide. A typical surf beach has a long, flattish stretch of sand at low tide, steepening gradually, and finally steepening abruptly around the high-tide mark and beyond. Sunbathers generally keep to the steeper, upper stretch because the sand dries out better and the slight elevation offers a better view. The lower, flatter sand stays wet.

Rips

Surf carries water shoreward. This water flows back out to sea as currents called rips.

At low tide look for shallow valleys running down the sand to the sea. These are the signs showing where rips ran when the tide was higher. At low tide these may be dry or filled with pools of water. Follow one of these valleys up the beach from the water, and you'll see it branch sideways at intervals as shallow pools or damp valleys running parallel to shore. If you walk up a side branch,

Identify where the rips are before you surf.

you'll climb to a flatter area of sand with no valleys. Instead, there is a smooth slope down to the water, and up toward the top of the beach. When the tide rises, this is where you'll find the most regular waves. It will be the best place to play.

Look again at the pattern of valleys, like a river with its tributaries entering from either side. The tributaries are separated by sandbanks. When the tide covers the beach, water from waves breaking over these banks will drain down the side channels into the main channel, then out to sea as a rip.

Close to the main rip channel, the sandbanks between the tributaries have a much steeper profile than farther up the side channels. Waves break abruptly and violently on the steeper slopes, reforming in the deeper channels just beyond. This area of dumping waves is not the best place to surf.

Once you've located a rip, watch as the tide rises to see how the water flows, and how waves look when they meet the current. In a rip, waves are choppy and chaotic, but much smaller than the surf on either side.

If you swim into a rip you will most likely be swept out to sea. Do not try to swim against the current. Instead, swim across the current to escape. Once you are clear, swim toward shore. Always locate the rips when you visit a surf beach.

Beach Profile

Storms pile sand toward the top of a beach, and onshore winds blow the sand into dunes in a natural process of deposition. As the tide rises up a beach, the gentle profile at low and midtide changes to a much steeper profile toward high tide.

On exceptionally big tides, the water will rise to the very steepest part of the profile. Waves will run all the way to shore without losing much power. When they reach shore they will steepen and break abruptly, usually dumping heavily onto the shore

Swell offers better-shaped waves to ride than windblown waves.

or surging up the steepest beach. These waves are explosively powerful and best avoided. If the tide is rising, land before it reaches this zone. On a falling tide, wait until the shore break is replaced by lines of gentler spilling waves before you play.

Often the best surf waves are found around midtide. Rips are strongest on a falling tide, so favor a rising tide. That way you have the additional advantage of a shorter distance to carry your kayak at the end of the session.

Direction of Swell

Depending on swell direction, you may find bigger waves at one end of a beach than the other. A bay partly sheltered from the direction of swell by a headland will experience waves at full strength at the end farthest from the headland, while swell refracting around the headland to the closer end of the bay will be reduced in size and cleaner in form. Likewise, a beach on one side of a peninsula may catch a huge, ragged swell straight on, while a beach on the far side has clean, manageable, refracted waves. Figure out the best surf location for the swell forecast or wind-wave direction. This means first locating the best beach, then finding the best part of that beach.

Other Places to Ride Waves

Beaches are not the only good places to find surf. Other options include point breaks and reef breaks.

Point Break

Headlands can create amazing places to ride waves. Swell approaching one side of a headland will wrap around. The wave on the other side can break progressively along the shore from the headland into the bay beyond, offering very long rides. This is called a point break. Because the wave breaks as it reaches shallower water, the break will constantly progress in one direction along the wave. You will either surf the wave toward the right each time, or toward the left, depending on which side of the headland you are surfing.

Reef Break

A submerged, isolated ledge of rock or reef causes waves to converge, forming a horseshoe-shaped wave that breaks from the center outward toward the edges of the reef. A reef break is typically very powerful compared to a beach break on the same day because of the effect of the convergence. Reef breaks are magical because you can usually paddle around them on deep water without meeting breaking waves on your way out. Once in position you can ride quite large waves away from the break into deep water. The downside is they are often farther from launching places.

Surf Zone Techniques

Take time to become comfortable in and familiar with the surf environment. Here are some guidelines and techniques to help you choose the easiest moment and place for paddling out, and others to complete your surfing maneuvers in a balanced and relaxed manner.

Paddling Out

Having decided exactly where to launch and surf, turn around and study the top of the beach before you paddle out. Choose landmarks that will help you locate your position from the water. Look

A reef break creates a steep, converging wave.

Always locate the rips before you decide where to surf. Farther down this beach there is a safer, flagged area.

for clearly visible landmarks, one closer than the other, that line up. If there are no suitable features, consider placing your own marks. You can use flags, upright paddles, spare kayaks, or mounds of gear. Ideally, you will use these landmarks to define the safe area in which you wish to surf. This will typically be between rips. It is easy to drift along the beach in wind or current, or by surfing diagonally, so reference points will help you recognize where you started.

Before you launch, watch the wave patterns for as long as possible. Identify rips and places with steep breaks. Gauge the wave size during lulls and sets, and get a sense of the duration of the lulls. That way you can time your launch to paddle out during a lull.

Paddle out between rips to learn how big and powerful the waves are. That way you don't need to go beyond your comfort zone. If you are confident, paddle beyond the break to wait for a set. Use your landmarks to make sure you are not drifting. Pick a wave and ride.

If you find a good place on the water to wait for waves, where the waves peak consistently, look for landmarks to triangulate your position. Using the same triangulation, you can then pinpoint exactly the same spot every time you paddle out.

Only if you are completely at ease with the wave size should you consider using a rip to help you paddle out. To your advantage, waves break less heavily in a rip, and the current will help you. Once you have paddled out beyond the break, you

Paddle out during a lull, and paddle hard through any breaking waves.

can paddle along the beach to locate your position from your landmarks. Don't use a rip until you are confident in the conditions and are ready: A rip can be a quick way to get delivered to a bad place beyond your ability and confidence.

Because rips are formed by the water carried toward shore by breaking waves, the more powerful the waves, the more powerful the rips. Rips run fastest following a set, and slower after a lull. It's convenient to ride the waves during a set when they are bigger, and then to paddle out during a lull when the waves are smaller and the rips at their most powerful.

Catching a Wave

Go for the unbroken part of a wave near the break. This is where the wave is steepest, so you get the best acceleration. Turn to face the shore, wait until the wave has started to lift your stern, then take a few (two to four) paddle strokes to accelerate. After your final stroke, leave your blade in the water trailing in neutral while you pause to see what happens. You should glide forward on the wave. Most of your steering strokes on the wave will be of a trailing nature, rather than in front of you, so your blade is in position to begin a turn in either direction, or to steer straight.

If you find you need more than a few paddle strokes to catch a wave, you probably need to pick

When the wave lifts your stern, use the fewest possible strokes to catch it.

Turning to one side using a stern rudder/brace will prevent burying your bow.

a steeper part of a wave face next time. If waves consistently go by without you, accelerate sooner.

When you take off on a steep wave, your bow will bury if you aim straight for the beach. Avoid this by angling your bow a little to one side when you catch the wave. This should prevent nosediving, but you will need to edge your kayak to the wave and apply a stern rudder on the downhill side to avoid broaching (broaching is being turned side-on to the wave).

Adjusting the trim of your kayak forward slightly can help your takeoff; sit upright again, or lean slightly back, as soon as you have caught the wave.

Experiment with Trim

Shifting your body weight forward can often help you accelerate, while leaning back can increase drag and slow you, and lightening the bow can help prevent it burying. Trim is very kayak-specific, so experiment to discover how best to trim yours. Leaning forward can speed a turn, but it depends on your position on the wave.

Zigzag Run

Your first control challenge is to steer a more-or-less straight course toward the beach, turning a little from side to side by using a stern rudder on alternate sides. As soon as you start to turn toward one side, switch the stern rudder to the side of the kayak that is becoming the down-wave (shore) side. Edge your kayak from the rudder, toward the wave. Use the stern rudder to stop the turn, and bring the bow back to aim directly at the beach. Sit upright at this point. Continue to steer toward the other side, shifting your edge again toward the wave, and bring your stern rudder to the new down-wave side to stop the turn. Limit your turns in either direction to about 20 degrees, otherwise it will be difficult to turn back.

Diagonal Run
To maximize the length of your ride, steer at an angle from the break. Turn a little using a low

brace/stern rudder. To avoid a broach, engage a stern rudder on the down-wave side. Edge down, into the wave (out to sea). This is the same as the first part of a zigzag, but instead of turning back, hold your direction and ease around a few more degrees. Your kayak will accelerate, tracking diagonally along the face as it heads for the beach. Aim for an angle of about 30 degrees, and try to hold that angle as you track from the break. As the wave steepens it will be increasingly difficult to prevent the kayak from turning side-on to the wave, so steer more directly toward shore as the wave steepens, or prepare to broach and brace into the wave.

The kayaker on the right is steering diagonally using a combination of stern rudder with low brace on the down-wave side.

Turning on a Wave

Ultimately, you will get a longer, more controlled, and interesting ride if you can change direction whenever you wish. If you surf diagonally from the break and reach a part of the wave that is less steep, you can return to the steeper part by making a turn. Turns are easiest when you are high on the wave and your bow is not locked in to the base of the wave.

Turn your stern rudder into a reverse sweep in a way that also slows you down. Put in a quick reverse stroke on the other side as well, if necessary. With the bow free, the kayak should turn readily on a reverse sweep. As your bow points straight to shore, sit your kayak upright. As your bow swings farther around, edge toward the wave and stern rudder on the down-wave side. Now you are in position to surf diagonally toward the break again. Be ready to turn again as soon as you reach the break. You can pivot on the break itself, or you can leave yourself a little more time and turn early. Once you have turned, aim to be in position to surf diagonally from the break once more.

This full, double-turn move on a wave is called a *cut back*.

You can change direction from a diagonal ride in the soup in a similar way. Stall until your kayak is riding high on the soup, and then make an assertive forward sweep on the high side of the wave to spin your bow toward shore and to accelerate

The bow is locked into the base of the wave, preventing a turn from the break. Back up to free the bow to turn.

you into surfing forward. As you drop forward, begin your turn to surf diagonally in the opposite direction.

Bracing into a Break

When a wave breaks broadside to your sea kayak, a huge weight of water pushes the kayak sideways. Edge into the wave and present your hull to the beach to avoid capsize. Balance on a low brace. Your offside hand should contact your spray skirt near your offside hip. Keep your onside elbow raised above your paddle shaft, and bent to push down if necessary. Your blade should be flat on the water skimming, not locked in the water. This position allows you to find your edged balance with

your hips, using minimal or no downward pressure on your blade.

The foam pile will hide your blade from view, but under the foam your blade rests on the slope of the wave as it skims toward shore. Your kayak will likely be locked in a sideways position until the force of the break diminishes, so as soon as you find your balance, look around to make sure you're not on a collision course.

A turbulent break can kick your kayak onto its side, throwing you off balance. Use a high brace here: Drop your onside elbow beneath the paddle shaft to turn your blade face down. Maintain contact with your spray skirt with your onside hand. Gently bring your kayak back into balance, and

A low brace near the stern is used to maintain balance, and also to steer along the wave. Note the bow is lower than the stern.

A high brace is used to maintain balance in a breaking wave. The paddle is close to horizontal to prevent the blade from grabbing. Bent elbows are held close to the torso.

then raise your elbow to return your blade to the low brace position again.

Caution: It is essential to keep your paddle more or less horizontal so the blade skims. If you raise your offside hand, the increased angle will make the blade grab and you will be pulled away from it by the wave. If pulled off balance onto an extended arm, you risk shoulder dislocation. To avoid injury, keep your elbows tucked close to your hips and your offside hand as low as possible, ideally touching the spray skirt.

Steering Along a Broken Wave While Locked in the Foam Pile

When carried sideways by a breaking wave, you can move forward or back along the wave by shifting the position of your brace back or forward.

To track bow-first along the break, move your brace back a little—about 45 degrees back from your cockpit—and lean your weight back. To track along the wave in reverse, brace in front of the cockpit (you'll find a high brace more comfortable than a low brace, but keep your offside hand low). Watch over your shoulder to see where you are going. Get the hang of this as soon as possible, because there are few other ways to avoid collision, except capsize.

Exit from a Wave

Riding a gently sloping wave toward shore offers easiest control, but once the wave steepens it is more difficult to avoid broaching. Take a short ride, then deliberately start a turn from the wave before it breaks. Once the kayak begins to broach, lean into the turn onto a low brace. As soon as the kayak turns enough to climb the wave, bring your low brace forward into a bow rudder and edge your kayak to the opposite side. This anchors your bow and frees your stern. You'll make a stylish and controlled exit from the wave.

A control tip: If you are in the soup zone (broken water) and are having difficulty turning out to sea quickly enough between waves, paddle forward along the beach. If you are having difficulty turning quickly enough toward shore, then reverse.

Controlled Landing on an Unfamiliar Beach

Playing in surf is fun, and it also develops skills you need for safe coastal touring. But to land safely at an unfamiliar beach you also need to be able to reverse through waves.

First, watch the wave pattern. Approach the beach during a lull for greatest control. Paddle between waves rather than surfing. Reverse to hold your position through a wave until your bow is higher than your stern, and then chase the wave toward the beach. When the next wave reaches you, repeat the procedure.

When you near shore, look for the best place to land, avoiding rocks and steep places where waves are dumping. If necessary, make your way parallel to the shore to a safer place.

When in position, pick a small wave, reverse through it, and immediately chase it up the beach. Sprint as high up the swash as possible before the wave begins to drain, then quickly exit your kayak and drag it higher.

Practice on a day when you are comfortable surfing. Try to reach the beach without surfing or losing control of the kayak. It will be more intimidating on a rough day in an unfamiliar place, so practice is important.

Caution: Avoid the temptation to surf onto an unfamiliar shore. Surfing usually ends with your kayak sideways to the beach. It may then be difficult to avoid being taken sideways into a dumping break, or onto rocks or logs on the beach, or onto swimmers. For safe practice, avoid crowded beaches, and be sympathetic to other water users.

Rolling in Surf

Capsizing in surf can be abrupt and somewhat violent, but if you wait underwater you will usually find everything settles down between waves. This is a good time to get into position and roll up.

Most often you will capsize toward shore. Tuck into your capsize and prepare to roll to seaward.

Once you are upright, immediately glance around to orient yourself and decide what to do next.

Broadside to broken surf, most often you will capsize toward shore, so set up to perform a complete roll, coming up to seaward.

This is because the sideways push of the wave against your kayak will drag you to the surface to seaward, making a roll on that side easy. Roll up gently with the wave's help, so you don't carry on over. Brace to stabilize until you can see what is going on.

Moves to Practice on Flat Water

Most paddlers don't have easy regular access to surf in which to practice. However, the moves you make on a wave incorporate sequences you can practice on flat water. If you are familiar with and fluent with these sequences on flat water, it will be easier to use them on a wave.

Catching a wave requires a few smooth, powerful strokes to accelerate, then a forward glide with the blade trailing in neutral after your last stroke. From here you can steer from side to side by engaging the back of the blade as a rudder while edging away from it, then switching sides to engage the other blade and changing to your opposite edge.

On flat water, build up to your maximum speed in four to six strokes (two to three on each side), accelerating smoothly to avoid flutter or blade turbulence. On a wave you may only need one or two strokes, but they too will need to be smooth and powerful. Now, make as many clear changes in direction as you can, edging away from your stern rudder to turn, switching sides to change direction, until you come to rest. Repeat this sequence on the other side.

When riding a broken wave sideways, you will occasionally find yourself thrown off balance.

Practice switching from a low brace (maximum edge toward the brace, with the back of your blade to the water) to a recovery using the face of the blade, and back to the low brace. In this practice, keep your kayak edged all the time as you switch back and forth. Then practice on the other side.

When you complete a ride and need to exit gracefully, turn toward the wave using a low brace. As the kayak begins to turn out to sea and climbs the wave, bring your low brace forward and engage the face in a bow rudder at arm's reach. Shift your edge and lean forward to weight your bow.

To practice this on flat water, accelerate in six strokes to maximum speed, which is good practice for your takeoff. Rest your blade in neutral behind you for a moment before gradually engaging the back of the blade, edging onto it, and bringing it gradually forward as a low brace. Turn about 90 degrees from your original track, then bring the blade forward, engage the face in a bow rudder, shift your edge, and turn on the bow rudder. As you approach the limit of your turn, draw the blade toward the hull, turning it into a forward stroke to power you in your new direction. In your practice session, make this the first forward stroke of six new accelerating strokes to set up for another turn in the opposite direction.

Tips: With the loose grip, you can feel how the water presses on the blade, so you can fine-tune the blade angle better. You might imagine needing to grip your paddle very tightly in surf, but most of the time you will benefit more from a loose grip.

The moves you make on a wave depend on your ability to feel the water against your kayak and against your paddle. On flat water, repeat practice sequences with your eyes closed so you can focus on feel rather than on seeing what is going on.

Safety

Safety is always an issue in surf. Check out the beach and locate the rips. Wear a helmet to protect your head, especially against the occasional impact you will sooner or later have with your own paddle or kayak. Wear suitably insulating clothing. Coordinate with other water users.

Learn about surf etiquette. A kayak on the loose can be a dangerous missile, so one person per wave is safer than two. Always make sure your way is clear before you take off. If you are on a collision course, the quickest way to avoid or reduce impact is to capsize. If someone else is approaching on a collision course, try to get out of the way. If that fails, be prepared to roll with the impact, when you know whether the approaching craft will go over or under yours.

Have someone spot you from shore, and be constantly aware of drift.

Rescues in the surf zone are rarely practical or safe.

It is easy to take just one too many rides when you are tiring. Better to stop when you are still reasonably fresh.

Any swim you take will be tiring. If you swim with your kayak, hold on but push from behind. Don't pull from down-wave.

It is often easier to empty a kayak in shallow water, where you do not have to lift so far, than on shore. When handling your kayak in the shallows, watch the waves and the water flow. Your kayak might wash up the beach but return on the backwash, and you may regret using your shins to stop it.

Tidal Rapids

Tidal rapids offer an exciting and challenging kayaking environment. The water flows in a complex three dimensional dance, often overlaid by wave patterns, themselves modified by the water flow. Here I will explain the features you might find, and some maneuvers to try in these dynamic places.

Tidal Stream and Current

Current is a steady flow of water in one direction, such as down a freshwater river, as a constant nontidal flow in the ocean, or as surface movement caused by wind. The currents that concern kayakers are horizontal surface currents.

Tides are different. They are caused by the gravitational pull of the moon and, to a lesser extent, of the sun. The change in direction of tidal streams is predictable, as it is tied to the lunar cycle. In practice, plenty of variables come into play to make the available information fall short of perfect, so temper any tidal predictions with observation.

Mariners usually make the clear distinction between tidal stream and current. It makes sense to calculate the effect of each individually. Commonly, people refer to any moving water as "current." I hope it is clear that I use "current" to mean moving water—for example, in the context of a tidal rapid.

The Effect of Constrictions

Pinch the sides together at the end of a hosepipe while water is flowing, and the water speeds to a jet. In the same way, when a headland or islands constrict a current or tidal stream, the water speeds up. The rate increases even more over shallows. Where the flow is accelerated tidal rapids form, which are either hazards or fun places for sea kayakers. You can predict where these rapids might form by looking for prominent headlands on a map, and at depth contours on a sea chart.

Tidal Rapids: Races and Overfalls

When a current or tidal stream is sufficiently constricted in width, the accelerated water creates a rapid, which can produce waves that steepen and move against the direction of water flow. This is called a tide race. Eddies form behind whatever created the constriction. As on a river, the rapid begins as water accelerating into a smooth tongue or "V" of water from the point of constriction. The fastest flow runs down the tongue to its very tip, where it breaks into waves.

An overfall is a similar effect produced by the reduced depth, rather than in the reduced width, of the channel. Reduced width would cause a tide-race. Some extra effects may occur in overfalls that are not found in tide races. For example, a ledge of rock across the flow of tide may cause a constantly breaking standing wave (a stopper) immediately downstream, and surface eddies occur close downstream of places where the seabed reaches close to the surface. Overfalls are often found at headlands,

When paddling downstream on a tide race, you will face the breaking waves.

When surfing waves in a tide race you will face upstream.

A tide race forms off a headland.

where erosion has cut back a cliff at wave level to leave a ledge with shallow water.

But some headlands have deep water close to land (these form races rather than overfalls), and some ledges occur offshore, producing overfalls where the water is constricted only in depth, not in width.

Features of Tidal Rapids

From slack water, a tide stream typically starts to run gently, picking up speed to reach a maximum flow before gradually slackening off. It then runs through a similar cycle, but in the opposite direction. Rapids caused by current only, and not by tide, maintain a constant speed and direction twenty-four hours per day.

With current, what you see is what you get, unless the weather or swell conditions change. You could play on a rapid all day, with the waves and features staying the same.

With tide, the dynamics of a rapid change constantly with the changing speed and direction of the water, and with the changing level. The rapid may be completely different in different directions, or may only form on a rising tide or a falling tide.

How rough a tidal rapid will be at any moment depends on the general sea state and swell

In a tide race, the waves break against the current, here running from right to left.

conditions, as well as the speed of the current. You will get fast water and turbulence on a calm day, but the wave action depends on the waves coming from elsewhere. Wind will produce waves, and so will the wake of a ship. In both cases the wave size increases as the waves move up against the current. Once waves have passed through the race and reach water that is flowing more slowly, the wave size will fall again. The sea upstream of a tide race often seems calm because the waves lose energy when breaking in the race. When the tide changes and the waves and water run in the same direction, the rapid will be much calmer.

Predicting Conditions in a Tide Race

Waves against the current will create rough conditions. The conditions will get more turbulent with wave size and with strength of current. To gauge a tide race from afar, look first at the tide tables. A big range (a spring tide rather than a neap) will have a stronger flow and a bigger rapid. A neap tide (on the half-moon) will have a gentler rapid. Look at a chart or tidal stream atlas to see the direction and speed of the flow hour-by-hour in relation to the times on the tide tables.

Next, check the swell direction. If the swell is against the direction of the tide stream, it will be rough. Also check the wind forecast. Any wind will produce waves, and when those waves run against the tidal stream, expect conditions much rougher than you would normally expect for the wind speed.

Eddy Line

Trace the midline of the tongue downstream, and you'll see waves angling in from either side toward the smooth water. These are called lateral waves. Lateral waves mark the dividing line between fast water and the eddy. The dividing lines are called eddy lines. The tongue narrows downstream as the lateral waves encroach on it, finally leading to a chaotic area of exploding, crisscrossing wave patterns.

Tide race eddy lines are more like wedges than lines. They begin narrow and clearly defined, but can widen down-rapid to extend several kayak-lengths across, and wider. To reach the eddy from the main stream at the top of the rapid, cross over the narrow line and burst into the eddy, changing direction very abruptly. To cross farther downstream, where the "wedge" has grown wider, you will need to first cross a pseudo-eddy line, then a no-man's-land of turbulent water, and finally another pseudo-eddy line into the main eddy. Although the no-man's-land is typically not moving as fast as the main stream, it does move downstream.

The main stream does not follow a straight line. It snakes along, and at times it meanders almost as far as the eddy to either side. It's not practical to plan in advance exactly where to leave the stream to enter an eddy in relation to the coastline. That would sometimes be easy and sometimes more difficult, depending on how close the meandering main stream is to that part of the shore at that moment. It's better to follow the main stream, watching the water and waiting until its meandering path carries you near the shore. Make your exit where the eddy wedge has, for the moment, become narrow.

Returning to my hosepipe analogy, when there is only a little water flowing through a long hosepipe, you can drop the end and pick it up from where you dropped it. The faster the flow, the more the hose snakes. With a powerful flow, it becomes difficult to catch the end at all, it snakes so widely. The flow in a tide race does something similar: more confined snaking at the upstream end, widely snaking farther downstream.

Whirlpools

Eddy lines spawn whirlpools. They start small and indistinct on the eddy line near the top of a rapid, deepen and intensify farther down, and finally fill and dissipate. As the eddy line widens into a wedge, you will see whirlpools spinning down both sides of the wedge.

Crossing an eddy wedge is most easily done by leaving the main stream immediately downstream of a whirlpool, where the rotating water will carry you neatly from the current into well inside the no-man's-land. You can then use another whirlpool to carry you across the final pseudo-eddy line from no-man's-land into the main eddy.

It's easiest to follow the main stream through a rapid if you can see whirlpools on both sides of the current and steer between them. In this case, the whirlpools on your left will rotate counterclockwise, and those on your right, clockwise.

If you feel like examining the whirlpools in more depth, watch for them farther down the eddy line. Here they will have grown in size, so you can get an idea of what to expect if you enter one upstream.

Whirlpools usually start small, as swirls of water between the eddy and stream. They can intensify quite vigorously before spreading in diameter. Finally they fill, to become a shallow dish before fading. Depending on the size you see, you might enjoy dropping into one near the top of the rapid and spinning downstream as it intensifies and then finally dissipates. Enter to one side of the vortex in the direction of spin, sit upright, and brace for balance. If one end of your kayak slopes down, paddle gently toward the low end to level your kayak.

Whirlpools can be dangerous. A quite friendly-looking one can take a swimmer in wet suit and PFD down for some time, so if you capsize, don't let go of your kayak.

Fastest Flow

The fastest flow will run through the biggest waves, which break where the lateral waves intersect from either side. This main, wave-rich area, often called the wave train, can be fun to run downstream, or to surf upstream. As the flow increases, the waves crowd closer and become steeper. Certain periods during a tide cycle will produce rougher conditions, so choose a gentler or more demanding experience by picking your time.

Eddy lines offer a fun play zone for crossing into the main flow and reentering the eddy, or for spinning on the spot. This is easiest close to the top of the rapid, where the eddy lines are narrow and distinct, but this is right above all the biggest wave action! When you cross the eddy line but don't make it back, you may have a Grand Canyon–style rapid to run, but without the river banks.

When the current is fast, any eddies will be powerful and extend for some distance. That means you can probably paddle downstream into the waves until the breakers are smaller before making your move to cross the eddy wedge at a point where the full strength of whirlpools has

already dissipated. Then you can use the eddy to return to the top of the rapid.

Overfalls may produce standing waves, which are static in position. When they become steep enough to break, they can do so continuously. The effect is like a breaking surf wave, except the intensity of the break, and its location, remain static. A beach break will eventually drop you on the beach, but a breaking standing wave on an overfall might hold you for an hour or more.

These are often called stopper waves because of their effect on kayaks. They can be fun to play in or can be dangerous, depending on how powerful they become. Such waves are not dependent on swell or wind waves, but will surge under the influence of additional waves. There is more opportunity to hit rock in overfalls, so it's good to check where the rocks are on a low tide, and note how they affect the surface currents as they cover.

Some Things to Try

Eddy lines can be fun places to play and to develop kayak control skills. They vary in intensity through each tidal cycle, so choose an appropriate time for your skill and comfort level.

Turn on the Eddy Line to Enter the Current

Cross an eddy line on a low brace, edging into your turn as on a bicycle. Your paddle blade should keep light contact with the water in a low brace position through the turn. To fine-tune the degree of edge you use, practice until you can make the turn without touching the water with your paddle. Time your edging to coincide with the push of water that turns the kayak. To fine-tune your timing and positioning, try this with your eyes shut. You will be more accurate when you respond to what you feel in addition to what you see, and more balanced when you position your brace but do not need it.

Cross the eddy line slowly enough to allow the current to turn the kayak.

Edge into your turn. Use a low brace on the low side of the kayak.

Maintain your edge while the kayak turns.

Sit upright after the kayak leaves the eddy and matches the speed of the main current.

Your kayak turns when you cross an eddy line because one end is pushed in one direction by the current, and the other end is pushed in the opposite direction by the eddy. Once you are fully in the current, those forces no longer turn you. If you cross the eddy line quickly, the kayak will turn very little before it is fully in the current. If you cross slowly, the kayak will make a fuller turn. Keep enough forward speed to fully exit the eddy, or your kayak will end up aligned along the eddy line.

To cross the eddy line into a ferry glide across the tongue, you need more hull speed and an acute angle to the current. Make your last stroke as you cross the eddy line a sweep stroke on the downstream side, finishing as a stern rudder in the draw position, with the upper edge of the blade closest to the kayak and the offside arm pushing across the kayak.

Spinning on the Eddy Line

Spinning on the eddy line, when done well, will keep you in the same spot as you spin. The trick is to keep your body centered over the eddy line while pushing your bow and reversing your stern into the current or eddy to keep yourself in position. Too much of a push either way will move your body from directly above the eddy line, and you will lose control.

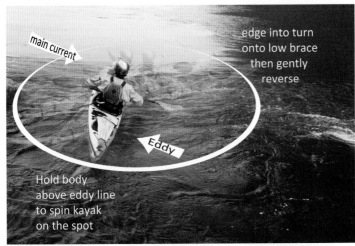

main current

edge into turn onto low brace then gently reverse

Eddy

Hold body above eddy line to spin kayak on the spot

To spin on the spot, keep your body over the eddy line and push one end of the kayak into the current and the other into the eddy. Top line of images are from left to right, and bottom from right to left.

Follow the Main Current

Try paddling all the way down the center of the rapid with the main flow. There are two guidelines to follow:

1. Keep between any whirls or vortices that indicate the eddy lines on either side.

2. Aim straight into the waves.

There will be some crisscross, but the waves always steepen against the flow, so it's a good way to keep on line. The line will meander, so watch the water for your line, not the shore. If you stray a little too far off track, you'll feel the water spin your kayak.

Rapids Caused by Current, Not Tide

Where a race is caused by current rather than tide, then the speed and direction remain constant and the conditions will only vary with wind or swell conditions. If there is also a tidal component, this will cause variation. But the tide stream might only reduce the speed of the current and not necessarily reverse the direction of the flow when it opposes the current.

Summary

When waves run against current, they build into considerably bigger waves. Wind will quickly build waves, so check the weather forecast for wind, and be watchful for changes. Swell builds big conditions as well, so check the swell forecast too.

The current will carry you far and fast. Keep your eye on landmarks, and be particularly watchful for your companions. If you do happen to exit your kayak, keep a hold of it, and hold your paddle in the air to attract attention. A paddle is much easier to spot from water level than a kayak or a person floating in a tide race. Rescues are more

Rescues in a fast current may be more difficult than you expect.

difficult than you might expect. Practice first in easy conditions and build on your skills.

Expedition Kayaking

What is an expedition? One of the more thought-provoking definitions I have heard is "An expedition is a group of paddlers who don't get on together, under a leader with an ego to maintain, on an extended trip. When they return you know it was a real expedition because it was hell, and nobody has a good word to say about anyone else. Otherwise it's called a holiday, isn't it?"

Having said that, here are a few ways to ensure your holiday goes well.

Expedition Planning

Who are you going with? Are your aims compatible? Are your shared expectations achievable? Will you get along together for the length of time and the activity planned?

These questions should be core in your mind when you start planning an expedition, or if you are invited on a multiday paddling trip. Even if the paddling trip is inviting, if you don't like the people it's probably not a good idea to accept.

Let's say one paddler intends to explore into every nook and cranny, and another intends to speed through as many miles as possible in the shortest time. That might not end well. One or both parties will be upset unless you agree to a compromise. There are paddlers around who share the same goals, so find those rather than going with paddlers who have opposing ideals. It is smart to be on the appropriate trip.

Next, if it was you who thought up the plan and brought together some other people, that makes you the leader, right? Well, not necessarily. Many really good trips work with everyone making group decisions around the original vision. It is always good to defer to someone who has better skill in a particular area. That way you maximize your strengths.

A lot of people have good planning skills but do not enjoy being a leader. Maybe being a planner is a better role to have. Leave someone else to be the decision-maker, even if the decisions are between the suggestions of other group members. Perhaps you need to designate someone to be ready to take over the lead if things go awry. Perhaps you need a group scapegoat, whose responsibility is to humbly take the blame for everything that goes wrong, no matter whose fault it is. That can take the sting out of many a situation, and it's not such a bad role to play. After all, if you know you are innocent of many of things you are blamed for, it's easy to take the flack.

That brings me to roles within a group. Sometimes people like to take on a designated role, and know that's what they are responsible for. Others like to be totally independent and self-sufficient. One person may love catering and hate washing up. Another might like to snack on power bars and never eat cooked food. The disparity is not a problem as long as you figure it out before you go.

It will not work if the power-bar person gets allocated daily washing-up duties. But is it a problem if three people cater together while another eats differently? That should not be, if it's agreed to beforehand.

The earliest stages of planning should be about goals, commitment, roles and personalities, strengths and weaknesses. Once you have a compatible group and a common goal, then you might just have the makings of a holiday!

Loading a Kayak

Loading kayaks for trips can be a source of frustration and conflict between paddlers if one finishes packing well before the other. When the first stands around getting cold and irritable while the other gets defensive, it's not the best start to the day. Figure out the best way to load your kayak quickly and efficiently. Here are some ideas.

Load Near the Water

Carrying a loaded kayak is riskier than carrying an empty one. Reduce the risk of injury to yourself or others by teaming up to carry the kayaks empty. Then carry your gear to the kayaks to load. If there

Many hands make a safer carry.

Agree on your strategy beforehand to carry kayaks loaded or empty. Here straps have been used under the hull to spread the load. Britta Johansson

is no option but to load first, the more people to help carry a single loaded kayak, the better.

Balance the Weight

When you have finished loading, your kayak should sit level on the water as it does when empty. Balance the weight evenly front-to-back, and side-to-side. Too much weight in the bow will make your kayak turn into the wind, and if the stern is too heavily weighted the kayak will turn downwind. Make sure the weight is evenly balanced side-to-side so the kayak floats completely upright: If the kayak lists to one side it is uncomfortable to compensate for all day.

Keep the Ends Light

Pack the ends of your kayak with lightweight items. Keeping the ends of your kayak light will keep them buoyant in waves, but will also make tracking easier. When the ends are heavy it is difficult to stop a turn once you have started.

Where Is Your Compass?

Make sure metal items that will affect a magnetic compass are not stowed near your compass.

Dry Bags

Large dry bags work fine if you have only a little equipment and plenty of space. Sticky fabrics such as vinyl also work OK when space is plentiful. But small, slippery dry bags (such as those made of nylon) slide into position more easily when space is tight. Avoid filling bags so tightly they become solid. Leave enough room for a little flexibility in each bag, so it can bend or change shape, to make loading your kayak easier. Use rigid boxes for fragile items so you don't crush them by forcing gear against them.

Think about the shape of the kayak. Long, narrow bags will likely fit into the ends better than fat ones, and big, bulky items will most easily fit in the wider part of a compartment.

Where to Start Packing

Fill the ends of the kayak first, then position your largest items so you can slide small bags past them to fill spaces. This is where small bags come in handy. Cylindrical fuel bottles, for example, torpedo more easily into spaces than box-shaped fuel cans, and a bag containing just your fleece sweater will slide into a space more easily than one holding your complete change of clothing. Work methodically from the ends toward the hatches so you don't leave voids that you cannot reach to fill.

Establish a System

Use the same bags for the same gear every day. That way you get used to each bag fitting in the same way into the kayak. You will also be able to find items more easily when you know which bag to look in.

Carry all your gear to the kayak before loading, then separate it into piles for each compartment. That way you can see at a glance everything you need to pack, and visualize where it goes before you begin. You won't end up forgetting that extra bag and having to struggle to fit it in.

It may help to lay the gear alongside the kayak so you can better visualize where everything will go. I've known people make diagrams and number bags at home so they know how everything will fit. Certainly any practice done at home will make it easier during the trip.

Finally, that extra fleece you were going to leave behind? Leave it behind! Don't add extra items at the last minute, or your packing will be difficult every day. One secret of quick packing is to restrict the volume of gear to an amount that will not completely fill your kayak. The other trick is practice, and that does not mean once a day on the trip—it means stashing your stuff in and out of your kayak at home or in your yard with the clock ticking until you are quick! It is better to practice beforehand than wait until you are on your trip. It could save hours of frustration in rain and with bugs, and make for more pleasant interpersonal relations!

Timing

Loading your kayak is just one of a number of routines you will follow before launching. These routines have a predictable timeline. Once you know the timing, calculate how long before launch-time you must start. If you need more time than others, don't wait until they start; start getting ready before they do. Be ready and relaxed, not rushed.

Cooking Arrangements

How you cook, and what and when you eat on a trip, should be a personal choice, but there are widely differing styles of group organization on expeditions.

Group Cooking

Group cooking is a style often adopted by commercial operations, and is also particularly common in North America, where it is necessary to find a cooking area well away from tents so food smells don't attract bears to a sleeping area. If everything associated with eating must be kept apart from everything else, it is a practical solution to do group cooking, with just one cooking place and time. Then everything is in the same place when it is time to hang food and eating equipment, or to cache bear-proof canisters.

In common with group cooking, at the start of a trip hardware such as stoves, cooking pots, cutting boards, water containers and filter pumps, cooking tarps and wind shelters, and shared equipment for emergency such as first aid, repair, spare paddles, towlines and such, should be distributed between the group. Likewise, the food should be distributed so everyone carries a share. At mealtimes all the cooking equipment and food is gathered together, the meal prepared and cooked, and everyone eats together. As a group activity, everyone is typically at the call of the cook to fetch water, fuel, or specific food items, or to chop food, find plates and cutlery, wash up, or whatever else needs doing, or is allocated as tasks on a roster.

There can be a rotating schedule so everyone takes turn as cook and at washing up, although plan to be as regimented or as loose as you like with how you apply this. Some individuals prefer to wash up, while some love cooking. Some prefer not to do anything, so to deter shirkers some groups allocate tasks down to the last detail.

Self-Catering

Independent style is more common in the United Kingdom, where sheltering beside a tent to cook is practical. Each person could carry, prepare, and eat what suits him or her best, even if everyone gathers together to do so, which is usually the arrangement of choice in Scandinavia.

In this case, each person provides for what is needed for food and also for cooking equipment. In practice, this frequently rationalizes itself with some collaboration in pairs or threes sharing a stove, and either planning meals together or taking turns to cook a meal. When two or three people share a tent, then it can be convenient to cater within that group too.

Independent style offers the best flexibility to accommodate different dietary needs. It also allows those who want to spend more time preparing and eating to do so, or allows someone to snack quickly so there is more time to explore, hike, or catch up on sleep.

Carrying Food

When you prepare food for a multiday trip, you will need to pack it. Remove and discard unnecessary wrappers, pack in appropriate portions, and wrap in resealable bags if possible. Do not forget to make a note of what is in each bag and, if necessary, how to prepare it. Some items look alike. It is discouraging to discover that the powdered milk you just stirred into the hot drink you are so ready for is actually mashed potato.

You should return with any wrappers you take with you, so think about the weight and bulk. Zipper bags take little space when empty, and can be resealed to carry unused quantities of food. Some watertight boxes stack when empty, while others do not. If you will end up

with garbage, then it is useful to carry a suitable garbage container that will not attract vermin, or worse.

Tips for Overnight Stays

A cockpit cover is a good way to keep rainwater, creatures, and insects from your cockpit. It can be comforting to find your cockpit dry after a night of rain, and largely free of roosting mosquitoes or nesting earwigs. You can store kayaking clothing and your paddles inside the cockpit before sealing the cover.

Secure your hatch lids as soon as you have finished unpacking anything. That will keep unwelcome intruders from your storage areas and ensure you do not lose a lid. Raccoons can open most hatch lids, so it may be prudent to turn your kayak upside down.

Dry your gear with care. Lichens, along with other bits of vegetation, can cling to fleece and wool, and can be difficult to remove. They can also be very scratchy if you do not remove every bit. Ticks not only lurk in the grasses, but also crawl around on rock. If you lay out your clothes on rocks to dry, check them thoroughly before you bring them into your tent or put them on. A hanging line is a better option if you have somewhere to tie the ends. Otherwise, spreading clothing across your kayak may be a good option. Use the deck lines and bungees to secure items so they do not blow away.

Tides and weather change. Be sure to secure your kayak and gear overnight well out of reach of the waves.

If you light a fire, make sure you have some way to extinguish it. If you have a bucket of water standing by, this will also serve as an immediate aid should someone get burned.

This location offers easy landing and sheltered camping.

Carry fresh water with you. Flexible water bags are more practical to stow than solid containers such as bottles. If you need to add to your water supply, then a filter pump or some other way to purify water may be essential, unless you are assured of a freshwater tap. A collapsible bucket can be used to gather water. Sediment will settle to the bottom. You can then filter-pump what you need when you need it, without having to return to the water source, and without pumping more than you need. Rinse you kayak and gear in salt water if there is no option to use

fresh. This will reduce salt crystal buildup, reducing wear and tear.

Keep your tent zipped closed when you are away. Your tent may be visited by animals, but more likely by mosquitoes, gnats, or ticks.

Nowadays you are likely to be carrying at least one battery-operated device that will need to be charged. Use a portable solar panel if you will spend time on land in sufficiently bright conditions. Some flexible panels can be spread across a kayak deck beneath bungees while you paddle, charging a storage battery that can later be used to recharge your devices. One gadget burns fuel to generate electricity. For overnight light, why not carry LED lamps with solar panels you can recharge while you paddle? If the lamp is on your deck charging, it will be ready to switch on should your trip extend into darkness.

Leave No Trace

Wherever you go you should leave no signs of your passage.

Plants, nesting birds, and seals on the beach all have a reason to be where they are. But they are all easily disturbed if you are clumsy. Be sensitive to the needs of other creatures.

If you must have a fire take care where you light it, so you do not damage plants growing there, and make sure you fully extinguish it afterward, removing all trace. If someone else chooses the exact same location next day to camp, they should see no sign except perhaps footprints in the sand and flattened vegetation from your tent.

Carry out all your garbage.

Follow the lavatory routine that is appropriate for the area you are visiting, cat-holing, carrying out, or making use of public marina facilities depending on regulations and common sense.

Paddling a Full Kayak

When it is full, your kayak will be slower to accelerate, less nimble to turn, and more difficult to stop. If you hit something you are more likely to damage your kayak. But extra momentum can help when paddling out through surf, and the extra weight makes it easier to reverse through waves when making controlled surf landings. A loaded kayak is often more stable than an empty one, and rolling, should you need to, is usually easier, if a little slower. You will be less affected by wind, but more by current. You'll find it an advantage to use a slightly shorter paddle than normal. It will require less muscle for each stroke and a slightly faster stroke rate, making acceleration easier.

Rescuing a Full Kayak

An unloaded sea kayak is fairly easy to empty of water after capsize. It can be quickly ready for reentry. Because of the bulkhead behind the seat, simply raise the front end and all the water drains out. Lifting the front end of a fully laden kayak is not impossible, but it is not as easy from the seat of the rescue kayak. It is easier to flip the kayak upright and empty it using a pump once the paddler is seated again.

There are several different types of pump. The quickest and easiest is a fitted electric pump that squirts out a stream of water at the flick of a switch. But electrics and salt water don't always mix well, and a fitted pump only works for the kayak it is installed in. Your kayak may be fine, but what if you need to rescue someone else?

Some models of self-contained electric bilge pumps can be dropped into another cockpit, but otherwise the options are manual. Hand-operated stirrup pumps are the most commonly carried solution. They work best when operated with two hands, so you need two people rafted together for stability, taking turns pumping. If it is windy and you are drifting in the wrong direction, you may need a third person, attached by towline to the raft, paddling to prevent the drift.

Pumping is time-consuming and can be hard work, so consider reducing the volume inside your cockpit by cutting foam spacers to fill extra space between the front bulkhead and your foot braces. You might find that your sleeping pad secured beyond the foot braces will do the same thing.

Getting Information for Your Trip

Sea charts: Research the area you'd like to paddle. Sea charts show relevant water information, including the direction and strength of tide streams and currents, the positions of rocks, underwater contours, and places that dry out at low water. Tide races and overfalls are shown, and the underwater gradient and depth offshore can be an indication of how powerful swell might get close to shore. Sea charts also indicate the land features most easily identified from the water.

Topographic maps: These show roads, habitation, and other points of interest on land better than sea charts do. Sea charts fall short when you want to explore on land.

Other sources: *Admiralty Pilot (Sailing Directions),* local sailing guides, and kayaking guidebooks all can offer general background information about an area, plus detail that may be useful on the water. You can also investigate online sources. For most trips, I jot relevant details from my research directly onto my chart, and leave the heavy books at home.

Sea charts show the appropriate information for on-water; topographic maps are the best for land use but reveal little of the sea.

Decisions to Make Before You Go

Some logistics are best left until the trip is under-way, but some need to be figured out beforehand. In early planning, agree with your paddling part-ners on the main purpose of the trip, and how far you would like to travel each day. This way nobody gets false expectations.

You might also discuss the conditions that make you uncomfortable, and when you would prefer to be ashore, so you can better anticipate trouble before it arrives.

There are a lot of safety aspects you should discuss before you go, from telling someone where you are going and when you expect to return, to distress signals you'll carry, to personal medical conditions.

Discuss issues specific to the area you are considering. Does the state of the tide matter? Is it better to go during spring tides (bigger range) or neaps? Maybe you can use the extra speed of a spring tide to go farther with less effort. Tide races will be bigger and more exciting with a spring tide. In that case, be careful if making surf landings at high tide, when the beach profile is more likely to cause a dumping shore break. Also, be aware that you'll need to carry farther from low tide landings at spring tides.

Perhaps a cliff coast would be more acces-sible and fun to explore during neap tides, and the water level in caves will remain within a more reasonable range. You need water in the caves, but you also need headroom. A spring tide may expose rocks at low tide and offer insufficient headroom at high tide. With a neap tide, conditions around headlands will be less challenging, and you'll find more room to camp above the neap high tide mark.

Using the Chart and Map

Adding notes to your map will remind you of points of interest. This can help you with your navigation, plus it might remind you of an oppor-tunity to land to see something special.

I like to add direction lines with distances to help me make decisions when I reach a bay I might choose to cross. The line gives me an easy start point, with a compass direction and distance, and the distance around the back of the bay also mea-sured out for comparison. I still need to factor in the effect of tide and wind, but I have an immedi-ate reference to basic information. Spending time doing this before you go on a trip makes you study the map more closely, visualizing every step of the way. The more familiar with the map you become before you go, the easier it will be to use on the water.

Finally, check if your map is waterproof. If not, use a waterproof map case or laminate your chart. If you decide to laminate, you can cut your chart into sections that will fit easily under your deck elastics. It's easiest to follow the coast if you can line up adjacent map sections edge to edge, so avoid sealing adjacent sections back to back. Leave a margin of laminating material around each map section to avoid leakage. Punch a hole through that margin so you can tether your chart, otherwise it may escape from under your deck elastics when you paddle through surf or breakers.

Maps can be aligned visually to a coastline, but some locations are confusing. When in doubt, use your compass as a backup. You'll need a compass anyway, in case visibility drops. It's easiest to use a compass mounted well forward on the deck for navigating. Dropping your eyes to a compass on your lap is likely to lessen your stability, and often causes seasickness. But it is useful to carry an extra compass you can use in your hand for taking bearings.

Keep Gear Handy

When you sea kayak a lot, you figure out what you need to have handy, and where to conveniently stow it. Some things can be waterproofed and carried in the pockets of your PFD or jacket. Consider emergency items such as a flare, perhaps a VHF radio or cell phone, a handy snack, a hat, sunglasses, sunscreen. I like to carry a waterproof camera, and I prefer to have my towline ready to use.

Other items are best stowed in your day hatch, accessible from your seat, but tucked out of the way: maybe a flask with a hot drink, a packed lunch, an extra wind jacket, a headlamp, and perhaps a simple way to repair damage to you or your kayak.

This isthmus offers a choice wilderness camping spot with easy landing, shelter behind an outcrop on flat well-drained ground and a stream nearby. Look for an easy landing: You need a way to get from the water onto land, ideally with as little difficulty as possible. Look for a place sheltered from swell, wave action, and current. Look on the sheltered side of an island, in a bay on the side where the wind is blowing offshore rather than onto shore, or where the prevailing swell has wrapped around a point diminishing its power. Look for a beach of small pebbles or sand rather than big boulders or rocks. Choose an area of ledges that offer easy access to shore, rather than cliffs.

If you are practiced in self-rescues and carry a hand pump and paddle float, stow these somewhere secure in your cockpit, maybe beside your seat. Here they will be easily accessible when you are out of your kayak and need them, but will not clutter your deck or risk being washed away.

It is smart to carry a spare paddle. Should you break or lose your paddle, you will have serious difficulty returning to shore. In rougher conditions, you may also have difficulty staying upright. It might be difficult to purchase a suitable replacement on a trip. Carry your spare where you can access it without exiting your kayak, which in practice means either on your deck or inside the cockpit. But make sure nothing you carry in the cockpit could keep you from exiting your kayak easily in an emergency.

Camping

Spotting a suitable place from the water: On a multiday trip your progress may depend on the weather, and you might need to choose where to stop each night while you are still on the water.

When you are paddling an unfamiliar coast looking for somewhere to camp for the night, how should you choose? Begin by looking for specific things. You may be able to choose simply by looking at the map, but not always. Sometimes you have to choose by looking at the land. Most of the following can be determined from the water.

Consider how easy it will be to launch: If the foreshore is rocky with a narrow strip of sand at the top, it might be a great place to land at high tide, but a challenging one to launch from at low tide. Or you may land easily in the shelter of rocks at low tide, only to find the rocks covered and the beach completely exposed to wave action at high tide. Try to leave yourself an easy launch option. If possible, choose somewhere you'll be able to sneak

away from if conditions get wild, rather than somewhere you could get pinned for a week. Consider the expected direction of wind and swell.

Room to camp: You need room to camp, not only beyond high tide, but beyond the reach of potential breakers.

Fresh water: You will need to find fresh water if you are not carrying all you need. From the sea you may be able to see streams or brooks, or imagine where water would flow across the landscape. Note these places so when you land you can run up to see if you're correct. Hints might include notches in the slope, different vegetation, and the gleam of reflected light. You may also see braided trails of water across the sand of a beach, or the gleam of a wet rock surface when elsewhere is dry.

A dry flat area for your tent: You can deduce how wet the land usually gets by the topography and vegetation, although knowing a bit about geology also helps. If you see a flat area with marsh grasses, it will get wet with the slightest rain! If it is a wet day already, you should be able to judge where the ground is least waterlogged, or drains best. Otherwise, imagine where water would run if it rained hard, and avoid the "low" spots where water will collect. Marram grass, on the other hand, prefers sand that drains more easily, but it is not a very comfortable grass for camping on, so look for edges where it runs into different vegetation. Get used to spotting the telltale detail from a distance. It can save a lot of landing to check out areas that turn out to be uncomfortably rocky, boggy, or bug-ridden.

Shelter: In a sheltered location your tent is less likely to be affected by the wind, but you are more likely to be troubled by bugs. On a long trip it may be more important that you do not damage your tent. A good view is always a factor, but should not be at the expense of an uncomfortable night.

Exposure to sun: Will you watch the sunset from your tent, or have the early sun to dry your tent in the morning?

Wildlife: You may be able to spot a bird colony from the water, and save yourself landing. Look carefully for signs of wildlife before you make your final decision to stay. I once had moles push mountains of dirt up under my tent in the night when I took a chance and camped on grass speckled with molehills. I would feel less inclined to take a chance camping on a well-trodden bear path.

When in doubt: Be prepared to paddle farther if necessary.

A Special Kind of Freedom

There is a special kind of freedom to heading out for a few days with everything you need packed inside your kayak. And it's a special kind of satisfaction when the plans go well, your training in wind and waves and current make the conditions you experience fun, not traumatic, and you find yourself a perfect tent site for the night, perhaps with a freshwater stream, some wildlife to watch, and a dramatic sunset. Take the time to prepare well, start with a trip that is well within your ability, and always watch for ways to make it a better experience!

Kayak Sailing

Like many aspects of kayaking, kayak sailing trends in and out. There has been a history of sailing kayaks since kayaking first became a sport. There are three main approaches: opportunistically sailing an unmodified kayak that was designed to

BE CONSIDERATE

Bear in mind the environmental impact of:

- **Frequent campers in the same popular spot**
- **Fires on the beach or on the rocks**
- **Camping too near bird colonies**
- **Paddling too close to nesting cliffs**
- **Paddling too close to seal colonies or rookeries for sea lions**
- **Cutting wood for fires**
- **Moving rocks to pin your tent**
- **Use of soap in streams where others might find water to drink**
- **Leaving fecal matter inappropriately**

A sail can reduce visibility ahead.

be paddled; modifying a kayak to make the sailing rig part of the fixed equipment; or using a kayak designed to carry sail.

The first time I saw someone sail a kayak, it was using an umbrella. When the wind grew too strong the umbrella simply inverted, and it was easily folded down for storage. On the beach, the umbrella offered shelter from the rain.

There are simple handheld sails, using two masts with a triangle of fabric between, and a handhold on each mast. These are held in both hands for sailing, so preclude paddling at the same time unless you go tandem. Holding the sail in position for any length of time is tiring, but

sailing like this can be a fun diversion. For solo use, the kayak needs a skeg or rudder. The sail can be deployed or dropped very quickly, and there are no lines to tangle.

Circular battened sails have straps and clips to fasten to your deck lines. These take a little more practice to set up, deploy, and fold away again, but the setup is minimal. A line (sheet) is used to control the sail, but this can be rigged to permit paddling while sailing.

Both sail types fold flat for storage, and with no other equipment involved you can pass your sail from kayak to kayak.

These 1970s-era sails leave little room for forward paddling, but can be quickly and easily set up and stored.

Sails using a regular mast do require some modification to your kayak—usually some kind of mast foot, and cleats for rigging and control. The sail is normally left in position on the mast. If the mast is to be lowered while you are afloat, the front deck must be long enough to stow it without affecting your paddling. The mast foot is normally as far forward as possible, and there must be a way to immobilize the rig once lowered. With the mast far forward there should be enough room to paddle while sailing. A paddle may be sufficient for steering, but a skeg—or better still, a rudder—will make this even easier.

An alternative is to have a mast foot, such as a vertical tube fitted between the deck and hull,

within easy reach, and a sail on a mast that can be dropped into the mast foot. The mast with sail can be stored in a pipe along the front or back deck for easy access and easy stowing.

Sailing canoes/kayaks of more traditional design are more likely to have a rudder, lee boards, or occasionally a liftable center board, and may have a fixed mast. The bias toward sailing and kayaking being about equal, this type of kayak usually has a fairly stable hull shaped for sailing efficiency. As with sailing dinghies, it is useful to be able to move around to balance body weight against the pull of the sail. Shifting from the standard sitting position is easier when a hand-operated tiller is added, freeing the feet from steering. Operating

The sail position close to the bow allows freedom to paddle.

Outriggers offer stability for a larger sail area.

the sail is easier because the kayak is stable, and the features are designed and built-in, rather than added. Kayaks such as John MacGregor's various "Rob Roy" models were probably the earliest of this style.

Currently, there is more emphasis on sailing accessories that you fit yourself than on ready-built sailing kayaks. Since most kayaks are narrower and tippier than boats designed to carry sail, instability issues often deter kayakers from rigging kayaks for sail. When sails are used with ordinary kayaks, it is usual to keep the sail area small.

Adding outriggers can offer an easy aftermarket solution. You are unlikely to choose to paddle far with outriggers installed, so set up on the beach when you decide to sail. With an outrigger you can comfortably carry more sail area than without, so you can go faster in the same wind.

From a safety angle, recovering from capsize in a sit-in kayak while sailing can be awkward. Be sure to understand the options for your rig, and test them out thoroughly before you need to use them. With a sit-on-top it is a little easier.

Night Paddling

Night paddling is not something everyone does by choice, but it can be a magical experience, with moonlit seascapes, or skies dense with stars. But darkness can be disorienting. Things we take for granted as easy in daylight can become challenging after dark. Occasionally kayakers end up still at sea after dark so a controlled trip at night can be good preparation.

Judging Distances at Night

Judging distances can be difficult enough in daylight, but take away our most useful guides and we're all in the dark!

We can judge position by lining up lights on known objects. The use of two of these fixed positions will put us somewhere on a straight line, but if we use an additional pair of marks off to one side we can pinpoint our position accurately on a chart.

Let's say you are paddling toward a light or pair of lights, but do not know how far you still have to go. Make your kayak wander off course to one side for a few seconds, then bring it back on course. If your closest light is distant, it will appear to move very little against the background light. If you are close, it will appear to move a lot in relation to the more distant light. The closer you approach the more movement you'll see when you "wiggle" your kayak in this way.

You can use the same technique to judge whether the lights on a boat are close or distant.

Keeping Together in the Dark

When you are paddling with other people in daylight, it is easy to start talking with someone and, before you realize it, you have begun to separate from the others. A glance around will remind you to group up again. But at night you might not see much! Lights offer one way to maintain visual contact, but they have to be visible through 360 degrees. And they must be white. Other colors are reserved for use as navigation marks.

The effect of a bright light will destroy your night vision, making it difficult to distinguish faint lights and the shadow of shore. Alternatively, you can assign a number to each person and periodically each person can call out their number in turn. Any missing number can be identified with a person. Occasionally you may hear extra numbers from passersby or anglers joining in.

Larger groups may be better off splitting into small groups of three or four, with one light per group. Paddlers can more easily keep together in smaller groups, verbally and around the light, and the different groups can keep visual contact by watching the lights but keeping their distance so the groups do not merge and mingle. Radio or

Anything reflective will increase your visibility at night.

phone contact between the groups offers the possibility of an extra layer of security.

Paddling in the dark can be a magical experience, with brilliant trails of bioluminescence sweeping from your bow and every paddle stroke stirring vortices of brilliant stars. In moonlight the effect is different. The ghostly light is often sufficient to show what might be around you but not the detail.

In inhabited areas, bright pinpoints of light nearby mingle with more distant ones, and it can be difficult to judge how far away they are without spending a little time becoming oriented. This is one reason you should allow more time for your journey at night. You will become aware of all kinds of lights, the glow in the sky above towns, flashing beacons, the lights of cars, boats and houses. You need to be able to distinguish between and identify them if they are to help you.

There is a maritime obligation for every craft to carry a bright white light to warn other vessels to prevent collision. You can use the light to reveal your position if you get separated from your paddling companions, and to scan possible landing places for dangers.

Should you need a brighter light—for example, to help illuminate the scene of a tricky assisted rescue—then a white, handheld flare offers a quick solution. It is not a distress signal but it will be visible for some distance and may lead to investigation, so it is best to use flashlights unless they prove inadequate.

There is no legal obligation to display a light constantly on a kayak. A "glow," rather than a "light," is really what we need when we display something to show our position. Chemical light sticks can provide such a glow. These consist of a glass tube containing one chemical sealed inside a plastic tube containing a second chemical. The light is activated by bending the plastic tube until the glass tube inside breaks, then shaking to mix the two chemicals. The light typically lasts for about one night. They are conveniently waterproof and need no batteries, so are a useful backup even if you normally carry a small waterproof lamp that will shine through your pocket, in addition to your regulation bright light.

Strobes have found their way from the dance floor into the outdoor activity world, especially for cyclists, hikers, and pedestrians, but strobe lights may not be used in international waters, either to attract attention or as a distress signal. This maritime rule makes sense because flashing lights are used for navigation markers, using a variety of flashing sequences, in the colors red, yellow, green, blue, and white. Misinterpreting your strobe for a navigation marker could steer a vessel into danger.

On inland waters of United States, an area classification that excludes most of the coast but does include some coastal bays, a strobe may be used as a distress signal. If you see a flashing light on the water in this region, unless from its position it is clearly a navigation marker, assume it is someone in distress and take appropriate action.

Navigation marks can often be identified at night by the color and flashing sequence of a light. Not all buoys have lights, but at closer range you may be able to discern the shape of a buoy by its silhouette.

Lighthouses, in addition to their identifiable flashing sequence, may have standing lights (lights that show constantly at night), with different color sectors visible from different directions. Prominent hills and steep cliffs marked on the chart often show at night as dark silhouettes against the sky, and can offer the opportunity to use transits to more accurately reveal your location.

Equipment
Detailed

Choose a kayak that suits your needs: paddling just the middle section of a modular sit-on-top kayak.

The chapter on Equipment Basics described the gear you needed for your first time afloat, and what the different parts are called. This chapter offers more detail. Choice of equipment is personal, but the better you understand the options and the advantages of each, the more likely you are to find the equipment that works best for you. The chapter also covers care, maintenance, and repair of equipment.

Kayaks

You may choose a kayak by chance but you can be more discerning. Take into account what you see yourself doing by kayak, the design features that will offer improved function for you, and the construction materials and fittings that will suit your paddling environment and budget. You will get better service from that kayak if you also learn how to best take care of it, which includes maintenance, repair, storage and transport, also covered in this section.

Choosing Your Kayak

Choose the best kayak for the kind of paddling you want to do most of the time. If you intend to paddle daily on a small lake, and once a year take a multiday trip on the ocean, find a kayak suited to your daily lake paddling. If you expect to use your kayak primarily for rolling, you might get considerably more pleasure from a short, narrow, low-profile Greenland kayak: You can always rent a higher-volume expedition kayak when you need it for your occasional trip.

What kind of paddling do you see yourself doing? Will you kayak for the sake of kayaking, or as the means to something else? When choosing a kayak, begin with your vision of why and how you will paddle; for example, to take photographs of wildlife on lakes, or to enjoy rolling.

Which other hobbies influence your choice?

Photography: A kayak can be a great platform for approaching and photographing wildlife, offering you a different viewpoint than from land. Choose a stiff-tracking, stable kayak with a rudder so you can glide and steer while holding a camera steady. A large cockpit offers easy access to bulky camera equipment, and a high-profile kayak lessens the chance of water entering the cockpit when your spray deck is open.

Fishing: For fishing, consider a stable, sit-on-top kayak that offers freedom to move around when landing a fish or accessing storage areas, and is fitted with rod holders and mounting positions for fish-finders and GPS. Should you fall overboard in the excitement of the moment, it is easier to get back aboard a sit-on-top without losing your tackle. Kayaks designed specifically for fishing are discussed in the Types of Kayak section (see page 248).

Sailing: Different kinds of sails may be fitted to kayaks. Some let you paddle at the same time as sailing, others do not. If you wish to sail and paddle simultaneously, you will need to mount your sail far enough in front of you to operate without interfering with your paddle stroke. Your front deck should be long enough for you to lower your mast. You can probably best achieve this with a kayak 17 to 18 feet long. Choose something stable. A rudder will make control easier.

Expeditions: For an expedition, you will need more cargo space than a typical day boat offers, so consider a longer kayak. Look for a high-profile kayak with glide, one that keeps tracking forward rather than one that stops quickly when you stop paddling. The position and size of the main hatches should make loading straightforward. Extra compartments are useful to separate items you wish to keep more accessible. Balance your need for speed and tracking against your need for maneuverability. A kayak with good secondary stability for turning may offer the best combination.

Day trips: How fast and how far will you want to go, and how much do you enjoy maneuvering? A short, maneuverable, stable kayak is fun for exploring where speed is not an issue, but the straight tracking and speed of a longer, narrow kayak is more practical for open water and crossings. For day trips you will not need much cargo space, so you can choose a lighter-weight, low-profile kayak that is easier to carry and transport.

Speed and/or racing: If speed is your primary objective, choose a longer, narrower hull. Consider the range of surf/racing skis as well as sit-in kayaks. Go for a rudder, and consider pairing it with a wing paddle. Look at carbon fiber composite or cold-molded veneer construction for the lightest and fastest options.

Rockhopping: A stable and maneuverable kayak with rocker (a banana-shaped hull from bow to stern) and a flattish bottom will offer the most fun. Rotational-molded (rotomolded) polyethylene is a robust material, in case you touch rock occasionally. Composite kayaks in the same design realm will have better performance, but you will need the handling skills and wave-reading experience to avoid impact.

Surf: The same type of kayak you might use for rockhopping will work for surf. Composite kayaks offer lighter weight and stiffer options than plastic, and you'll notice the difference in performance on the wave. Generally, if the cockpit and seat are set back from center, the kayak will be easier to control in surf than if the cockpit is farther forward or near the center. If you want a kayak for surfing only, then a surf kayak or a wave ski is the ideal option. This is a short, flat-hulled craft with rails and fins, and shaped like a surfboard. The seat is

A surf kayak hull is shaped like the underside of a surf board. Notice the small size, the fins, and how far back the seat is positioned.

located close to the stern. A surf kayak or wave ski performs on a wave in a similar way to a surfboard, but is very activity specific: It is not much fun beyond the surf zone.

Moving water: Look for a stable, maneuverable kayak with rocker, and a more centrally located cockpit. Rounded gunwales are more forgiving than low-profile decks with sharp gunwales.

Rolling: Rolling is easiest in a narrow, low-profile kayak. The lower your hips sit to the water level, the easier your kayak will be to roll. For this reason, a narrow kayak with a short waterline will be easier to roll than a similar kayak with a longer waterline, or wider beam. Likewise, a kayak with a low seat or no seat will be easier to roll. Choose a kayak with a low back deck if you wish to roll in the lie-back position. Greenland kayaks often offer the features you might want for rolling. Choose between a more traditional, skin-on-frame style, plywood, or composite. Of these options, given identical dimensions, the skin-on-frame will generally be the most stable because the skin sags a little

For easy rolling, this kayak is narrow, has low profile, is highly rockered and has a small cockpit.

between the ribs and stringers, although it will also have the smallest inside dimensions due to the enclosed frame.

Types of Kayak

Choose a kayak type to fit your paddling needs, then select a model with the appropriate features.

Traditional Kayaks

Greenland kayaks have experienced a renaissance. Many enthusiasts build their own kayaks in the Greenland style, with wooden frames covered in canvas. There is also an increase in availability of similar designs in wood and composites. Much of the interest in Greenland kayaks relates to rolling, with some kayaks being built specifically for that purpose. Baidarkas, traditional kayaks from the

northwestern United States and Canada, have also seen resurgence in popularity, but for touring rather than rolling. Baidarkas have more end-to-end stringers along the hull than Greenland kayaks. This creates more chines, enabling a rounder hull section.

Sit-on-Top Kayaks

Sit-on-tops are built so the paddler sits on the deck rather than inside a cockpit. If you fall off or capsize, it is more straightforward to flip upright and climb back onto a sit-on-top than to reenter a swamped sit-in kayak, and there is no need to bail. For that reason, sit-on-tops are great confidence builders. Kayakers can develop skills without fear of capsize. They are also great in the surf zone, where accidental capsizes happen constantly. There is no need to return to shore to empty every time you spill.

The deck of a sit-on-top is often molded to include a well in which the paddler sits, surrounded by a perimeter wall or gunwale. Because the seating area remains above water level, any water drains away through scuppers; drain holes that pass down through the hull.

Sit-on-top kayaks are popular for warm water paddling, are easy to self-rescue after a spill even in the surf zone, and are commonly used like this one in California for fishing.

Replicas of historic Greenland kayaks offer design insight.

The open nature of a sit-on-top can be a drawback in cold places, and when the water is cold. Additional clothing becomes essential. A sit-in kayak with a spray deck is warmer.

Rotomolding is a good way to manufacture sit-on-tops because there is no need to join the hull to the deck; the molding is done in one piece. It is more challenging to make a good seam between hull and deck using composites because there is rarely good access to the inside. If seamed only on the outside, the join will be weaker than that of a sit-in kayak, which is typically seamed both inside and out—although there are some good composite sea-touring sit-on-tops.

The biggest market for sit-on-tops is for recreational kayaks and fishing, with a smaller number specifically for touring, which is where the distinction blurs between a sit-on-top and a surf ski.

Recreational and Touring Kayaks

This is a huge category. Generally, recreational kayaks are friendly, stable, open cockpit craft, mostly 9 to 13 feet long, of rotomolded or thermoform plastic. They may or may not feature one or two hatches with bulkheads. Touring kayaks are longer, from 13 to 17 feet, and usually have two hatches, sometimes more. (Expedition kayaks are usually 16 to 18 feet, and commonly have three or more bulkheads and hatches, as well as more carrying capacity.)

Although there are no clear boundaries between categories, recreational kayaks, while great for sheltered water, are less suitable for exposed or open water. Touring kayaks are faster, and cover distance more easily. Most sea kayaks are touring kayaks designed for sea and ocean touring, with those promoted as expedition kayaks tending to have greater carrying capacity and ease of loading.

Surf skis are sit-on-top racing kayaks often used for touring on saltwater. In places like Australia they are commonly used in waves and in the surf zone, and they are used for racing. In some countries, such as South Africa, sit-on-top

Surf skis, fast sit-on-top racing kayaks, are better suited than racing kayaks to awkward launch sites and rough water. Surf skis are most common in Australia (shown) and South Africa, on warm water.

This tandem touring ski was used for an Iceland circumnavigation in 2011. Notice the short deck shield over the feet.

247

expedition kayaks are used for coastal exploration. These sometimes have a half-deck to shield the legs, while still permitting easy mounting and dismounting. Like other sit-on-tops, skis have a deck sealed to the hull to form a single floating part that cannot fill with water. Most surf skis are composite.

Fishing Kayaks

Fishing from a kayak has grown in popularity, to the point where now there are many kayaks designed specifically for fishing. At the most purpose-specific end of the spectrum are wide, stable kayaks, usually sit-on-tops, with raised seating options that allow easier casting and clear vision down into the water. Look for provisions for holding rods and accessories such as a fish finder or a GPS. Options include molded-in recesses and attachments that clip onto rails. If you need to anchor your craft to fish, look for provisions that make this easy.

What will you do with your catch? If you intend to catch and release, you will not need to carry a cooler, but if you catch for food then maybe you will. Look to see if this is possible on the fishing kayak you consider.

If you intend to use your kayak mostly for journeys, but to fish fairly often too, look for a kayak that offers reasonable speed and tracking but also a way to carry fishing rods and tackle, and possibly your catch. You will sacrifice some stability in standing to cast, but will be able to travel farther with less effort. Some touring kayaks come with built-in rod holders and gear mounts that will be adequate unless you are a really serious angler, but you can modify any kayak to make fishing easier.

Most fishing kayaks are plastic. Fishing kayaks tend to be heavy, so question how you will handle your kayak on land. Will you need a road trailer?

Will you be able to load it onto your vehicle? Will you need wheels to get it to and from your vehicle? There are many kayak fishing groups happy to explain how they tackle these issues.

Sea Kayaks

Sea kayaks for touring usually range from 15 to 18 feet long, and are designed to cope with waves and open water, and to cover distance efficiently. Shorter sea kayaks, between 13 and 15 feet, are coming into fashion for short trips, rockhopping, and surf. These fill the niche once well served by whitewater kayaks, in the days when these were 13 feet and longer. Nimble, stable, easy to manhandle, and fun in rough water, these are a good compromise where speed is less important than maneuverability.

Expedition Kayaks

Expedition kayaks are designed to carry a load easily and quickly. They typically have several sealed compartments accessed via hatches, and handle well on the water when loaded. Lengths are typically from 16 to 18 feet, occasionally longer. Most

Expedition kayaks are designed to carry weight well and may have several easy-to-load hatches.

expedition kayaks are composite. Plastic kayaks can survive abuse from awkward landings, but commonly have mini-cell foam bulkheads that reduce carrying capacity.

Play Boats

A whole range of kayaks fit in the day boat/play boat category. Designed for stability, waves, rolling, rock gardens, or playing in currents, many of these designs work fine for short distances and day trips, but are less suitable for long distances and multiday trips. Although exceptions include some great expedition boats biased toward rough water play, this category of sea kayak is largely shorter, from 13 to 16 feet, with the trend toward greater maneuverability and stability. Plastic is forgiving for use in rocky areas, but many high-performance designs are composite, perhaps because it is more cost-effective for small production runs.

Solo or Tandem

A tandem kayak offers a less-experienced paddler the chance to join a more-experienced paddler, or allows two paddlers to travel faster than either would be able to alone. Tandems are often used in groups as a safety option. A tired or incapacitated paddler can rest while a stronger paddler maintains speed, so a group can maintain a schedule. Some tandems are incredible load carriers, enabling groups to be self-sustaining for long periods of time, or to carry luxuries.

However, tandems suffer in the hands of conflicting personalities, and are often referred to as "divorce boats" because they demand a degree of agreement and coordination between the two partners. The paddler in the stern has more control over steering, although rudder controls can be extended to allow the front paddler to steer.

A tandem with a short midsection requires paddlers to synchronize their strokes to avoid hitting blades. A longer midsection allows paddlers to operate independently.

Tandems have a bigger volume, usually drift faster in crosswinds than singles do, and are often faster, so extra care must be taken to keep kayaks together in a mixed group.

It is possible to roll a tandem, but it takes coordination. There have been plenty of failures when each paddler attempts to roll on opposite sides. Yet one partner can roll unaided if the other tucks forward to hug the deck, so neither need exit if one can roll.

Kayak Features

Within any chosen category of kayak, there is a lot of room for design variation. Each design feature has its own performance implications. Here I will identify the main features and explain what they mean to the paddler.

Stability

This is a relative term. What you find stable or unstable depends on your own balance, body build, and experience, in addition to the characteristics of the kayak.

Primary or initial stability is the stability you feel when the kayak is level and upright. When you edge the kayak, you experience another position known as edged or secondary stability. Recreational kayaks tend to have high primary and high secondary stability. Racing kayaks tend to be tippy. A combination of less primary stability with greater secondary stability will offer a sea kayak easy edging for turning and control in wind, and will feel most comfortable when held with one hip lower than the other, but will feel wobbly when held completely upright. Kayaks with good primary but little secondary stability are not comfortable to edge for turning, so work best steered by rudder.

Stability is also influenced by body shape. If you have a narrow upper body but heavy hips, your center of gravity will be lower than someone with narrow hips and broad, heavy shoulders. A lower center of gravity makes balancing easier.

Be confident in your ability to master the kayak you choose. You may choose a kayak that feels tippy to start, and master it as your skills improve. It will not take long to develop the same degree of confidence in a slightly tippier kayak than the one in which you already feel relaxed. Adding cargo can make your kayak more stable, so try this when getting used to a new kayak. You can reduce the ballast as your confidence and ability increase. Also, try some of the balance exercises in the section on balancing (page 39).

Length

For touring and exploring in a solo kayak, select a boat that is 11 to 18 feet long. You would only need something longer for a special project. Whitewater kayaks and surf kayaks are shorter than 11 feet, but they are designed for going down rivers with the current, or riding waves. They lack sufficient hull speed for easy touring.

In general, given similar construction, a longer kayak will be heavier to carry than a shorter one, but the shorter one will have less hull speed. Questions to consider: Will you kayak with someone else to help you carry, or will you carry alone? Is there a maximum length you can safely carry on your car? If you intend to store your kayak in a garage, how long is the garage?

Tracking

This is a measure of the ease in which you can paddle a straight line. Maneuverable kayaks such as play boats require more course correction than less-rockered kayaks. The design of the hull determines how well a kayak tracks, but weight distribution is also crucial. With weight too far forward, in calm conditions a kayak will track poorly. It will also turn strongly into any wind. With weight too far back, a kayak will track well on calm water, but will turn from any wind. A good seating position and load distribution is crucial for tracking in wind.

A kayak that tracks well empty for one person may not for someone else: The crucial element, trim, is personal. Someone with long legs will trim a kayak down at the bow more than someone with short legs, and there will be a difference based on how heavy those legs are too. In general, heavy paddlers and tall paddlers trim a kayak down at the bow more than short paddlers and lightweight paddlers.

To a point, you may be able to adjust the seat forward or back to improve tracking. Or you can carry an appropriate weight of cargo in the bow or stern to similar effect. Otherwise, choose a kayak that really does suit your height and build. Tracking and trim is important.

Keel

Many kayaks have a keel. This is usually a V-shape in the hull from bow to stern. A keel offers stiffness along the hull, and is one way to achieve straight tracking. It also creates a prominent area that will be most subject to wear from launching and landing. Composite kayaks with a keel often come with a "keel strip," an externally applied strip of fiberglass laminated from bow to stern along the keel. This sacrificial layer may be replaced when worn, protecting the integrity of the hull underneath. A keel strip will add drag along the hull.

Some kayaks are designed without a keel. The hull shape is a shallow arch in cross-section. Any wear from launching and landing is spread over a larger area of hull. Such a hull gains little benefit from a protective strip.

Chines

Chines are creases or angles along the hull from end to end; they offer secondary stability when a kayak is edged. They also add stiffness. A hard chine is one that forms a sharp angle. When the angle is rounded, it is known as a soft chine. Some kayaks have a rounded hull section without any prominent angles. These have no chines. Racing kayaks and skis typically have no chines.

A hard chine may act as a keel when a kayak is paddled on edge.

Weight

Weight is more of an issue for lifting and carrying on land than it is when you are afloat. However, lightweight kayaks do handle more responsively on the water. Lightweight kayaks typically cost more than heavier ones because of the materials used. Thermoform kayaks are lighter than rotomolded

This fast lightweight racing kayak is easy to carry, has an easy-access cockpit, understern rudder. It is also tippy so requires good balance, and is not best suited to rough water.

ones, but cost more. Carbon fiber kayaks are lighter than fiberglass ones, but they cost more.

On the other hand, a smaller kayak will be lighter than a bigger one in the same material, so the solution to the lifting challenge may be a compromise between size, material, and cost.

Cockpit and Seat Size

Both cockpit size and seat size must be appropriate to your build.

Small cockpits offer the best spray deck seal because they are closer to circular in shape. The greater the cockpit curvature, the better the spray deck elastic will grip, so the better the spray deck works. Conversely, a long cockpit sacrifices the seal along the side of the cockpit, which being straighter will leave the elastic slack.

A small (ocean) cockpit offers a wider range of useful leg and knee positions when seated than a large cockpit, especially when combined with a full-plate footrest. But it is not as easy to get into and out of as a larger one. Getting into a small cockpit requires sitting on the back deck and feeding both legs into the cockpit at the same time. A cockpit that angles up from the back deck is easier to slide forward into, while a cockpit with no rise from back to front will require more depth at the cockpit. If your legs are too long to slide into an ocean cockpit, you can kneel on the seat and corkscrew in. Reverse the action to get out.

Individuals vary in proportions, not only between torso and leg length. Being the same height as someone else does not mean you will fit in the same cockpit. Likewise, one person may find a cockpit long enough to sit in and bring his or her legs in afterward, while someone else with the same leg length cannot because of a longer upper leg.

Seats vary in width, and in distance front to back. A good seat width will let you slide a finger between each hip and the side of the seat. If you are wedged into the seat you will lose some of your paddling power potential, and if you have much more free space you may slide sideways when you edge.

The seat width is restricted by the beam of the kayak at the level of the seat bottom. Given the same beam, a hull with vertical sides will accommodate a wider seat than a hull that narrows from the gunwale down.

For edging, you may get the greatest control when you straighten one leg, pressing it down along the hull, while lifting the other. Ideally your seat will allow this. Long seats that rise to the front generally prevent this. A shorter and flatter seat offers more options. For more on seats, see page 262.

Cargo Capacity

Most touring kayaks have a cargo capacity equivalent to or greater than that of a large backpack, and for many paddlers this is more than adequate. If you wish to carry more bulky equipment, or make extended self-contained tours, then you need to look more closely at cargo capacity.

Kayak manufacturers sometimes, but not always, suggest maximum load weight. Add your own weight to that of your load to see if you come within the suggested range. Some manufacturers reveal storage compartment volume. But you also should check hatch sizes and position, and the shape of the storage space. Compartments with similar volume may be long and narrow, or broad and short. There is little to be gained from a large compartment if what you wish to carry will not fit through the hatch. If you need to carry a bear-proof container for your food on a multiday trip,

it should fit through the hatch, and the compartment should have the dimensions to receive it.

Rolling Suitability

For some paddlers, difficulty of rolling is a deal breaker. Some kayaks can be rolled more easily than others for a variety of reasons, including body shape and size, and the kayaker's ability. A kayak with a low back deck may be preferable to a roller with a lie-back finish roll, but of no significance to someone who finishes a roll from the side. It is personal.

Glide

Glide refers to how a kayak continues to move forward when you stop paddling. A kayak that quickly stalls and stops is said to have little glide, while one that continues to move forward for a long distance has good glide. Play boats tend to be so maneuverable they will spin off course when you stop paddling. This does not necessarily mean they have poor glide. With a skeg dropped, some will show good glide, others not.

Color

The color you choose for your kayak may depend on what is locally available, but there are some interesting criteria to consider given a wider choice.

Do you like the color? We are psychologically affected by color. One color may make you feel uplifted and confident, another may make you feel serious and clear-minded, while yet another may make you feel insecure and timid. If you are to spend time with a particular color, you had better feel comfortable with it.

How visible will your kayak be? The deck color may differ from the hull color, so consider how visible it will be when upright, and when overturned.

Red and yellow kayaks here show well from a distance.

Do you want your kayak to be easily spotted by powerboats and other watercraft, or in an emergency? Or do you want to avoid attention so you pass unnoticed?

Kayaks become more visible when they contrast the surroundings. The important aspects are color contrast and brightness contrast. Fishermen often use black flags on their pot floats because black contrasts best against a bright background, but helicopter pilots searching from above do not see the contrast between an upturned black kayak

hull and dark water. A white hull may not show well when surrounded by whitecaps, but otherwise contrasts against a dark sea. Colors in the yellow–orange–red spectrum generally show well and contrast against typical sea colors, so are often considered "safety colors," but bright pale blue often contrasts just as well.

Translucence affects visibility. A translucent surface reflects only parts of light, letting the remainder pass through. This makes it less visible than an opaque surface of the same color. Dark colors absorb more light, reflecting less, so they too are generally less visible.

If you want a kayak to be readily visible, choose a light, opaque color for the deck and hull that will contrast the waters you paddle. If you want to be unnoticed, choose translucent colors similar to the water color in a pattern of slightly lighter and darker shades, which visually breaks up the shape of the kayak. A woman I met who prefers not to be noticed when she paddles and camps solo in north Germany chose kayak colors specifically to blend in. The hull is the color of the sand on the banks where she upturns her kayak to camp, and the deck is dark brown to blend with the water. If you are choosing a kayak for fishing, or wildlife photography, you may want a camouflage of some sort.

Kayak Construction

Many different materials are used to build kayaks, each a compromise of strength, stiffness, weight cost, and design constraint. Here are the more common options.

Skin-on-Frame

This revisits the traditional method of kayak construction, creating a frame and then stretching a skin over it. This became highly popular again in the 1950s and 1960s, when a massive number of designs were produced with plywood sections and wooden stringers covered in cotton canvas. Nowadays similar methods are used, sometimes with heat-shrink Dacron as a lighter-weight and easier-to-handle skin material, and sometimes with aluminum instead of wood. Resurgence in more traditional construction and design brought back timber frames hand-tied with line, with oiled or painted canvas in place of animal skin. With some guidance, a skin-on-frame kayak may be built in one week or so.

Folding

Folding kayaks are mostly skin-on-frame, and are designed to be taken apart after use, then

A folding kayak is easy to store and transport.

Here the skin is laid out ready for the frame to be inserted.

With a folding kayak it is easier to plan trips using public transport including ferries.

reassembled. This offers a realistic option for people who live in apartments with limited storage space, or with access limited by stairwells or elevators. They also offer a solution for people who rely on public transport. Frames for these kayaks may be wood with metal ferrules and clamps, or aluminum with nylon sections. The frame is assembled and tightened on the inside. Skins are usually one piece; waterproof man-made fabrics are normally used.

Another style of folding kayak uses a stiff, lightweight, plastic skin folded origami-style to create kayaks that most closely resemble plywood designs. This diminishes the need for a full frame.

Wood

Wood is a pleasing material for kayak construction. It insulates well, and is strong, lightweight, and biodegradable. It must be finished with varnish, paint, oil or a coating of fiberglass to prevent waterlogging and rotting. There are two main methods of construction. Wood strip kayaks are made from many narrow strips of wood glued together across sectional frames. The frames are

removed completely or partly once the skin is complete, and the hull joined to the deck. Wood strip is a good way to build rounded hull shapes.

Kayel or "K L" construction is named after Ken Littledyke, who pioneered the method of stitching and gluing panels of plywood to build kayaks. The panels are first held together with copper wire threaded through small, drilled holes along the edges. The seams are sealed using fiberglass tape with resin before the excess copper wire is removed and any holes filled. Finally, the kayak is painted or varnished. This is a simple way to build a hardchine hull, although it is possible to create curved sections by bending the plywood. Marine plywood is more durable around water than standard plywood, but costs more.

Building a Kayel plywood stitch and glue kayak can be a home project.

Composite

Composite kayaks can be made using a variety of fabrics embedded in plastic. The plastic, in this case, is a two-part mixture applied in a mold. The reaction between the two components causes the liquid to set solid, trapping the fabric. The plastics used are polyester, vinyl ester, and epoxy resins. Often more than one type of fabric is embedded.

Choices include fiberglass, made from microfibers of glass bonded into fibers either matted or woven into cloth, carbon fiber, and Kevlar. In addition, stiffening panel or ribs of foam core, core mat, or wood are used. With a relatively much lower cost to produce a mold compared to plastic kayaks, manufacturers often test new designs in fiberglass before making the heavy investment in a mold for a plastic version.

Heated Plastic Molding

There are several different methods for manufacturing plastic kayaks that require heat, and each has a different result. All might be called "thermo"-form, but that term is generally applied to only one, the others being described by other specific aspects of manufacture.

Rotational-Molded Polyethylene

These kayaks are made from polyethylene granules inside a heated metal mold that is rotated and also tipped end to end. The melting plastic spreads over the inside of the mold. Once the mold is cooled, the kayak may be removed. The cockpit

An open "rock and roll" oven awaits a mold. The heavy aluminum two-part kayak mold is seen hoisted open.

and hatch openings are cut out, and deck fittings etc. are added afterward. There is a lot of structural integrity to a rotomolded kayak because no seam joins the hull to the deck. The plastic is durable and affordable, but the surface is resistant to glue. Because of this, the industry-standard foam bulkheads tend to leak in time.

The surface of a rotomolded kayak is fairly soft and liable to scratch, but the skin is thick, tough to puncture, and wears well. The plastic is flexible so internal structures are added to help keep the shape. Flattish surfaces are prone to "oil-can," especially in hot weather. Whitewater kayaks are usually rotomolded.

Some rotomolded plastic kayaks are made in sections that interlock and buckle together. Modular kayaks are easier to carry and store, and offer the option to add sections to make a single into a tandem, or even longer.

Blow-Molded Polyethylene

In extrusion blow molding, a tube of extruded polyethylene is sealed at each end into a sausage-shaped balloon, which is captured in a two-part mold. Compressed air is blown into the balloon to force the plastic to conform to the mold shape. The mold is cooled to harden the plastic before the kayak is taken from the mold.

Thermoform Plastic

Thermoform kayaks are made from sheets of plastic laid over or into molds under heat and pressure to create the deck and hull separately, which are then glued together. The original sheets can be made as laminates using several different materials, so the properties of the plastic will vary between manufacturers. They usually incorporate an ultraviolet-resistant layer. The surface of thermoform plastic is generally harder than that of rotomolded plastic, making it more resistant to surface scratches, and the stiffer material allows for a thinner and lighter-weight molding. The material can retain a highly polished appearance, similar to a fiberglass kayak. This type of plastic can be glued to, making it easier to fit watertight bulkheads, hatches, and stiffening ribs.

Fixtures and Fittings

Kayaks are fitted with a variety of add-on features to improve performance or for safety. Knowing what is available before you buy a new kayak may help you make a better decision, although some features may be easily added later.

Foot Braces

Your foot braces stop you from spinning in your seat and allow you to push your kayak forward when you lever against your paddle. They also help you sit upright. Without well-adjusted foot braces, you must hold your position inside your kayak using your thigh or knee grips, or you will lose power. It is much easier to use your feet.

The ideal position for your foot braces will position your hips, knees, ankles, and feet in comfortable alignment. In practice many sea kayaks have

Position foot braces so you can straighten your legs without tension.

cockpit shapes and thigh braces that force your knees down and apart, with your heels together and your toes pointing out, froglike. This is not ideal for powering your forward stroke as it strains your hips, knees, and ankles. If possible, bring your knees closer together so they bend upward rather than outward.

A bulkhead foot brace, sometimes known as a "full-plate foot brace," offers the widest range of placement for your feet. This is especially valuable when you paddle for any length of time without getting out of your kayak.

You might consider having a bulkhead installed in a custom position for your leg length. If so, leave enough space to wear shoes with a thicker sole. You can fill the extra space with a thin foam pad when you wear a thinner sole. A custom-fit bulkhead will also limit who can paddle your kayak. It will, however, maximize your dry cargo space, and minimize the cockpit volume that could fill with water in event of capsize.

Otherwise, you can modify the standard bulkhead position by using foam spacers until you have a good fit. This also reduces the space that could fill with water in capsize, but does not add dry storage.

Deck Fittings / Deck Rigging

Most kayaks have a variety of anchor points for attaching lines and bungees. Lines offer easy grab points for handling the kayak on and off the water, including after a wet exit, when a kayak without grab points can be slippery to hold. You should be able to work your way from end to end of the kayak passing from handgrip to handgrip. Your cockpit serves for one section, but how you break up the line between there and the ends is up to you. A series of carrying handles appropriately spaced will do the same job as lines, and may be easier to grab.

Bungees are useful for temporarily holding items. You will lose things occasionally in rough seas if you don't tie or clip them to your deck. You can use them for charts, spare paddles, a bilge pump, or a windbreaker you have just taken off. Bungees function poorly as grab points. Grab points are important; bungees are useful.

You should always carry a compass in case of sudden fog. Most can be hooked onto deck lines when needed, but you will never forget to take one if it is fixed to your deck.

Skeg

A skeg is a fin or plate that extends into the water under the stern of the kayak. It improves tracking in a straight line. A skeg is most useful when paddling across the wind or downwind, and is counterproductive when paddling against the wind. Most skegs nowadays are retractable, but early versions were strapped over the stern when needed.

A retractable skeg will stow inside a slot in the hull. Small stones, sand, or mud often lodge in the slot and jam the skeg, so it is a good idea to tie a short tail of line through a hole drilled in the back corner of your skeg so you, or another paddler, can

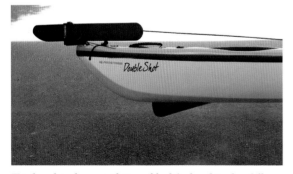

This kayak is shown with its rudder lifted and its skeg fully deployed.

The control to raise or lower the skeg is usually beside the cockpit.

easily pull the skeg out when it jams. This is especially useful afloat because it is easy to get stones lodged when you launch. Some paddlers prefer to launch stern-first for this reason. Otherwise check that your skeg operates smoothly as soon as you are afloat, and get assistance to free it before you set off so you know it will work when you need it.

There are many types of skeg control. Some kayaks use a sliding cable to push the skeg down. Pushed cable is liable to kink, so avoid forcing when stuck. Some skegs are spring-loaded and are pulled up using a cable or line. Others work using a hydraulic system. Familiarize yourself with the system on any boat you paddle before you leave shore.

On multiday journeys, carry a repair kit and spare parts if you rely heavily on your skeg. At the least, you must be able to remove your skeg should it become jammed in the down position, as this will cause problems in wind, and make landing and launching awkward.

Why a Skeg Works

When you paddle a kayak forward, you create higher pressure where the bow pushes against the water, and lower pressure where water fills in behind the kayak as turbulence. A side wind will push the stern into the turbulence more quickly than it pushes the bow against the pressure holding it, pointing the kayak into the wind. We call this "weathercocking," after the traditional wind vane in the shape of a rooster that always turns to face the wind. A skeg under the stern will grab the water beneath the turbulence and help slow the sideways drift of the stern to match that of the bow.

A skeg should be most effective close to the stern, but in waves the stern is often lifted from the water, and the hull at the stern is often too narrow to accommodate a skeg box. In practice, the best compromise is locating the skeg somewhere between the cockpit and the stern. Because the skeg is resisting a sideways movement, it makes little difference whether it lies along the center line of the hull, or to one side.

Kayaking downwind can be the most challenging direction to keep a straight track. The stern can wander to either side, and control can seem as tricky. The skeg helps in this direction by stopping the stern from being blown around.

How to Use a Retractable Skeg

When paddling straight into the wind, the skeg should be raised. Otherwise, the skeg is useful in any direction. To angle across the wind, start with the skeg about halfway down. Once at cruising speed, check to see the effect, and trim up or down as needed. When paddling downwind, begin with the skeg fully down, get up to cruising speed, and then raise the skeg a little to reduce drag. You'll soon discover if you need it fully down or if you can manage with less.

Rudder

A rudder acts similar to a skeg, equalizing the sideways drift of the bow and stern in the wind. Fine adjustments may be made by steering. Paddling into wind, a rudder may cause problems because when the bow is caught by the wind and the rudder anchors the stern, the kayak will turn across the wind. For this reason it is best to raise the rudder when paddling into the wind. Maintaining direction into wind is easier anyhow.

Rudders are almost always positioned behind or very close to the stern, so they are frequently out of the water in waves, especially when surfing downwind.

On flatter water and in little wind, a rudder offers an easy way to maintain and to change direction using the feet to steer rather than the paddle, which can then be used for propulsion only.

Rudders are controlled by the feet, but the controls vary. Best is a system with a fixed foot brace, with steering at the toe, or between the feet. With standard rigging and a toe control, press with the left foot to turn left. Press the tiller toward the left side if you have a "T-bar,"

Note: If you edge your kayak and use a rudder for turns, toe control can be easier when the rudder lines are switched over. Extending the left leg to edge the kayak down on the left side, which also involves pressing with the left foot, then steers the kayak to the right. The controls are most easily changed by crossing the lines at the stern of the kayak. You will need to practice with the new arrangement for a little while before it becomes natural.

Skeg, Rudder or Both?

Whether to use a skeg, a rudder, both, or neither is an entirely personal decision. A rudder offers an alternative to edging and steering with a paddle, reducing the number of strokes needed to maintain or change direction. A skeg makes a maneuverable kayak track more stiffly, reducing the need to correct a course. In waves, a combination of the

A tombolo offers a perfect landing beside a camping spot near Lysekil, Sweden.

two works well because when the rudder is clear of the water at the stern, the skeg still aids tracking. Otherwise the rudder can be used to steer. Of course, with practice you can achieve the same control using only a paddle, so use whatever suits you.

End Grabs

End grabs let you take firm hold of the end of your kayak, either to carry it or to keep contact with it if you are in the water. You will see a lot of alternatives, including handles, toggles, and straps. Most times, all you'll use an end grab for is to lift one end of your kayak, but imagine other situations, such as tumbling in surf, when you will need a firm grip and yet don't want to get a finger trapped. Safe solutions make it impossible to trap a finger. If you think your end grabs may cause problems, modify or replace them.

Hatches

Most modern sea kayaks have bulkheads and hatches. These create flotation compartments that keep your kayak afloat even when the cockpit is awash, and offer easy access to dry storage inside the kayak. How waterproof the compartments remain depends on the integrity of the deck and hull, bulkheads, hatches, and any fittings that pass through the deck or hull. Leaks do occur, so it is never a bad idea to carry flotation bags inside sealed hatches, and to carry your cargo in watertight containers.

Hatch lids are typically made of rubber, synthetic rubber, or stretchy neoprene, or are molded from composites or plastic with a rubber seal. Tether your hatch lids to your kayak so you cannot lose them by accident. Some lids sink in water.

Care of Hatches

Ultraviolet light will prematurely age your hatch lids, so store them away from direct sunlight when not in use. An occasional application of a protective spray, such as "303 Aerospace Protectant," will extend the life of rubber hatch lids while keeping them pliable and easy to seal.

Bulkheads

Bulkheads are the walls inside your kayak that create watertight compartments. In composite kayaks they are usually made from the same materials as the kayak. Plastic kayaks more commonly use mini-cell foam, which also adds flotation.

Knee Tube

A knee tube is a storage tube running under the front deck all or partway between the cockpit and the front bulkhead. In a kayak with an ocean (small) cockpit, one end of the tube will be between the knees of the paddler, offering a way to grip the deck while edging and rolling, hence the name "knee tube." With a longer cockpit, the knees do not reach the knee tube.

Early knee tubes were accessed beneath the deck. The end of the tube was usually open, or closed with a foam stopper, with the far end being sealed. There was no way to access the compartment with the spray deck sealed. Nowadays, a more common arrangement is to have both ends of the knee tube sealed, with access via a small deck hatch, sometimes called a "whisky hatch."

Seat

For some people, choosing a kayak comes down to choosing a seat. But there are two types of seat: those for selling kayaks, and those for kayaking. We imagine ourselves having to sit for quite a long time and look for the most comfortable seat to relax in. However, a seat that is comfortable to relax in on the shop floor isn't necessarily the best, or good, for kayaking.

Sit on the floor facing a wall. Position yourself so your heels rest lightly against a wall, with your toes upstretched, knees fairly close together. Now bend your knees and bring your heels from the wall, keeping just the balls of your feet against the wall. Hold your torso upright and imagine creating a plumb line from the top of your head to your tailbone. This is a good starting point for a paddling position. Fold your arms so they don't get in

One leg is straightened and the other relaxed and bent to help fully rotate the torso.

When the torso is rotated in the other direction, the previously bent leg straightens while the other bends.

the way, and rotate fully to one side, straightening the leg on the side toward which you rotate. Now rotate in the opposite direction, straightening your other leg and allowing the first to bend.

If you find it difficult to sit upright, as you see happening in the second image, position a small cushion or pad beneath your tailbone, so it tips you forward a little. See how that affects your posture. Now move the cushion forward until it is under your thighs, and see how that feels. It is easier to sit upright when you are tipped forward rather than back.

When you use your legs to drive your torso rotation, you'll find your hips move forward and back by a couple of inches as your knees move up and down. Think about that movement in the context of a kayak seat. Your seat should tip you forward if you are to sit upright easily, and there should be room at the sides of the seat for your hips to move forward and back without rubbing when you rotate. There should be freedom for your knees to move up and down a little as you press on each foot brace. Ideally, you should have little or no contact with your back support while you paddle, or it will interfere with your torso rotation. But the back support can be right there, ready for when you stop paddling and want to relax. If you do have constant contact, it should be limited to support in the lower back region, where there will be less body movement, otherwise there will be constant rubbing.

Kayak seats are all-too-often designed to tip you back against a substantial back support, with support under your thighs holding your knees up to the deck or into knee braces. Then, with some padding at the hips, you'll be securely wrapped in your kayak. You could probably watch TV comfortably from this position, but it is a weak position for paddling.

If you need to make changes to a seat, try the simple options first. A small pad under your tailbone, for example, might give you a more powerful paddling posture. If you have narrow hips, add hip pads so you don't slide sideways in your seat when you edge. Leave about a finger width on either side so you can still rotate without restriction. Only change your seat if you cannot make the adjustments you need in another way.

Backrest

The function of a back support should be to rest against when not paddling. When you sit upright to paddle, you should just clear your back support, and not rub against it when your torso rotates during your forward stroke. Your back support may also serve to protect your back if you lean back during a roll, preventing contact between your spine and the cockpit rim behind you.

Kayak Transport, Care, and Maintenance

A kayak can last a lifetime if you give it a little care and attention, so here are a few tips on handling and storage.

Transporting a Kayak

Roof racks are a good way to transport kayaks. Cars no longer have a standard "gutter" to which you can attach a universal roof rack. Instead, there is now a different adapter for almost every car. You will need a roof rack specifically for your model and year of manufacture.

A roof rack will not necessarily always stay on the roof of a car, even if you want it to. Use locks to deter theft.

Occasionally, a roof rack will fly off anyway in a crosswind, taking a kayak with it, and sometimes part of the roof. Check the maximum roof load weight and any other relevant information in your vehicle manual, and make sure the roof rack is secured correctly on your vehicle. Even if the weight is within the limits specified by the car and roof rack manufacturers, the torque on a kayak from a strong gust of side wind when you are traveling at speed may be enough to twist a roof rack free. Strap your kayak securely to the roof rack, and then tether the bow and stern to the front and back of your car as well. The end lines are primarily a safety measure in case the roof rack leaves the car. They should be lightly taut, not tight, or they may bend the kayak. If the roof rack does detach, your kayak will still be attached to your car, which should minimize damage to your kayak and could prevent a much more serious accident.

If you normally have to load your kayak onto a roof rack by yourself, but have lifting difficulties, then consider a side-loading rack. This has a frame that slides along your roof rack until it rests alongside your car. You secure your kayak to it at a low level before raising it and locking it in place on the roof. The lifting part is made easy by design, often with the aid of hydraulics.

To prevent your kayak from twisting to one side during transport, use kayak cradles that conform to the shape of the hull, or stacker bars (upright bars) against which you can secure your kayak.

Use padding on your roof rack to protect your kayak from metal bars. Cradles and pads spread the load well, but a narrow bar can cause dents or cracks. Tie your kayak down firmly, but not tight enough to cause damage.

A kayak can get very hot on the roof of your car in the sun, especially when you are parked. Roads tend to radiate a lot of heat, and a dark car roof will make a kayak even hotter. A composite kayak can heat up enough to cause surface wrinkling, or "orange-peel" cosmetic damage, and the heated air will pressurize any sealed compartments. In hot sun, consider a white cloth travel bag for your kayak. Remember to remove hatch lids when you expect a temperature change, and also when you change altitude.

Regional regulations govern overhangs in front of and behind vehicles, and any necessary warning signs, flags, or lights required. Always check when you travel farther afield for different regulations that might influence the kayak or vehicle you use, or how you carry your kayak.

Otherwise, hang a red flag at the back to alert other drivers to any overhang, to remind you where the end is when you reverse or maneuver in tight spaces, and to help pedestrians see the kayak should they walk behind your car.

After paddling, rinse your kayak and gear to reduce salt buildup. If you paddle freshwater, thoroughly rinse to avoid buildup of mineral and plant matter, and to reduce the possibility of transporting invasive species from one water body to another. Your car may get salt, sand, or other water contents on it when you carry your kayak after paddling, so rinse that off when you rinse your kayak. On a similar theme, carry a plastic box or an extra-large dry bag in your car to hold your wet kayaking gear, to protect the interior of your vehicle.

Tip: On multiday paddling trips in hot, salty environments, you will find salt builds up quite rapidly with evaporation. Rinsing your kayak inside and out in saltwater at the end of each day to remove salt crystals will prevent excessive build up. You can use freshwater when you get home.

If your vehicle is capable of towing, a trailer may be a good way to carry your kayak and gear without having to lift onto a roof rack. It is also a way to carry more kayaks and gear than your roof will take. If your loaded trailer is as low as or lower than your vehicle, you may get better fuel consumption than when you carry kayaks on a roof rack.

There are a number of small, lightweight trailers for kayaks that fold away and stand vertical for easy storage, so you will not necessarily need a large storage space.

A side-loading roof rack makes loading and securing kayaks easier. The rack is designed to make the final lifting onto the roof easy.

A kayak cart makes easy work of carrying your kayak and gear.

Kayak carts are another option for transportation. Kayak carts consist of a small frame with two wheels. Strap the cart under the kayak close to its center. Lift the low end of the kayak to push to where you need it. You will have more control and be able to spot any potential problems more easily when pushing rather than pulling. Most kayak carts are not safe for highway use. If you want to tow a kayak behind a bicycle, find a trailer designed for the road.

On Water: Launching and Landing

You can slide down the beach to launch and run your kayak up onto the shore when you land, but both will wear your hull. Master the techniques to get in and out of a floating kayak, and you can save that scraping whenever conditions permit.

Carry your kayak instead of dragging it. I wore through the keel of my kayak on my first solo multiday trip in less than a week by dragging it on sand beaches. Two options I might have used when solo: Unload the kayak to carry it empty, or use a kayak cart.

Winter Maintenance and Storage

If you break from kayaking in winter, this could be a good time for a full maintenance check. Examine your deck lines, bungees, and end grabs, and replace any that look tired or worn. You should find appropriate supplies at your local kayak store, or at a marine chandler. Make sure all the cables and lines for skegs and rudders are intact, and then flush the cable sleeves with water to dislodge any sand, salt, or silt that might dry and solidify over winter. Check that cables run freely. Examine the security and condition of your backrest and seat, rinse adjustable foot braces, and remove hatch lids to allow compartments to air.

Scrutinize your hull, deck, and seams for deep grazes and impact fractures; you can repair these when the kayak is thoroughly dry. If there are no repairs needed, you might wish to take the time to polish a fiberglass kayak using a buffing and polishing compound. Use one that removes 600-profile scratches from the surface. This will also take off the dull surface discoloration that, in time, affects the gel coat. A final protective layer of wax polish, and your kayak will have a fresh gleam for the new season.

For a plastic kayak, apply a light spray of ultraviolet (UV) shield, such as 303, and rub it in before storing.

If your kayak will be stored in a place that could drop below freezing, make doubly sure you have sponged out any remaining water. Spray rubber hatch lids with a UV shield to keep them fresh and pliable, and order replacement lids for any showing signs of cracking. Changes in temperature will cause pressure changes in the compartments, so lids will constantly suck in and stretch out if you leave them on the kayak, aging them unnecessarily. Remove the lids and store them inside the kayak. You can deter vermin by sealing mosquito net across your hatch rims and cockpit, using bungee cord. Mesh/netting is better for the kayak than using hatch covers and waterproof cockpit covers because it permits airflow.

If possible, store your kayak away from direct sunlight in a cool dry place, perhaps a basement or garage. If storing outside, try to find or create shade and shelter. Support the kayak at each mid-deck, rather than at the very ends, to avoid sagging.

Repairs

If you use your kayak, expect it to get a few knocks scratches and occasionally greater damage. While some minor damage is of no consequence, it helps to know how to make basic repairs. Different materials are susceptible to different types of damage so the repair techniques vary. I will describe some common repairs. Some of the preparation and also some repair materials can be hazardous so always use protective clothing, a mask and goggles when appropriate, and follow the safety recommendations of the supplier for all repair materials.

How to Repair Gel Coat

Gel coat is the hard, water-resistant outer skin on a fiberglass kayak. If you damage this skin the glass fibers exposed will absorb water. Applying a gel coat repair will seal the wound, shielding the fibers from water. Gel coat damage can be repaired with fresh gel coat.

Gel coat is a resin that hardens with a chemical reaction between two liquids mixed in the correct proportions.

Laminating gel coat will remain sticky if exposed to air while it hardens. In a mold, the surface that will become the outside of the kayak is sealed from air against the mold, so it sets hard.

This damage needs a gel coat repair. First, roughen the surface.

In manufacture, the glass fibers applied next will adhere to the sticky layer that was exposed to air. When you repair gel coat from the outside, you will be left with a sticky surface if you do not exclude the air. Tape a sheet of acetate or plastic wrap directly across the repair, or add liquid wax to your mix. Topcoat gel coat has wax already added. The wax floats to the surface after you have applied the gel coat, sealing out the air, so leave the gel coat alone once applied until it has set.

Prepare your damaged gel coat for repair by removing loose or shattered fragments and sanding the area and the immediate surroundings. Fresh gel coat adheres to old gel coat and the fiberglass under it with a mechanical bond, not a chemical bond, so it is essential to roughen the surface. The repair will flake away from any shiny or waxed surface, so prepare the area thoroughly.

Check the temperature range for the chemical reaction and make sure you are in a warm enough place. Gently premix top coat gel coat to distribute the wax that otherwise separates out before taking the amount you need for the repair. Avoid introducing bubbles. Gently mix a little gel coat with the hardener and, if necessary, add wax. Again, avoid introducing bubbles when you mix.

Spread the gel coat across the repair area so it covers a little deeper than any depressions, to allow for shrinkage as the gel hardens. Once thoroughly hard, use a block with wet and dry sandpaper to blend your repair to the surrounding surface. Careful sanding with progressively finer grades can make your repair almost invisible.

If you do not feel up to the job, look around for someone who specializes in kayak repair. In the meantime, seal damaged areas against water damage with duct tape.

Note: Color matching for gel coat repairs is seldom completely accurate. Each manufactured batch of gel coat will vary slightly in color, even with the same color name, and gel coat on a kayak will gradually discolor in time, making it challenging to find a match. Expect your repair to be at best almost invisible, and at worst a healed scar. Accept your repair as a badge of honor, proving you use your kayak. Blemishes are normal, both as a result of the kayak being hand-built and from any repairs.

How to Repair Fiberglass

Following collision damage, the split fiberglass must be repaired from inside, the gel-coat replaced from outside and the broken hatch rim replaced. The first step when clean and dry will be to remove the deck line and hatch rim. Replacing it will be the last part of the repair.

Structural damage to your fiberglass kayak may require a fiberglass repair. Direct impact with a rock, for example, may crush an area of fiberglass even if it does not leave a hole. You may suffer a tear in the skin, or a split seam. Most damage can be repaired with care.

First, remove any damaged fabric. If you see an eruption of soft fibers inside the kayak around the point of impact, this is damaged fiberglass that should be carefully cut away. Stop when you reach an undamaged edge.

Holes are best repaired from inside the kayak if you have sufficient access.

You will need a temporary structure against which to create the repair. A sheet of acetate will bend around the curve of a deck or hull, conforming reasonably well to curves and providing a stiff surface to work against. Cut the acetate so it overlaps the edges of the repair by about an inch, and tape securely all around the edges to the outside of the kayak. This is, in effect, your mold. The better you manage to make your mold conform to the original shape of your kayak, the better your repair will look. Plastic wrap sealing a piece of card can be used instead of acetate.

First, apply a generous layer of laminating gel coat against this surface from the inside. Do not use topcoat gel coat or the wax will prevent the fiberglass from sticking.

Cut at least two patches from fiberglass mat to the size of the hole, and one or two a little larger than the hole. The final layers of repair will need to overlap the damaged area on the inside. Once the gel coat has set, mix laminating resin with hardener and thoroughly wet the fiberglass patches using a stiff laminating brush. You can do this against a sheet of cardboard. A roller is useful if you have one. Paint the area of repair on the inside of the kayak with resin, then carefully lift each patch in turn into position, stipple with your brush to flatten, press it to remove bubbles, and blend each layer into the next. Last, smooth the surface so there are no fibers sticking up. Let the resin set.

Once set hard, lightly sand the repair inside to remove any sharp points and carefully remove the dust. Peel off the tape and the acetate from the outside. Tidy the edges of your repair with a block and sandpaper if necessary. If the repair is in a position where it will contact your skin when paddling, seal the fresh surface with a thin layer of resin or topcoat gel coat (mixed with hardener) to prevent the fiberglass from irritating the skin.

You can repair minor damage by applying a fiberglass patch to the outside of the kayak. This will be necessary anywhere inaccessible from inside. Rough up the area around the repair site with sandpaper to give the patch something to grip onto. The first layer of repair will be fiberglass patches wet through with laminating resin, applied directly to the damaged area and the area immediately surrounding it. Wait until this repair has set hard, and then sand it lightly to remove any sharp points. Finally, apply topcoat gel coat as a water-resistant seal. The wax in the topcoat gel-coat will allow the surface to set without remaining sticky. Any further attention needed will be for cosmetic purposes only.

Repairs on an expedition may require a dry, warm environment. Use hot bottles of water inside the kayak if necessary to keep temperatures high enough.

How to Repair Carbon Fiber

Carbon fiber kayaks are built using epoxy or vinyl ester resins, and should be repaired using the appropriate type of resin. They are often built without a gel coat, so are sometimes sealed on the outside with automobile paint. Repair with a patch from the inside if possible.

Cut away damaged material and sand the surface within 2 inches surrounding the hole. Remove all the dust from sanding and wipe clean with acetone.

Mask the outside of the hole using a patch cut from a sheet of acetate or card covered with plastic wrap, with an inch or so of overlap all around the hole. Tape this patch over the hole using masking tape. Acetate and plastic wrap will separate easily from the finished repair.

If you are replacing a gel coat layer as well as the carbon fiber skin, then mix and paint gel coat over the hole on the inside, barely overlapping the edge onto the surrounding kayak skin, and allow to set.

Cut four or five patches of carbon fiber, with the first one the size of the hole and the rest progressively bigger. The largest should be just smaller than the sanded area.

Mix the epoxy or vinyl ester resin to the manufacturer's instructions. Thoroughly soak each carbon patch in mixed resin, stippling with a stiff brush, then transfer in order of size, smallest first, to the repair site. Smooth each layer carefully with the brush before adding the next. Smooth any air bubbles out to the side. Spread a piece of plastic wrap over the patch area inside the kayak and gently smooth again to squeeze out any remaining air bubbles and leave to set.

Finally remove the backing mask from the outside and sand the repair smooth as necessary.

How to Repair Polyethylene

Polyethylene (polythene) is used for rotomolding kayaks, and is notoriously difficult to glue. Nothing sticks to it. The most reliable repair is a weld, similar to a metal weld using a heat gun and a plastic rod. The surrounding kayak material is also heated before the weld is applied, but the repair material must be melted more. For a neater repair of a split, cut a V-shaped channel along the split to take the repair material.

Bulkheads

Bulkheads in polyethylene kayaks are commonly sealed in place using a sealant in factory conditions, often after "flaming" the surface to be sealed. Resealing afterward is less effective. Strip out the old sealant, if possible, before applying a complete new bead of sealant around the bulkhead. New sealant will not seal well onto a cured sealant surface.

Deforming

Rotomolded kayaks are prone to deforming in heat, or when poorly stored. Often you will see a flat or inverted area in the hull near the seat. This deformation is known as oil-canning. Usually a kayak will revert to its proper shape if left in a cool place without any pressure on the distorted area. If not, leave it to warm up in the sun with no pressure on the distorted area and it will likely pull itself back to shape. If neither method works, gently warm the area using a hair dryer and press it gently back into shape. If necessary, add a weight to encourage it, then leave it alone. It may take a day. Avoid overheating.

How to Avoid Deforming

When storing or transporting a rotomolded kayak on your car, use shaped cradles spaced by about half the length of the kayak. Otherwise, use broad supports and store on edge. In hot weather the plastic becomes softer the hotter it gets, so when you land for lunch choose grass, or wet sand, or somewhere in the shade to leave your kayak, rather than on dry sand or hot asphalt.

How to Repair Thermoform Kayaks

A variety of plastics are used in thermoform kayaks, including ABS and acrylic. These plastics can be glued, so a patch may be glued over a hole, or a protective strip glued along a keel if it is wearing through. The kayak manufacturer or supplier should be able to recommend the most appropriate glue. A leaking bulkhead may also be sealed using glue.

Paddles

There are several styles of kayak paddle, with a lot of subtle variation between blade shapes. Most paddles function just fine but you'll find specific

Kayak paddles with blade faces up. Types shown from the left: dihedral, dihedral, Greenland, fiberglass flat curve, spoon, spoon, wing.

blade shapes function better for certain tasks than others. No single blade will score highest for every field, so your paddle choice should prioritize what you want to do best. You will frequently hear the terms Euro paddle and Greenland paddle used to differentiate between short wide blades and long skinny blades respectively.

Wing Paddle

This blade, shaped like the wing of an aircraft set on end, offers better traction through a paddle stroke than any other. When placed close to the hull at the catch and sliced away from the hull through the forward stroke, the blade works on the principle of a wing. The flow of water across the curved back of the blade travels farther than the water across the face, creating lift toward the bow. This stops the blade from slipping back when you pull against it. Grip in the water is important, for the principle is to plant the paddle in the water and pull the kayak past it, rather than pulling the paddle past the kayak.

Not only does the blade grip well, but as indicated by lactic acid measurements in the muscles, the paddler uses less energy for the same speed over a given distance compared to other paddles. The difference is so significant the wing has become the blade of choice for racing.

A wing paddle is less versatile for maneuvering and steering strokes, and is mostly used in combination with a rudder.

Spoon Paddle

The wing is an extreme example of a spoon blade. The blade is shaped like a spoon, so if you hold it flat with the face up, you could carry a pool of water on the blade. The shape grips the water well, so until the development of the wing, the spoon was the most powerful blade for racing. Spoon

blades are more forgiving for maneuvering than wings, but when guided edge-first through the water, a spoon has no neutral position, instead turning in the direction of the curve of the face. For example, when the blade is held close to neutral in preparation for a bow rudder, the blade will be pushed against the hull, potentially tripping the paddler. In the same way the blade, face-down, is more liable to dive when sculling for a roll unless held at the perfect angle. But that same shape makes the spoon great for maintaining balance using a low brace on the move, as the back of the blade is shaped to skim easily in this position.

Dihedral Paddle

A dihedral blade has completely different priorities. Paddlers tend to grip a paddle more tightly when it flutters, and this can limit your reach and also lead to wrist problems. The dihedral blade is designed to reduce blade flutter. Flutter occurs when the blade is under load and shifts angle slightly under the pressure; the shift in angle causes the blade to move sideways through the water. It then stalls, reverses its angle, and wobbles in the opposite direction. It's the same type of movement you see in a falling leaf.

The face of a dihedral blade slopes away either side from a central ridge that runs from end to end. This V profile guides water toward both edges of the blade with an even flow, reducing or eliminating flutter.

The cost is reduced grip on the water. When you pull on the paddle your kayak moves forward but your blade moves back. The greater the load the more the blade slips, so a dihedral is not as good for accelerating, or paddling against wind or current. But because the blade slips more under load, you are less likely to strain yourself if you pull too hard.

The angle of the face makes the dihedral a forgiving blade to roll with, but less suited for the low brace positions used to maintain stability once upright, as the edges catch in the water and easily trip. Narrow dihedral blades are less liable to trip you than wide ones.

Greenland Paddle

Greenland paddles have long skinny blades. These tend to be dihedral or oval in section, and are most often symmetrical from face to back. The blade favors a low-angle stroke. The whole blade area grips most quickly when dropped into the water edge first rather than end first. Even with a dihedral shape, a Greenland blade will flutter a lot if pulled directly back, but with a wing style of movement it will grip really well. The blade is taken deeper into the water through the stroke, and then back toward the surface, constantly finding still water to pull against rather than grabbing water in one place, which soon moves aside.

The Greenland paddle can be used in a more upright way, as with a wing, but the catch must be modified to bury the blade far enough to the bow for a full stroke. This can be done by sculling the blade into a vertical position from the side before each stroke.

Greenland paddles were used at a low angle while hunting, so were not feathered. The low angle is very energy efficient. The paddler need not raise an arm to shoulder height and lower it again with every stroke. Also, with the upper arm against the torso throughout the stroke, there is little heat lost from under the arm; useful in the Arctic. Finally, there is little water run-off onto the hands and up the sleeves.

Greenland paddles work best with a low-profile kayak with a low front deck. The narrow blade and the oval or dihedral section make it possible to grip the blade close to the tip, enabling a whole range of extended paddle strokes for greater reach and leverage.

Enthusiasts love Greenland paddles, claiming they are easy to roll with. I prefer a flat curve paddle because it helps me stay upright, so I rarely need to roll.

Flat Curve Paddle

This is typically curved from shoulder to top, with no curvature from edge to edge across the blade. A short flat curve blade with good grab near the tip offers the most precision for maneuvering. It can be placed in a neutral or near neutral position in the water, either upright or flat on the surface beside a moving kayak, with the blade neither pulling nor pushing the water. Slight angle changes will engage either the face or the back of the blade.

The flat curve is probably the blade with the fewest bad habits. You can roll easily with it and brace easily with it. This makes it an excellent choice for rough water and for finessing maneuvering strokes. Pulled straight back in a paddle stroke it will flutter under load, but used as a wing paddle it offers a powerful forward stroke without flutter.

Although my personal favorite all 'round, the flat curve is less powerful than a wing or spoon for the forward stroke, and with high angle requires more energy than a Greenland paddle when used with a low stroke. Compared to a similar-size dihedral, it feels powerful. It feels as if you have to work harder than with a dihedral: Your kayak moves more because your blade slips less.

Paddle Features

Paddle lengths change with kayaking trends. Historically, a paddle in Labrador was as long as 11 feet. In Greenland they were usually shorter. When I began sea kayaking in the United Kingdom, the recommended length was in the region of 230 to 240 centimeters; longer than 7 feet 6 inches. Nowadays the trend is shorter, with 200 to 210 centimeters being common (6 feet 6 inches to 7 feet).

The trends match paddling styles, types of kayak, and paddling skills. Longer paddles are great for general touring, work well with a low paddling angle, and work with wide kayaks. This perhaps accounts for why low-priced paddles tend to be long, as they are often marketed toward beginners touring in stable kayaks. Paddlers who get used to a long paddle will often upgrade to a better one of similar length, so there are plenty of high-quality long paddles available.

Shorter paddles work better for high-angle paddling. They work best with narrower kayaks and offer quicker acceleration and easier maneuvering. The use of a narrower kayak and a high paddling style often comes later, as skills and experience accumulate, at which time a paddler can usually see the benefit of investing in a more expensive paddle. You will find fewer short paddles at the budget end, but a greater variety of short paddles to choose from in the more expensive price bracket.

When both your paddle blades are in the same plane they are **nonfeathered.**

Most historic kayak paddles from the Arctic and subarctic are nonfeathered, including those from Greenland, and several factors came together to make this a good idea not worth changing. One was that the kayak was primarily a hunting craft, and to creep up on prey without alerting them, it was better to keep a low profile to the water. Raising a paddle high in the air would be counterproductive. When you use your paddle in a near horizontal position it is ergonomically advantageous to have no feather. Your hands remain comfortably thumbs down, while any attempt to feather results in excessive wrist twisting. There is no question; a nonfeathered paddle is best for a low stroke.

A high-angle stroke is good for power. It is easy to keep the nonfeathered alignment and use a high-angle stroke, but it is also easy to feather the paddle, so the upper blade slices through the air cleanly. With each paddle stroke one blade is anchored in the water. The other blade swings forward 5 or 6 feet as your kayak glides past the blade in the water. If, on a still day, you paddle at 4 miles per hour, you will experience the resistance of a little more than a 4 mph wind against your upper blade with every stroke you make. You can diminish or almost eliminate that resistance by feathering the blades so there is an angle of 60 to 80 degrees between them.

Adopting a high-angle stroke with a loose grip, your hands will naturally stay in line with your wrists, so you have no repetitive bending that might cause wrist problems. The higher your stroke, the closer to 90 degrees the feather can be. In competition racing it was found that reducing the maximum angle from 90 degrees to 85–80 degrees resulted in a lower incidence of wrist injury in athletes. This, in theory, adds a little wind resistance, but not much. A 45-degree angle will result in about a 50-percent reduction in resistance.

Of course, it is not always calm when you paddle. If you paddle with a tailwind and a nonfeathered paddle, you will gain some help from the wind as compared to a feathered paddle. But paddling against the wind, which is when you must work hardest—or with no wind—there is a clear advantage to feathering.

You can change the feather to suit each situation, but in challenging conditions you are likely to regret doing so. You become accustomed to how your blade is aligned in your hand and sooner or later you will go for a stroke and find the blade is at the wrong angle completely. It is best to choose one angle of feather and stick to it.

Switching between a nonfeathered Greenland paddle and a feathered Euro paddle is the exception to this. The handgrip for each is so different that you are much less likely to make a mistake.

Feathered paddles with blades shaped to have a specified face and back are controlled by one hand only. This hand maintains an alignment to the shaft, while the other changes its alignment with each stroke, often with a looser grip. If your right hand maintains position, your paddle is said to have "right-hand control." You can tell the control of a paddle by standing with the paddle upright in front of you, and the face of the blade at your feet toward you. If the face of the upper blade is to the right, the paddle is for right-hand control. If it faces left, it is for "left-hand control."

A paddle with flat blades having no specified face or back, when set at 90-degree feather, is equally easy to control with left or right hand. But as soon as you set a feather of less than 90 degrees, you must use the appropriate control hand.

Most **paddle shafts,** with the exception of Greenland style, vary in diameter by just 2 millimeters, from very narrow to very wide. Rarely is a paddle shaft narrow or wide enough to fall far outside that range of variation.

However, there is a huge difference in performance within that range. A broad shaft spreads the load across the hand better than a narrow one, easing the jarring impact that is most noticeable when you paddle hard with a stiff paddle shaft. A broader shaft also offers greater precision for strokes such as the bow rudder, where fine control is needed over the angle of the blade. A narrow shaft will be lighter and marginally less costly to produce.

There is a lot of promotion of narrow shafts for small hands, but it would be rare for an adult, with all the range of hand sizes, to need or benefit from a narrow shaft any more than they would need or benefit from a narrower steering wheel in a car.

Ultimately your choice should be made on performance and comfort. No matter what your hand size, if you have a paddle with a narrow shaft you will probably gain better control by adding a broad handgrip.

There was a period when most good paddles were in one piece. Nowadays most paddles come as two end sections with a joint in the middle. This is much more convenient to carry, store, and keep from harm when you are ashore.

Manufacturers have come up with a variety of mechanisms to join paddles. Wooden paddles typically use a simple external ferrule system around each end, so one end fits inside the other. Hollow shafts use a narrower tube glued inside one end, which slides inside the other. The sections then lock together using a spring-loaded button through a hole, or by one of a range of more complex mechanisms.

The simple button-and-hole style offers a limited range of options for feathering your paddle, since too many holes weaken the shaft. Other methods variously allow a paddle to be extended within a range of length options, and/or adjusted through a range of feather options.

Crank-shafted paddles were promoted in an attempt to reduce wrist injury from repetitive strain.

The wrist problem arises through gripping the paddle shaft tightly. Reaching forward for the catch, you make a sharp bend in your wrist, upward on the thumb side. At the end of the stroke the bend is in the opposite direction. By repeating this with every paddle stroke you set yourself up for wrist injury.

If, at the catch, you were able to straighten your wrist by bending the hand-grip part of the shaft but leaving the rest of the shaft straight, you would have a crank shaft.

Different types of crank shaft vary in how the blade aligns to the main part of the shaft. A simple double bend will bring the blade parallel to the main shaft, but closer to the paddler at the catch. This, the first configuration released, also had a slight sideways bend. It was known as the "Double Torque." The pulling hand position relative to the blade can sometimes cause blade instability.

To address this instability an extra (third) bend was used to bring the blade back in line with the main part of the shaft. This configuration is known as the "Modified Crank." Now the blade is farther from the paddler at the catch than it would be with a straight shaft, so the blade is very stable in the water. This worked well in the United Kingdom when it was introduced, because the fashion at that time was for feathered and fairly short paddles used with an upright stroke. But in the United States, where it was more common to use a longer, nonfeathered paddle and a lower stroke, the blades tended to roll face up because of the crank. This led paddlers to grip more tightly on the shaft, negating the desired effect.

The third configuration addressed this issue, adding a fourth bend in the shaft so the hand is in the same position relative to the main shaft as it would be on a straight shaft, except the grip part of the shaft is at an angle. The blade remains in line with the main shaft. This can be used with a low or high paddle style, and the blade is stable.

With a straight shaft you can avoid the repetitive wrist bending. Simply keep your wrist straight at the start of the stroke by maintaining a loose handgrip.

Setback is a subtle detail you find on some paddles, less obvious unless you look for it. This is where the blade is aligned parallel to the main shaft but farther from the paddler at the catch. This has the effect of stabilizing the blade, which makes it easier to control with a loose grip. As there is a tendency for the blade to roll face up with a low-angle stroke when not feathered, the same as with the modified crank, setback is best matched to shorter paddles designed for a high-angle stroke.

Paddle Materials

Material costs and labor costs are the reason some paddles are more expensive than others. Some of the simplest and most cost-effective paddles are home-crafted from a single piece of wood. Some of the most expensive are handmade, laminated, composite and wood paddles with hollowed wood shafts. You would probably notice the difference.

The least expensive paddles have plastic blades on an aluminum shaft. Plastic blades vary in price depending on the material, from simple ABS, to nylon, and to nylon with glass or carbon fiber added for strength and stiffness.

Composite blades are solid, hollow, or have a foam or wood core. A core offers stiffness, strength, lightness, and flotation. The contoured shape that can be constructed using a core can reduce blade turbulence and improve the performance of a lot of maneuvering strokes. Each step adds performance, benefit, and cost. This applies to paddle shafts too, with aluminum, wood, fiberglass, carbon fiber and carbon-Kevlar being the major options.

Metal is cold on the hands: Wood is probably the best insulator for cold water and weather.

Generally, you get an increase in blade stiffness, lightness, and performance as the price increases. The least costly paddles tend to have the most flexible blades, are heavier to handle, and function less well. Although you pay more for a better paddling experience and performance, most paddles on the market do serve their purpose, and you are unlikely to go far wrong with whatever you buy within your budget.

Clothing

What you wear when you kayak depends on what kind of paddling you will do, and where you are. Dress for protection against the elements, whether that's the sun and heat, rain, wind, or cold, and dress against likely knocks and abrasions.

In addition, consider what will happen if you fall in the water. Even on a warm day you might want to dress for the possibility of immersion in cold water, where your strength and ability to help yourself will rapidly dwindle if you are inadequately dressed. You might want to wear skin-guard protection against jellyfish. Anticipate the possible scenarios and dress accordingly. Here are some ideas.

Outer Shell Layer

Kayakers commonly wear a paddling jacket, sometimes called an anorak or cagoule (cag for short). This is a waterproof outer shell to keep you dry. Lightweight paddling jackets have elastic or Velcro seals around the wrists, and some way to close the neck. Latex seals around the wrists will keep most water from coming up your sleeves. For warmth and to protect the latex from sunlight, the sleeve usually covers the seal and closes over it. If the jacket also has a latex neck seal, it is called a "dry cag."

A hood can be useful in rain and wind. For convenience, some hoods fold into a collar when not needed.

For your lower body, waterproof or windproof leggings can be used against wind and water.

One challenge when wearing rain pants with an anorak is the two layers end and overlap right where your back support makes contact with your back. You may find resting against drawstrings or elastic uncomfortable. You can avoid this by wearing a slightly longer anorak together with a chest-high bib. This will also better keep out water that might otherwise get between top and bottom.

A dry suit solves the problem by sealing you in a coverall with watertight gaskets around the wrists, neck, and ankles, sometimes even enclosing the feet.

Part of your outer shell layer is your hat. A rain hat with a wide brim, or sou'wester, can make a huge difference in a deluge; a wool hat can keep your ears warm on a chill day; and a sun hat can shade your face. They are small to carry but can make a big difference to your comfort.

Taking a break, the man with paddle in a full dry suit expects to stay dry when immersed. The man pouring tea wears rain pants and paddle jacket and expects to get wet when immersed.

There are good reasons to wear gloves. They protect the back of your hands against excessive sun exposure, they keep your hands warm, and they protect against blisters. You will lose some of the sensitivity of paddle control. The thinner the fabric over the palm and fingers, the more sensitivity you will retain.

Pogies, gloves, and palmless mittens are all options. Pogies are gauntlets that fit around the paddle shaft. You slide your hands into the sleeves so your bare hand holds the shaft. You keep your normal handgrip on the paddle while protected from the cold.

Board sailors developed a neoprene palmless mitten that hooks over the fingertips. For kayaking, this allows you similar protection to a pogie, but more freedom. You can let go of your paddle without having to thread your hand back through a sleeve. And it is easy to use your fingers without removing the mitten.

Some paddlers enjoy wearing rubber dishwashing gloves, which come in a range of bright colors to make a fashion statement. They wear them when kayaking, and perhaps for washing up too. Otherwise, try lightweight neoprene gloves or palmless mittens.

Inner Insulating Layers

Outer shell layers may keep you dry and shield you from the wind, but they will not keep you warm in cold water unless you wear suitable insulating layers underneath. Choose layers of wool or synthetic fleece that help retain body heat even when wet. A neoprene wet suit is another cold water option. Your body warms a layer of water between your skin and the neoprene so you stay warm when wet. Neoprene is a good insulator that works well in the water, but evaporation from the outer skin will chill you. For kayaking, wear it as a base layer under a windproof shell layer.

Avoid cotton garments, as they offer poor insulation when wet.

Shoes

Your kayaking shoes should help protect your feet from cuts, stings, and abrasions, and protect your heels from abrasion in your kayak. Be sure it is not possible for straps or laces to catch on a foot brace to trap you.

There are all manner of things liable to hurt your feet if you step out of your kayak in shallow water, or walk up an unfamiliar beach. Broken shells, especially when they are hidden under the surface in soft sand and mud, can slice deep cuts. Oyster shells are particularly known for this, but even scraping a barnacle-covered rock can cause a bad abrasion, with a risk of subsequent infection. Stingrays love shallow water, as do weeverfish and stonefish, not to mention jellyfish. In other places you may encounter broken glass, sharp stones, or coral. Your kayaking shoes should be sturdy enough to offer protection.

There are many water sports-specific shoes on the market, including neoprene boots, but you can get by with a pair of running shoes. Wool socks will help keep your feet warm even when wet.

Sun Protection

Covering your skin to protect against sun exposure can be really important on the water, where you will be exposed to reflected light as well as direct sunlight. You will burn more quickly than you will on the beach. The backs of your hands, your face and neck, and even under your chin, can be particularly vulnerable to sunburn if you are not careful, so be sure to use sunscreen on these areas.

The best way to avoid direct sun is to stay in the shade, and you can carry your own shade with you in the form of a long-sleeved shirt or jacket, sun hat, and lightweight gloves or pogies, potentially covering most of your exposed skin. In hot weather, a light-colored long-sleeved shirt with a collar and built-in sun protection will keep you cool and protected.

A hat with a wide brim offers a good deal of shade, while a baseball cap or visor may shelter your face but does little to help the back of your neck. Wear a bandana or a shirt with a collar to protect your neck. A bandana can be pulled up around to protect your face too.

Even if you wear a brimmed hat, unless you cover your face it will catch reflected light. It is sensible to apply waterproof sunscreen and wear sunglasses. Polarized lenses will allow you to see down into the water, where otherwise the reflected glare would be too great. Tether your sunglasses so you cannot drop them into the water. Remember to reapply sunscreen periodically.

Carry cover-up garments, hat, sunscreen, and sunglasses even if you do not start out wearing them. It is distressing to burn when you are unable to do anything to protect yourself.

The sun can be reclusive, hiding behind cloud, but the harmful rays will get through the cloud. Take care even on cloudy days.

Safety Wear

Regardless of where you paddle, prioritize the following items. They will make you look good but they also contribute to your safety.

Personal Flotation

A float jacket (personal flotation device, PFD, or buoyancy aid) is essential. People drown in very benign conditions, and they could easily have been saved by companions had they floated. You may not fall out of your kayak often, but if you do, you know your PFD will float you even if you are too tired to swim. That frees you to focus on rescuing yourself, rather than just staying afloat. A PFD will also help keep you warm in the water.

Use a PFD that fits well. Fasten it on fully and cinch any adjusting straps. If you raise your hands in a distress signal from the water, or try to get back into your kayak, you do not want your PFD to float up around your ears.

Spray Deck

A spray deck (spray skirt) is a fabric seal between your body and the cockpit. Its purpose is to prevent water entering the cockpit, swamping the kayak. It is commonly made of neoprene, waterproof nylon, latex, or rubber. Important factors to consider are how the spray deck seals to the cockpit, how it seals around your body, and how much it will prevent sagging hence water pooling. For safety there should be a release tab.

The seal around the cockpit is usually an externally sewn bungee cord, bungee or elastic sewn into a sleeve, or a stout rubber rand. A rubber rand or externally sewn bungee is used for plastic kayaks when a reliable seal is needed, but these are more difficult to stretch into position and to release. Other forms tend to slip on the plastic coaming, but work fine if you don't have waves dumping on your lap. The thinner edge of a composite coaming will accommodate most types of spray deck, but avoid the thick rubber rand.

The seal around your body can potentially let in a lot of water. A close-fitting neoprene tube provides an excellent seal once you have wriggled into it, and a well-fitting neoprene deck will stay taut, shedding water rather than allowing it to pool. Other stretchy fabrics work in this way too.

Nylon is not stretchy, so the deck needs to be well shaped for the cockpit, with little excess fabric, and the seal around your body must be secure, or the weight of water on your deck will cause it to invert like a funnel. A tight waistband or shoulder straps can help avoid this.

Your spray deck should have a release tab. This may be a short tab of fabric extending from the front, or to one side of the front, of the spray deck. It may be a grab cord, or tape running from side to side and attached to both sides.

This paddler is dressed in a full dry suit with hood. He is also wearing a well-fitting PFD, neoprene spray deck (spray skirt), neoprene shoes, helmet and sunglasses.

A good head is worth protecting! Wear a helmet when there is any chance you might hit your head while paddling. In surf with breaking waves, paddlers commonly hit their heads against their own paddles or kayaks, and occasionally in collision with other water users. Think about your head in surf, around rocks and cliffs, when you intend to practice rescues, and when landing in rough conditions on an unknown shore.

Your helmet should remain in the correct position over your forehead even when grabbed at the front by a wave. It must fit well. Find a style that fits your head, offers good impact and abrasion resistance, and is comfortable.

How will you access your helmet if you are not wearing it? Will your helmet fit into your day hatch where you can access it? Will it interfere with paddling if it is strapped to your deck? Are you paddling with someone who could retrieve it from another hatch for you? Might you be comfortable wearing it all day?

Your head may be the most visible part of you when you are floating in the water. Consider a bright color with reflective tape if you want to increase visibility.

Ear and Nose Protection

The human body responds to repeated inrush of cold water into the ears by producing bony growths called osteomata or exostoses, which gradually close the ear canal to block out cold water, but also sound. Evaporation of water in the ears in windy conditions can cause the same growths, even when the water is warm. Surfers suffer from this problem enough for the condition to be commonly known as "surfer's ear."

The condition is progressive and directly proportional to the time you spend in cold, wet, and windy weather without protection, but is slow. Most people seeking medical help are in their midthirties to late forties. Older paddlers may spend too little time in the cold, wet conditions to develop the problem.

If you think you might be at risk, ask your doctor to check your ears. If you discover you do have an osteoma developing, you can protect your hearing by wearing ear plugs, a neoprene hood, or a swimming cap when practicing rolling, kayak surfing, or paddling on rough, windy days.

As for your nose, your nasal channels and sinuses can hold a lot of liquid. If you are upside

A NOTE ON RINSING AND VINEGAR

Some kayaking clothing—polypropylene and neoprene garments, in particular—can get smelly after a while. Bacteria multiply rapidly in these fabrics under ideal, moist, warm conditions, and produce noxious odors. A quick and easy way to get rid of the smell is to rinse your garments in water with a little added vinegar. You don't need much vinegar to make conditions too acidic for the bacteria—perhaps a teaspoonful in a gallon of water. You will be left with a slight vinegar smell. Rinsing afterward with fresh water will get rid of that too, but don't expect a permanent fix. As soon as the acidity falls, the bacteria will be back and the smell will follow.

On multiday trips I carry a small bottle of vinegar with me. If my neoprene boots start to smell, I seal them in a small dry bag with a little vinegar and some water, give them a good shake, and leave them to soak for a few minutes.

down in the water frequently, you might find it uncomfortable to have all that water there, and it might not be very healthy, depending on the water quality. You can purchase nose clips at kayak stores, and sometimes at general sports stores. A soft rubber pad presses on each side of your nose to close your nostrils to the water. Otherwise, after rolling or capsizing in dirty water, you might consider flushing with a nasal saline solution.

Safety

A well-prepared kayaker will carry enough equipment to be self-sufficient on the water, able to cope with likely situations without calling for outside help. There is no single list for a kit to cover every contingency, and if there were the kit might not fit in a kayak. The best approach is to imagine likely scenarios and figure out how you would deal with them. If the solution requires you to have equipment with you, consider carrying it. For example, you might carry water in case you get thirsty, or a snack in case you get hungry.

HOW TO CHOOSE WHAT TO CARRY

Here is a process you can use to decide what to carry, and when.

First, think up possible scenarios; situations that might arise or things that might go wrong during the trip. For each:

- Consider all the possible ways you could prevent the situation from arising.
- Consider all the alternative ways you could deal with the situation if it arises.
- If the solutions require extra items for a kit, compare options and choose the most practical kit you could carry.
- Assess the risk of that scenario arising on a particular trip. Carry the kit if you consider the risk to be sufficiently high.
- Consider the consequences of the scenario if you do not have the gear necessary to deal with it. If the consequences are serious enough, then carry the gear even if the risk of the event happening is low.

Anticipate Problems

Try to anticipate and prevent problems rather than curing the effects, and if you carry a kit, be sure you know how to use it.

Here are some situations that do occur, and some ideas about how you might deal with them. In the first example, the steps outlined above are followed.

Example Scenario: Imagine someone in your group is unable to continue paddling; perhaps they are injured, sick, or too tired to make it to shore.

1. How could I prevent the situation arising? Maybe before I leave, I should ask my paddling companions if they feel fit and healthy. Are they liable to suffer from seasickness? Is the distance in the expected conditions well within their ability and experience? If I am left in doubt, I still have time to change my plans.

2. How might I deal with the situation? If someone cannot paddle farther, I might tow them. I would need a towline (page 105). How might I stabilize someone while I tow? I could raft them, or use sponsons. Can I deal with seasickness? Ginger helps. Can I deal with an injury? First aid kit needed. Can I call on outside help for quick evacuation if needed? Will I need a radio or cell phone? What if my companion is tired? Perhaps they need food/drink, or if towed, some way to keep warm.

3. What kit might I carry? A towline, inflatable sponsons; although these are of lower priority when there are more than two in the group, as two could raft together while the third tows. First aid kit, ginger candies in case of seasickness, some emergency snack/hot drink, a warm hat, an extra-large anorak or storm cag that will fit over a PFD, a marine radio or cell phone.

4. How great is the risk? Is this a bay trip along the shore with easy landing? A headland trip with few landing possibilities?

5. If the risk is low, which, if any, of the items would I still consider essential to carry?

A few common scenarios with some suggestions as to how to deal with each follow. I have not included every possible solution, or how to avoid the situations, or the risk of the event happening, or the level of risk if you are not prepared. Make your own assessment for each.

Scenario 1: Someone in your group—maybe you—damages a kayak away from any landing possibility.

You need a pump, but even a small hole can fill a kayak faster than you can pump water out. You also need a way to block a hole in a wet kayak. Plumbers' mastic tape will stick to a wet surface. It is messy to use, so cut sections beforehand from the roll, stick them to a strip of heavy-gauge polythene, fold the polythene, and seal it in a ziplock bag. The flat side of a plastic gallon milk container would bridge a hole or a splintered area of hull, so maybe something like that would be useful in a repair kit. Duct tape is a good standby if you can dry the surface enough to make it stick, but how will you dry it? If water leaks into a sealed compartment, then an inflated air bag, sponson, or paddle float would help fill the compartment to limit flooding.

Kit list: Repair kit; pump; air bag, sponsons, or paddle float

Scenario 2: You become separated from your group.

How will you communicate, and if all else fails how will you find your way back alone? Communication options include a whistle, a cell phone, a marine radio, a signal mirror, and a flashlight. You would be wise to carry a compass and your own chart or map of the area, and to know how to use them.

Kit list: Ways to attract attention and communicate; chart or map; compass; GPS

Scenario 3: Somebody is shivering, showing signs of cold.

You should think about carrying additional warm clothing, a hot drink, and some emergency food as part of a standard kit. You can also carry some kind of shelter, whether an exposure bag, storm cagoule, poncho, or emergency shelter, as a way to retreat from the weather if you need to. It is much easier to keep someone warm and comfortable than it is to deal with someone suffering from hypothermia. That applies to you as well as the people you paddle with. You might experience a sudden squall with a drop in temperature, strong wind, and heavy rain, and find yourself getting chilled. Even if you land, to sit it out you will get cold unless you have something extra to wear and something to shelter you from the weather. You will be a lot warmer if you sit on an insulating pad.

To do list: Attend a first aid course

Kit list: Spare clothing; emergency shelter of some kind; insulating pad/seat; hot drink; emergency food

Scenario 4: You cannot deal with an emergency and require outside help.

Attract attention using radio, cell phone, satellite phone, distress signals, or some other international signal of distress, such as raising and lowering both arms. But remember, there is no guarantee you will be able to attract attention, or that if you do, help will arrive soon, or that if help is on its way, it will be able to find you. Radio contact offers the most direct link to rescue services and to boats in the vicinity, and probably has the most reliable marine-area reception. Flares may

attract attention, but that depends on visibility, and also on whether someone spots the flare, realizes its significance, and alerts the authorities.

A useful sequence to follow is:

1. Attract attention by your best available means.

2. If possible, relay information about your location and time, the nature of your problem, and your planned course of action.

3. If and when you see or hear rescuers, make yourself visible and audible.

4. What you do while you wait will depend on the nature of the emergency. You might be able to start resolving the situation. I know someone who spent a night clinging to a buoy, failed to attract the attention of passing boats, and eventually waited for a favorable tide and swam 4 miles to shore. You also may be able to use a towline in order to move toward safety. Be resourceful.

Handheld flares, mirrors, laser flares, and flashlights, are possible tools you can use to alert searchers to your position. Another way is to wave an extended paddle in the air, especially if you tie on a bright-colored garment to act as a flag. Smoke flares are useful to helicopter pilots as a way to see the wind direction, as well as seeing you. Finally, if rescuers do come to your aid, follow their directions.

If you have to wait, you could get very cold, so expect everyone in the party to need spare clothing, shelter, warm hat, hot drink, and emergency food.

To do list: Learn how to use a marine radio, flares, etc.

Kit list: Ways to attract attention and communicate, which may include radio, cell phone, flares, flashlight, mirror, and laser flare; spare clothing; hot drink and emergency food; emergency shelter; towline.

Scenario 5: You break or lose a paddle.

You are at a serious disadvantage without a paddle. I rarely kayak without carrying a spare. When you paddle as a group, you can decide whether it is necessary for everyone to carry their own spare, or if one or two within the group is sufficient.

Ironically, very few paddles are broken or lost compared to the number of spare paddles lost from the decks of kayaks. Waves can easily release paddles from under deck bungees, and if you stow a spare on your back deck you will likely not notice when it goes. Deck bungees offer quick access, but in all probability you will have plenty of time to access your spare paddle should you need it. It is better to clip a paddle bag to your deck lines, or use some other secure system, leaving your bungees for short-term convenience.

Kit list: A spare paddle

Make It Appropriate for Where You Are

By thinking of possible scenarios that could occur in the places you paddle, you should be able to devise action plans and lists for kits that are far more appropriate than any generic one I could offer. Paddling estuaries in South Carolina, you might consider the risk of cutting yourself on oysters, suffering sunburn, or dehydration to be quite high. Florida kayakers suffer a higher incidence of hypothermia than paddlers in other states in the United States due to seemingly benign and warm conditions and the sudden appearance and chilling effect of summer storms, which brings me back to the subject of risk assessment.

Risk Assessment

What are the chances of needing spare clothing, a hot drink, and an emergency snack on a cold-weather coastal day trip? The chances are high enough for me to carry them. The chances of needing the same items while exploring a city pond for an hour in summer are low enough, and the consequences of not having them handy are so minimal, that I would probably not carry them.

What are the chances of someone suffering a heart attack on a trip along a remote coastline? The risk is low. But the consequences of not being able to call for emergency services might be fatal. Perhaps I should carry a radio.

What if someone lost a hatch cover? I could carry a spare, but what size? Perhaps I could improvise with some deck bungee and some fabric, maybe using a spare jacket, rain hat, or a dry bag. Perhaps I could fill the compartment with air bags. Having identified the possibility, I should make sure my own hatch covers are tethered to the kayak, and I could visually check my companions' kayaks to see if their lids are securely sealed when they are afloat. I could also carry an air bag, a way to improvise a lid, and a bilge pump, just in case. It is good to think up solutions to potential problems, but much better if you can also avert the problems before they need remedy.

Kit to Consider Carrying

You should know how to use anything you carry, or have the person who will use it with you.

I hope you know what you might need, what to carry, or how to find out. I hope, for example, you will remember to take a map or chart, and a compass, and will consider attending a first aid course. Choose suitable first aid and repair supplies to carry when appropriate. Here are a few items to consider, their limitations, and why you may find them useful.

Bilge Pump

A pump is a useful tool for getting water out of the cockpit or flooded compartment. There are different kinds of bilge pump available, such as these:

Hand pump: A hand-operated, stirrup-type bilge pump is the most common, affordable, reliable and versatile solution, but it works most easily when operated using both hands. This means, in a rescue situation, a second paddler is usually needed to stabilize the waterlogged kayak while it is being emptied. Stirrup pumps are versatile; they may be passed from kayak to kayak to drain a cockpit or a waterlogged storage compartment.

A stirrup pump is easiest to operate with two hands. Normally you will pump water from the kayak. Roland Johansson

In a self-rescue, the pump may be held between the legs and operated using one hand, while the other holds the paddle as a brace for balance. The

fitted foot pump, or an electric bilge pump, are better solutions for self-rescue as they leave the hands free to paddle, or to brace for balance while emptying the kayak.

Other hand-operated pumps mount onto the deck and become a fixture of the kayak. These are most useful for draining a flooded cockpit without having to remove the spray deck. However, they are not easily useful for pumping a flooded hatch or another kayak.

Foot pump: These are available as high-volume pumps for clearing a swamped cockpit, and low-volume pumps to keep a cockpit dry by pumping out any small amount of water that gets in. A low-volume pump is usually inadequate to cope with a swamped cockpit, while a high-volume pump generally falls short of completely draining the cockpit. For day-to-day sea kayaking, where some water comes in through the spray deck, a low-volume pump is a convenient alternative to occasional sponging, as there is no need to remove the spray deck. For self-rescues, a high volume foot pump is appropriate.

Electric pump: Fitted electric pumps generally have a secure watertight housing for the battery, often in a compartment, while the pump, intake, and outlet are located in the cockpit. The switch is typically on the deck, allowing access when the spray deck is secured. The advantage of a fitted electrical system is that it is always there when you need it, at the flick of a switch. Saltwater environments present a particular challenge to electrical apparatus, and the pump will remain in your kayak throughout seasons of storage, so carry out regular maintenance checks. Also, check that you have plenty of battery power for your needs before you go afloat.

Portable electric bilge pump: These are contained in a waterproof housing, along with batteries. When needed, the complete housing is set in the water with the outlet aimed out from the kayak. The advantage of a portable system is that it can be used to empty any kayak, and can also be dropped through a hatch to drain a flooded compartment. Portable pumps may be stored indoors, and so are easily checked for integrity and battery power before you set out.

Compass

For the benefit of the GPS-dependent paddler, a compass is an instrument that shows the direction of magnetic north by means of a free-swinging magnetic "needle." It is a simple tool that, with the addition of a graduated card, can show the direction you face in degrees from magnetic north. You can use a compass to align a map to features in the surrounding landscape or seascape, or to help you find shore in fog if you know the compass direction in which it lies.

I always carry a compass when I kayak on open water because I have been caught out many times in sudden fog, and have become disoriented in mangroves, forested island chains, and rocky archipelagos. You may not know exactly where you are, but you are not lost if you know which way to go.

A magnetic compass can be used in creative ways for more complex navigation (see page 154), but there are a few key concepts worth remembering. The first is that magnetic north and true north do not necessarily lie in the same direction. Magnetic north is part of Earth's magnetic field, and that moves. Currently, magnetic north is somewhere in arctic Canada. The true North Pole lies on Earth's axis. Draw a line across the globe from true north through magnetic north at any given time, and anywhere along that line south of magnetic north, your compass will point to true north, and between magnetic and true north it will point south. Anywhere east of the line, you will have to

A compass positioned closer to your bow will be easier to refer to when your eyes normally rest around the horizon. But you must be able to read the compass at that distance.

add to your magnetic degrees to get true north. West of the line, you will need to subtract. The farther north toward the latitude of the magnetic pole, when you are not on the line, the greater the variation will be, until at the same latitude it will reach 90 degrees of variation. Magnetic north was at King William Island in 1831, so back then, if you were kayaking at Pond Inlet on Baffin Island, your compass would have pointed south and west. By 2014, magnetic north had migrated north far beyond easy kayaking water.

A compass must be fluid-filled to be useful on the water. An air-filled compass will let in moisture and its parts will rust, rapidly becoming unusable.

Finally, a compass needle is magnetized and will be attracted to objects containing iron. Stow items that may be attracted by a magnet well away from your compass; this could include canned food, your stove, electronic equipment, and your camera. Otherwise your compass will indicate where you stored your metal items rather than magnetic north.

A simple, fluid-filled, orienteering compass will serve for emergencies, but a permanently mounted deck compass will be easier to read and always there for you. The closer toward your bow the compass is mounted; the easier it will be to refer to without lowering your eyes far. The closer to your lap, the more challenging it will be to keep a compass course, especially on choppy seas when looking down may cause seasickness. Wherever it is mounted, you must be able to read the numbers. A compromise may be a compass you can secure to your deck lines with bungees when you need it.

Dry Bag

Even if your kayak has watertight storage compartments, sooner or later you'll land through the surf and open the hatch to find water pouring from your sinuses or from your sleeve into the hatch. Or, you may have to unload your kayak in the rain. Everything you want to stay dry needs to be sealed in a dry bag or watertight container.

Dry bags are often not completely watertight, as you'll probably find out if your hatch leaks and your dry bags lie in water all day. Most bags are sealed by rolling the ends and clipping with a buckle. These are fine for items you prefer to keep dry, but that would not be damaged by water. If your clothes got damp, it would be an inconvenience. But you might be more upset if your camera or phone got wet. It is worth investing in a bag or box with a secure seal for those special items. There are soft containers available for phones and small electronics, and sturdy waterproof boxes with O-ring seals that work well to waterproof and protect camera gear. In addition, some heavy-duty, ziplock-type dry bags seem to be reliably watertight.

Float Bag

Float bags are inflatable bags (air bags) used for additional flotation. If your kayak has no bulkhead

A float bag is employed in a compartment after a leak has been discovered.

in one or both ends, it will have flotation in the form of fixed foam blocks. Even so, a swamped kayak may be difficult to handle and to empty. Float bags can be used to reduce the amount of water that can get in, and to make a kayak float better. They should be tethered in place and inflated. Float bags can also be used as backup in case you should damage your kayak or lose a hatch, causing a compartment to flood. Attach inside the compartment and inflate.

Float bags are a practical addition to an emergency kit. While it may be challenging to make an adequate on-the-water repair to a damaged kayak, by inflating an air bag inside you can ensure that a punctured compartment will not completely flood with water.

Flashlight

You are required, under international maritime law, to carry a bright white light at night with which to attract attention to prevent collision. To be reliable for kayaking it should be waterproof, and have a sturdy tether to your kayak. I once lost my light during a night crossing of the English Channel when the attachment broke and the flashlight sank. Would you carry a spare?

Strobe Light

Strobe lights may not be used in international waters, either to attract attention or as a distress signal. This maritime law probably arose because flashing lights are used as navigation markers, using a variety of flashing sequences, and in the colors red, yellow, green, blue, and white.

In inland waters of the United States—a classification that does not include most of the coast but does includes some coastal bays—a strobe may be used as a distress signal. If you see a flashing light on the water in this region, unless it is

clearly a navigation marker, assume it is someone in distress.

Glow Stick

Glow sticks are chemical lights. A transparent sealed plastic tube containing a chemical encases a thinner glass tube containing a second chemical. Bend the plastic tube to snap the inner tube, shake to mix to the two chemicals, and the stick will emit light. The glow fades in intensity over a period of hours. Glow sticks offer a reliable backup for battery-dependent lights, although they are not bright enough to use for attracting attention, so they should not be your legally required light source. They are useful to maintain visual contact within a group at night.

Mast and Flag

Waterways busy with small boat traffic can be hazardous for kayaks, which have a low profile and can be difficult to spot from the driving seat of a powerboat. A tall, flexible mast, like a fishing pole, with a bright flag, will increase your chances of being seen. The mast can attach with a rubber sucker to

A flag may be easily seen by other water users, and makes a pacesetter easier to see in a group.

your deck with no modification to your kayak. A flag also serves as an easy way to identify the pace-setter in a group on open water.

Reflective Tape

Kayaks show up clearly at night under a light if they have reflective surfaces. Deck lines with reflective fibers woven in will show clearly, and you can add patches of reflective tape to your hull and deck to make it show up better when upright and upside down. If you want to see how effective the result is, take a picture of the kayak at night using a camera flash.

Your paddle is more easily dropped at night, especially when you raft up with someone else. In the dark you may not see it go, and you may not be able to spot it floating. Reflective tape on the paddle will show up brightly under a flashlight.

GPS

I have a Swedish friend who always carries a GPS unit. He drags his kayak ashore over it when landing to protect the hull from the rocks. He uses it as a cutting board, and pounds it into the beach to tether his kayak in case of wind. Along with seventy or more alternatives, GPS, of course, is the acronym for "General Purpose Stick."

GPS also stands for "Global Positioning System." This is the system by which you can locate your position on the planet using signals from satellites. A waterproof floating set is best; otherwise seal your device in a waterproof case. You can choose an instrument that will display your position on a map, or as a position of latitude and longitude, and, depending on the device, a GPS unit can calculate your speed over the ground.

Positioning technology is popular, with ongoing improvements to devices and batteries, but a GPS will suffer from drained batteries far sooner than a chart or map. Consider GPS an additional aid. It is a great way to verify your position if you are unsure where you are.

Maps and charts are fundamental to navigation. You will find information on managing maps when afloat, map cases, and waterproof notebooks on page 162.

Skills
Breakdown

A special kind of freedom: cruising with the current down the Weeki Wachee River, Florida

In this chapter, I will break down skills into their component parts. The chapter is intended for instructors, but is applicable to anyone.

Breaking down a paddle stroke into its component parts is a useful way to see how it works. By being aware of, and working on each part, you can improve the whole stroke. Once a technique has been deconstructed, by evaluating each component in terms of its importance to the function of the whole stroke, you can also structure a smooth, logical teaching progression. For the individual, it offers an analytical path toward more precise self-assessment.

You may have noticed that, throughout this book, I admit that a stroke works best one way for some people and another way for others. We figure out what works best for us by comparing, and the more detail we use when comparing, the more finely tuned our results.

This chapter offers one way an instructor can analyze and present information. It doesn't matter if you are an instructor or not, you should be able to follow my reasoning and find some benefit.

Each technique explained in this book is made up from more than one element. The more complex maneuvers have many elements, some executed simultaneously and others sequentially. While it is possible to learn a complex move by mimicking someone else, it is easy to miss components that would improve the outcome. This is why it's good to deconstruct a technique, to examine all the elements, before building it up again. When you fully understand the technique, you can include all the important elements in your teaching, and won't miss anything significant.

Avoid choosing between correct and incorrect. Very few things in paddling are incorrect, but there are those moves that might cause harm or pain. Judge instead along a scale of effectiveness and efficiency. It is not incorrect to paddle forward with no torso rotation, although it is less effective, and less efficient. If you cannot or do not rotate, but can still paddle and complete a trip, you are doing something right. Success is doing what you set out to do. If that is to go forward, you can have success without torso rotation. You compensate in some way for not using your torso; you probably develop bigger arm muscles. You most likely tire more quickly than you need to.

By deconstructing an ideal forward stroke, you can identify torso rotation as an element. If you don't already use it, you will see your performance improve when you reconstruct your stroke from all the elements, including torso rotation. Addressing each element in turn ensures you do not miss one.

Deconstructing a Technique

Throughout the book I have drawn attention to the different elements of each technique. You should be able to take a description and list the different parts as they appear. Refer back to the section on the sculling draw (page 73). I will use this as an example, extracting the elements mentioned in the text. For convenience, I will group those elements into the three arbitrary categories below:

1. Elements of body position: Straight onside leg; bent offside knee; torso rotated toward your bent knee and direction of travel; top arm held straight, perpendicular to the kayak, at shoulder height. Paddle held vertically, so the bottom arm is probably also straight. Head turned to face sideways direction of travel. Edging will depend on the type of kayak and how heavily it is loaded. Hand-grip is relaxed, fingers open.

2. Elements of blade position and movement: Blade held upright in the water, on end to start, blade face toward the kayak. Blade is swung pendulum-style; blade is aligned in three different ways: 1) in neutral; 2) with leading edge away from the kayak; and 3) with leading edge toward the kayak. The top hand remains static and the bottom hand guides the blade forward and back parallel to the side of the kayak. Depending on how much you open the blade, you will get different effects. Open a lot and the kayak will move forward (bow first) and back (stern first) a lot. Open very little and you will get very little movement at all, forward, back, or sideways. In between is a range where you get good sideways movement without much movement forward or back.

3. Desired effects: In neutral, the pendulum effect should not make the kayak move. Otherwise, the desired effect is to push or pull the kayak sideways in a straight line without moving in the direction of the bow or stern. Why do we not want the kayak to move forward or back? It wastes energy. Steering while moving sideways is achieved using a greater blade angle at one end of the kayak than at the other.

Teaching the Stroke

There are many component parts to the sculling draw, and it would be unrealistic to expect someone to learn them all at once. Can we break them down into a learning sequence, introducing them step by step, just one or two elements at a time? If so, how should we single out the elements we should start with, and how best deal with the rest? First,

Success using the essential elements is when the kayak moves as intended. Next work on refinements.

define what you consider success at a sculling draw. I would like my kayak to move sideways.

Identify the Essential Elements

Each technique typically has components you might group together as "essential elements," and others you might group together as "refinements." From a teaching perspective, essential elements are the ones that offer the basic parameters for a working technique. For the sculling draw to work, what can you get by with at minimum to achieve what you define as success?

Take the list you made when you deconstructed the technique, and cross out items that are not essential to making the stroke work. Does the sculling draw work if you do not straighten one leg and bend the other? If it does, then cross off that item. Is torso rotation essential? If it is not, then cross it off your list. You might need to redefine some of your items to simplify this process. I came up with the following:

1. The paddle must be held upright (let's specify at 45 degrees to the water or greater when viewed from the bow, or you won't go sideways).

2. There must be some kind of pendulum blade motion forward and backward along the side of the kayak.

3. To pull the kayak sideways, the blade should be open a little to the direction of swing, and open about the same amount with each swing or the kayak will turn. How much should it be open? Too much and the kayak will move forward and backward without going sideways. Let's specify that, from being flat to the side of the kayak (that is neutral), the blade should open less than 45 degrees.

Do you need more? If not, then let's call these the essential elements. All the other elements of the sculling draw are now in the category of refinement, and these can be introduced later, or on another day.

Choose a Location to Eliminate Variables

Start by teaching the essential elements without any of the additional refinements.

Try to eliminate variables that would affect the stroke. What variables could affect a sculling draw? Wind, current, and waves for certain, so a calm, sheltered area would be ideal. It is a deep stroke, so consider depth. You need water deep enough for a paddle held vertical in the optimum position to not reach the bottom. You do not want water weed to catch the blade.

When practicing in a kayak, it is good to have a target, preferably something fixed and straight-sided nearby to pull toward, such as a dock or a steep shore. That way you can easily see if the

kayak turns, or if the stroke keeps it correctly aligned. This is more difficult to gauge when floating free in open water or drawing toward a small float or buoy. For a short distance sideways you might use another kayak as a target, but this will be complicated by drift, and at this stage you should try to eliminate variables.

Using Land Drills

On dry land, stand beside a straight line and swing the blade gently forward and backward along that line. Control the blade angle with each swing. When standing it feels natural for the blade to be positioned in a way that on the water would be "deep," so this is good practice.

Some people will find it challenging to keep the blade angle constant all the way through each swing. Practice without the water eliminates water resistance and increases visibility. This reduces anxiety, and also makes it easier for you to see and offer feedback. You might try something similar while sitting on a dock or standing in knee-deep water, with the blade partially or fully immersed.

Walk along a dock trailing a blade through the water with a loose handgrip to learn how to steer the blade to neutral. A slight change of angle makes the blade climb to one side or the other. An increased angle creates more drag. There are no distracting balance issues. It is easy to compare the effect of a tight grip to a loose grip. Try using just a fingertip grip.

Feel how, when the lower blade pulls sideways away from the dock, the upper blade pushes toward the dock. Offer pushing resistance with the top hand, arm straight, to prevent the blade in the water climbing from upright. When the blade in the water is in the pushing mode, the upper end of the paddle tends to swing out from the dock. Your top hand now needs a retaining grip.

On a dock, we can compare the effect of sculling with a vertical paddle to sculling with a less-than-vertical paddle. A vertical paddle blade pulls sideways powerfully from the dock, while a sloped blade climbs toward the surface. As it climbs it loses sideways pull. For a draw stroke, we need optimum sideways pull.

It is an advantage to be familiar with several alternative ways to teach each stroke. Then you can choose the most appropriate for the situation, or switch between them when one approach is not enough.

Modeling the Stroke

The better you demonstrate a stroke, the more likely your students will end up with a good working stroke. Even if you only direct attention to three essential elements, it does not hurt if additional refinements are visible. Your students will retain a mental image of the big picture and may adopt such extra details unconsciously while trying to mimic your performance. In the same way, it is possible to impart bad practices inadvertently, so be meticulous with your demonstration.

Assessing Success

If moving sideways is the goal, your students have success when their kayaks move sideways. Next is how to introduce refinements, such as turning and steering, to enable them to keep straight when they move sideways.

Refinements

All the elements you discarded as not essential can now be introduced as refinements. Each one should improve the effectiveness, control, or efficiency of the stroke. As such, your students should notice the difference.

To be able to explain why each element you introduce will make a difference, evaluate the effect for yourself first, to appreciate the difference. Work down the list you have made. Compare the stroke with and without each element to pinpoint the difference, and add your own refinements along the way.

When you decide in which order to introduce refinements, some will fall together very naturally. For example, to straighten one leg and lift the other knee helps you rotate your torso to face the direction of travel sideways. When

Add refinements one at a time to see the effect of each. Try a more upright paddle for example.

you do this it feels natural to turn your head to face that way too. This creates a logical sequence of three elements to group together when you teach: first the leg positions, next the torso rotation, finally the head. Try that in the opposite order too: first, turn the head, follow with the torso, and finally, adjust the leg positions. In addition to sequencing them in a particular order in the overall progression, you could also introduce some or all at the same time. However, the fewer new elements you introduce at once, the more likelihood of success.

A natural sequence of refinements is easier to remember and implement. It makes sense to adopt the torso rotation before you straighten and extend your top arm perpendicular to the kayak. It makes sense to emphasize open fingers of the top hand after the arm is extended, so you can see and feel the difference it makes. Adopting the approximate position then presents an appropriate moment in which to add the refinement. It makes sense to practice with the more straightforward neutral blade before you open it. It makes sense to achieve a reliable sculling draw before you experiment with how edging affects the results. Steering, ironically, is an essential component of the sculling draw, yet it requires quite a lot of skill. You will almost certainly need to return to this.

A sculling draw isn't a technique in isolation. Many of its component parts are shared with other techniques. It can be useful to step sideways during your teaching progression to focus attention on one element or group of elements, and this can be done afresh by bringing in another technique that shares that element.

For example, take your normal forward stroke, rotate, and perform it as if the side of the kayak were now the bow. Which elements are shared with the sculling draw? These include the legs,

torso and head, and the top arm stretch out from the side of the kayak. It also includes balance, which I have not mentioned till now. You could introduce this exercise and use it to focus on particular elements of the sculling draw.

Likewise, you might refer back to elements of the sculling draw when you introduce or refine other techniques. For example, when you scull forward, the blade finishes in a bow rudder position before you change the alignment to scull it back. When the blade reaches the end of its scull toward the back, and changes alignment for the scull forward, the blade is aligned as for a stern draw. You can skip a few stages in a progression toward a bow rudder or a stern draw if the body position with rotation, legs, finger grip, arm positions, and so on are already familiar from previously working on the sculling draw. A complete set of components grouped together is now implicit, and you can focus on the differences and the additions.

Variations on a Theme

Another positive step is to evaluate all the possible variations. Let's take the sculling draw, and let's say you distilled everything I wrote, added a few extra points, and came up with a great teaching plan. How will you respond when someone asks: "Why keep your top hand in one position and pendulum the blade? Why not move both arms together and use the power of your torso?"

This is not the only example I could use, but it is perfect in this case. There are many ways to perform most of these strokes. Paddlers develop easily distinguishable individual styles, recognizable by the different ways they perform strokes. Is anything wrong with using your top arm in this way with your torso? Could it be better than the other way? The way to find out is to compare them back to back. If you find a difference, then decide why one works better than the other. If it is a style with equal merit, decide which to teach. Introduce one, the other, or both.

Perhaps choose one to start, which would be your preference, and keep the other as a backup for someone who doesn't easily grasp the first.

Do you personally use both styles when you paddle? If so, are there particular situations when you would choose one over the other? Be curious enough about the possible variations in different strokes to figure out your reasoned opinion for when someone next asks you.

I might teach just one variation for simplicity. Most strokes have multiple variations that work similarly well. Ultimately, I choose between and decide which to teach, as I have chosen what to include in this book. But being practiced in all the variations is a valuable asset. Switch from one to another to help someone better understand a move that was initially challenging. Match a style to a particular body shape. Help someone succeed in a way that is easier on a damaged body part. Use different variations to accommodate different paddle shapes.

Were you taught that some variations are wrong? Question those statements. It may have been the right thing to do at the time to steer you in one direction at a certain stage of your learning, but now you need to be open-minded. When someone turns a paddle over to use the blade face to push backward, or engages the back of a blade to perform a bow rudder, is it wrong? Is it another correct way, or perhaps the correct way? Are there advantages or disadvantages that might make it good or poor in a given situation? Come back to the performance comparisons. Which is the more effective and efficient, and why? Does that depend on what you will next do with your paddle?

Strategies for Instructors or Leaders

Improving your own paddle skills once you are an instructor or leader usually requires a different approach. Paddlers often consider it presumptuous to offer helpful tips to someone in authority. Turn your analytical skills inward, critique your own demonstrations, and question your long-held opinions of what makes every stroke work. Start by thoroughly breaking skills down into their component parts, to analyze the significance of each part. Compare the effectiveness of a stroke with and without each refinement so you know what difference it makes.

Whenever you see paddlers on the water, be analytical of their strokes. Try to deduce from their paddling how they are using their legs. Spot three things they could do to improve the effectiveness of each technique you see them use. As an observer, it may seldom be appropriate for you to say anything; this exercise is to improve your skills, not theirs.

When you see someone performing a stroke ineffectively, or with a reversed hand, or the opposite side of the blade, try it like that yourself to figure out exactly what that paddler is doing, and why. When you understand the problem, figure out ways to solve it. The more you look for mistakes, the easier it is to spot them. Experiment with details on the water as well as off to refine everything you do.

The same goes not just for flat-water technical paddle skills, but also for how your kayak responds to waves, or wind. Tune in to the nuances. Notice when a particular shift in your weight in a particular position on a wave makes a difference in how your kayak picks up a following sea. It is easier to consider the effect of your weight shift when you have first isolated everything else that goes

Analyze what you see. Try to identify positive points to improve effectiveness and efficiency.

together to make the kayak catch a wave. Can you repeat the move, isolating that part again? What is the effect when you do the same thing in a different kayak?

It's a way to learn: discovery learning. Question everything, analyze, experiment, and play.

Expanded Glossary

Acceleration rate: the rate at which a kayak picks up speed. Not related to top speed: A kayak with quick acceleration may not have as fast a top speed as a longer kayak with slower acceleration.

Anchor point: a fixed point usually on deck to or through which lines and bungees are threaded or tied

Back: a weather term for when the wind changes in a counterclockwise direction, as from south to southeast (opposite to "veer")

Backrest: a support you can lean back onto when you want to rest, as opposed to a "back-support" for use while paddling

Back strap: a back support in the form of a strap fixed from side to side behind the seat

Back support: a support of any kind to help hold you in a good, upright paddling position

Beam: the width of the kayak at its widest point

Boomer: a wave that breaks occasionally over a submerged rock, but only when a larger wave arrives. Otherwise the water appears calm because there is enough depth for smaller waves to cross without reaction.

Bow: the front end of the kayak (same as "stem")

Broach: an unintended turn broadside to the direction of travel, usually caused by a wave

Bulkhead: a dividing wall inside the kayak, usually watertight

Buoyancy aid: a flotation vest, sometimes called a personal flotation device (PFD). Some buoyancy aids are also life jackets.

Cam cleat: a quick-release fitting to hold a line consisting of two toothed, oval-shaped parts that tighten on the line when it is pulled from one end, and slip when it is pulled from the other

Canoe: a small watercraft propelled by a paddler kneeling or sitting with bent knees and using a single-bladed paddle. Canoes were traditionally crafted by first making the skin, and then adding an internal frame. In United Kingdom the term is often applied to the kayak, with "Canadian canoe" or simply "Canadian" being used for the canoe.

Carbon: (see Kevlar) Carbon is a very stiff and lightweight bonding material often used for light-weight kayaks and paddles. Carbon alone tends to be brittle so it is often used with other types of fiber.

Carrying handle: a handle specifically placed and shaped for carrying, as in a suitcase handle. In singles, handles are usually found on deck near the bow and stern; in doubles, often several handles are positioned for multiperson carrying.

Carved turn: turn in which the paddler edges or leans into the turn, as on a bike

Chine: the lengthwise crease line in the hull of a skin-on-frame kayak, where the skin folds over a lengthwise frame

Chined hull: typically, a hull with a single chine along each side, making the transition between the more horizontal hull midsection and the more vertical sides

Clam cleat with fairlead: a combination used to attach a towline to the deck with a quick release. The fairlead prevents the rope lifting from the cleat accidentally.

Cockpit: the enclosed space in which the paddler sits

Cockpit coaming (also cockpit rim): the rim around the entrance to the cockpit, around which a spray skirt may be attached to keep out water

Compass recess: a recess in the deck shaped to hold and often protect a compass for navigation

Contoured bulkhead: a bulkhead shaped at the edges to curve around to meet the deck and hull face-to-face rather than edge-to-face

Cruising speed/top speed: Typically different; cruising speed is usually slower than top speed, because close to top speed, water resistance makes it increasingly difficult to raise the speed by each small increment. Cruising speed is a compromise between the energy expended and the speed achieved.

Day hatch: a hatch, usually small and positioned within reach of the paddler when seated, through which supplies may be easily accessed while afloat

Deck bungee: elastic lines, usually crossing the deck, to pin down items such as a map, chart, or spare paddle

Deck fitting (also anchor point, recessed deck fitting): usually refers to anchor points for deck lines or bungees

Deck line: fixed deck rigging mostly used as hand-holds when moving kayak around on land, but also used to maintain contact from the water for a swimmer

Dihedral blade: a blade with a ridge running from end to end on the face, with the face sloping backward toward each edge (the face looks like an open book placed face-down)

Draft (also draught): the depth of water needed to float without touching the bottom. A shallow-draft kayak needs less water than a deep-draft kayak.

Edge: to angle the hull of the kayak, pushing down one side and lifting the other using a shift of body weight, while also keeping in balance. Edging is used to control a kayak across the wind and to aid when turning. (The term came from slalom and surf kayaks, which truly had "edges," but it's rather an odd term for a sea kayak, which has a somewhat round cross-section and is usually lacking any form of edge.)

End grab (also toggle): usually a loop or handle at the bow or stern for carrying, towing, or retaining a kayak

Fairlead: a loop or ring to channel a line, allowing the line to run through but not otherwise escape

Fiberglass: very fine threads of glass usually bonded into white fraying bundles and compacted together in a loose mat, or woven into cloth. These fabrics serve as the reinforcement in fiberglass kayaks. The plastic used to bond the fibers is applied in liquid form. It sets around and between the fibers to form the tough, slightly flexible shell of the kayak.

Final stability: the stability of a kayak when edged

Fish-form hull: a hull that is wider near the bow than at the stern

Fixed skeg: a plate fixed under the hull at the stern to aid tracking

Flat curve: a paddle blade with a face that is flat from edge to edge, but curving from end to end

Foot pedals (also steering pedals): used to steer a rudder

Footrest (also foot pegs, foot brace; used interchangeably): typically adjustable to fit a paddler's leg length; used to brace against when paddling

Gel coat: the material used for the outside surface of a kayak. In the building process, gel coat is applied as a liquid to the inside of the mold and allowed to set before the fiberglass layer is added. Gel coat is clear, but becomes opaque and colorful once pigment is added. It is tough and waterproof.

Glide: the continued forward movement of a kayak after the paddler has stopped paddling. A kayak with "good glide" will continue to run forward for some distance before stopping.

Gunwale (also gunnel): The outer perimeter of the deck, where it joins the hull; the seam or join line. Originally it was a short strengthening wall around the outer perimeter of a gun deck to stop cannons rolling overboard. I rarely carry cannons.

Hard chine: a chine with a sharp-edged fold

Hatch lid: a lid that seals onto the hatch rim

Hatch recess: a recess or dip in the deck so the hatch does not protrude from the line of the deck

Hatch rim: a rim, usually attached to the deck, onto which the hatch lid seals

High brace stability: the stability of a kayak when the kayaker is lying in the water. A wide kayak that lifts the kayaker's hips high in relation to the water surface will have less high brace stability than a narrow and short kayak that allows the paddler's hips to sink lower.

High water (HW): The level of average high tide

Indexing: the oval-shaping of a paddle shaft to aid blade control

Initial stability: the stability of a kayak when held upright

Jamming cleat: a quick-release fitting with teeth or ridges to grip a rope for towing, etc.

Join line (also seam line): In a composite or thermoform kayak, this is usually where the hull is joined to the deck, along or close to the sheer line, although it is sometimes along the keel and from end to end along the middeck.

Kayak: a small watercraft in which the paddler sits facing forward with legs outstretched. Kayaks are propelled with a double-bladed paddle and were traditionally crafted by stretching a skin over a wooden frame.

Keel: a downward protruding ridge or "V" running along the center of the hull from end to end. Some kayaks have a keel, others do not.

Kevlar: Carbon and Kevlar are bonding materials used with or instead of fiberglass. Carbon fibers are very stiff and lightweight, but tend to be brittle, while Kevlar is tear-resistant. A combination of both in a cloth offers a strong, lighter-weight alternative to fiberglass.

Knee braces: shaped braces to maintain contact with inside of the deck to aid in edging, etc.

Knee tube: a lengthwise-aligned tubular structure in the cockpit under the front deck used variously for kayak control, as knee braces, or for storage, with access either from the cockpit or via a deck hatch

Life jacket: a personal flotation jacket designed to turn an unconscious wearer face up in the water

Liftable rudder: a rudder that may be lifted from the water, usually via a line from the cockpit, to avoid damage on landing

Low water (LW): Low tide (more accurately, mean low tide at mean atmospheric pressure)

Multichine hull: a hull with more chines than the minimum of two (one each side). Historically, multiple chines were used with skin-on-frame kayaks to create a curved hull rather than a chined hull; as more chines are added, the closer the result resembles a curve.

Mean high water springs (MHWS): Mean spring tide high tide level at mean atmospheric pressure

Outside-edged turn: a turn in which the paddler edges from the direction of turn, allowing the tail to skid

Overstern rudder: a rudder hung from the back of the kayak. The position permits a rudder to be sprung, making it less vulnerable to damage than an understern rudder.

Paddle: A kayak paddle usually consists of a paddle shaft with a blade at each end. A canoe paddle has a blade at one end of the shaft and a handle at the other.

PFD (personal flotation device): a buoyancy aid worn like a vest. Some PFDs are also life jackets.

Primary stability: the stability of a kayak when it sits upright on the water

Recessed deck fitting: a fixed anchor point for a line or bungee positioned in a custom-shaped indentation in the deck

Resin: the plastic used to bond glass fibers. Initially a liquid, it reacts when mixed with a chemical "hardener," and after a short time sets hard. Different kinds of resin are appropriate for use with different bonding fabrics. For Kevlar, epoxy resin works more effectively than polyester resin, which is used with fiberglass.

Retractable rudder: a rudder that can be withdrawn into the hull when not in use to avoid damage

Retractable skeg: a skeg that may be withdrawn up into the hull. A partly dropped skeg will have less lateral resistance than a fully dropped skeg, so a retractable skeg may be "trimmed" to the best position for control in different conditions.

Rocker: usually refers to the end-to-end curve of the hull as seen from the side; the "banana" curve. A kayak with no rocker has a straight keel line, a kayak with reverse rocker (also known as a "hogged" hull) sits deepest at the ends.

Round bilge hull: a rounded hull shape with no chines, more semicircular in profile; often used on racing kayaks and wave skis

Rounded hull: a hull with no chines, curving smoothly between the horizontal hull and more vertical sides

Rudder: a flat plate or shaped foil at the stern of the kayak used for steering

Rudder lift line: a line pulled from the cockpit to raise a rudder from the water

Rudder lines: the lines (or rudder cables) linking the foot-steering controls to the rudder

Rudder pedal: a foot control deploying a movable pedal for each foot to control the rudder

Scupper holes: holes between the deck and hull of a sit-on-top kayak to drain away water

Seam line (also join line): In composite and thermoform kayaks, this is usually where the hull is joined to the deck (along or close to the sheer line), but is sometimes along the keel and the center of the deck.

Secondary buoyancy (also secondary flotation): the flotation that comes into effect when the bow or stern plunge deeper into the water (same as secondary flotation)

Secondary stability: the stability of the kayak when edged

Sheer line: the line defining the widest part of the top of the hull before it turns inward as deck

Skeg: a flattish plate that sticks down from the hull near the stern to aid tracking

Skeg box: the recess in the hull into which a skeg is retracted

Skeg control: the means by which the skeg may be raised or dropped by the seated paddler. This is typically by line, cable, or hydraulic control.

Skeg slide: the sliding button that is used to pull or push a hydraulic plunger or cable to lower or raise the skeg

Skid turn: a turn in which the paddler edges from the direction of the turn, allowing the tail to skid

Soft chine: a chine with a blunt-edged fold

Spoon: a blade shaped like a spoon, the face being the hollow side

Spray deck (spray skirt): a fabric cover to seal the paddler's waist to the cockpit to keep out water

Stem: the front end of the kayak; same as bow

Stern: the rear end of the kayak

Swede-form hull: a hull that is broader near the stern than near the bow

Symmetrical hull: a hull that is the same width near the bow as near the stern

Thigh braces: shaped braces to hold the thighs when rolling, etc.

Toggle (also end grab): usually a bar tied to the bow or stern for carrying, towing, or grabbing to prevent separation after a wet exit

Top mark: the shaped and colored plate or sign above a buoy denoting the type of buoy below it

Towing point: an attachment point or fitting near the cockpit to which a line may be fixed for towing another kayak, or the point of attachment on a kayak being towed

Tracking: this refers to how straight a kayak tends to go. A stiff-tracking kayak goes straight easily and resists turning, a loose-tracking kayak requires more directional control by the paddler. A loose-tracking kayak will benefit most from a skeg or rudder, yet will be more easily turned than a stiff-tracking kayak.

Trim: This is how the kayak floats: level, down at the bow or stern, or to one side. When trimmed to one side a kayak is edged, so the term is more commonly used for forward or backward adjustments, either by loading the kayak more heavily at one end, or by leaning the body.

Understern rudder: a small rudder positioned beneath the hull near the stern. The understern rudder is more efficient for steering than rudders placed farther back (overstern rudder). Despite its vulnerability, the reduced drag makes it the rudder of choice for racing kayakers, especially on flat water. A small fin is often fixed immediately forward of an understern rudder to protect it from impact.

Vacuum bagging: a technique in which dry fiberglass or other laminates in the mold are covered and sealed with a membrane before air is sucked from one end to draw resin through to wet the fibers

Veer: a weather term for when the wind changes direction clockwise, as in south to southwest, (opposite to "back")

Waterline: the line between the water surface and the hull. The waterline will be lower when a lighter paddler sits in a kayak and higher with a heavier paddler.

Waterline beam: the maximum width of the kayak at the water surface. This may be less than the beam of the kayak.

Watertight compartment: Often a misnomer, this is the space accessed by a hatch, and is typically sealed from the cockpit by a bulkhead

Wing: a blade shaped somewhat like an aircraft wing held on end, with a deep hollow face and a back that scoops deeply from edge to edge. Used primarily for racing.

INDEX

ABOUT THE AUTHOR

Nigel Foster began kayaking on the south coast of England as a teenager. His hobby took him on sea kayaking trips, down whitewater rivers, into surf competitions, and into travel. A 400-mile solo trip along the south coast of England gave him a thirst for kayaking adventure that led him to circumnavigate Iceland at the age of 24. Later, after exploring Newfoundland, he made a solo crossing of the Hudson Strait from Baffin Island to Labrador in 1981: an uncompleted trip he barely survived, and which he returned to complete in 2004. This story is told in his book, *On Polar Tides*.

As a schoolteacher, he taught geography and environmental studies in preparation for a career in outdoor education. He worked with schoolchildren and adults in residential outdoor centers and at the National Water Sports Center for Wales. By 1986 he had started his own kayaking business in Wales, running technical courses and tours, primarily in sea kayaking. Nowadays he is well known and in demand around the world for his classes in kayak technique.

His design curiosity led him to produce the Vyneck, his first production composite sea kayak, with Keith Robinson in 1976. He and Geoff Hunter used Vyneck kayaks for the first circumnavigation of Iceland. He has since brought many more models to market, both in composite and rotomolded plastic, together with paddles and accessories, produced under license. He has worked with a range of companies as a consultant and/or designer, currently collaborating with the Swedish company Point65.

Nigel has published a number of books and has written regularly for magazines.

He continues to balance his time between instructing around the world, writing, designing, and finding excuses to play guitar. He lives in Seattle with his wife, Kristin Nelson, an accomplished kayaker who makes her living as a ceramic artist.